Faith Bytes

365 Daily Connections with Jesus

Steven B. Angus

Faith Bytes

Copyright © 2023 Steven B. Angus

All rights reserved.

ISBN: 9798868270512

Unless otherwise noted
All Scripture references are taken from the
New King James Version of the Holy Bible

Common English Bible (CEB)
Copyright © 2011 by Common English Bible

English Standard Version (ESV)
The Holy Bible, English Standard Version. ESV® Text Edition: 2016. Copyright © 2001 by Crossway Bibles, a publishing ministry of Good News Publishers.

Living Bible (TLB)
The Living Bible copyright © 1971 by Tyndale House Foundation. Used by permission of Tyndale House Publishers Inc., Carol Stream, Illinois 60188. All rights reserved.

The Message (MSG)
Copyright © 1993, 2002, 2018 by Eugene H. Peterson

New King James Version®. [NKJV] Copyright © 1982 by Thomas Nelson. Used by permission. All rights reserved.

New Living Translation (NLT)
Holy Bible, New Living Translation, copyright © 1996, 2004, 2015 by Tyndale House Foundation. Used by permission of Tyndale House Publishers Inc., Carol Stream, Illinois 60188. All rights reserved.

New Revised Standard Version Updated Edition (NRSVUE)
New Revised Standard Version, Updated Edition. Copyright © 2021 National Council of Churches of Christ in the United States of America. Used by permission. All rights reserved worldwide.

Cover Photo: stock.adobe.com

Faith Bytes

DEDICATION

To *Cheri Clyde Angus*
My wife and best friend
Finding you has proven it is possible to love again.

In memory of
Steve Clyde
and
Gretchen Angus
Your faithfulness and unconditional love were so precious
Cheri and I could not help but love again.

In appreciation to
The Legacy Tennessee Annual Conference
and
Kingston Springs United Methodist Church
For Providing an Opportunity to Share the Love of Jesus as a Pastor.

This Book is Offered in Gratitude for
Our Friends and Family
You remained at our side in the darkest days.
You rejoiced with us when God brought new light into our lives.

Faith Bytes

Steven B. Angus

CONTENTS

Preface	
January	1
February	26
March	48
Holy Week	65
April	71
May	93
June	115
July	138
August	163
September	188
October	212
November	237
December	259
The Author	283

Steven B. Angus

Steven B. Angus

PREFACE

If we were responding to a survey about faith, most would enthusiastically declare its importance. However, we are less specific about how we nurture its growth. We tend to approach it with an all-or-nothing process. Like the person who begins a new lifestyle of healthy eating and an exercise program, we tend to adopt the notion that "If a little is good, more has to be better." Whether it is the lack of time or pushing ourselves to the extreme, we abandon our goal. Our faith becomes lethargic.

During my years as a pastor observing those who have grown in their faith, I realized it usually occurred not by gorging on spiritual exercises but by taking consistent byte-sized morsels of time spent with Jesus. Yes, I am aware that it appears I have used the incorrect form of "byte" in this incident, but allow me to assure you that I have chosen the word intentionally.

In our technology-driven society, the byte represents information in its most miniature and simplest form. The byte is a unit of digital data that most commonly encodes a single text character in a computer's memory. A byte appears on our electronic device as one letter, punctuation mark, or number while encoded on its memory drive. You may remember, as I do, inserting a five-and-a-quarter-inch floppy disk into the computer's drive and marveling at the ability to store 256 Kilobytes of data. Realizing 1 kilobyte represented one thousand keystrokes, we wondered if we remembered something we had viewed on an episode of Star Trek. The progression soon went from byte to Kilobyte. Followed by Megabyte, Gigabyte, Terabyte, etc., to the Yottabyte. In case you are wondering, there are 26 zeros in 1,000 yottabytes. The point for us is it began with the byte and grew.

In this book are three hundred and sixty-five byte-sized faith builders gleaned from my fifty-plus years of ministry. You will encounter individuals from scripture, Church history, and United States and World History. Some were presidents, saints, Kings, Prophets, and prisoners, and others were just notorious. We will discuss the Lord's Prayer, the Fruits of the Spirit, the Golden Rule, Apples of Gold, and what it means to be Branded for Jesus, each in byte-sized servings. Each day's Faith Bytes also includes space for us to interact or for you to make personal notes to yourself or Jesus. This Devotional aims to create a "Connection" with Jesus to form "Memories" of his great love for you.

Steven B. Angus

Steven B. Angus

JANUARY

January 1
New Year—Happiness?

We are presented with a New Year as if it were a newborn child. Before we can become accustomed to cradling our new blessing, we hear the temper tantrums of her older siblings. Do you remember those embarrassing scenes waiting at the Walmart checkout? Yes, those. With screaming and kicking, they remind us who was here first. Like the adult child who refuses to leave home, the decisions of years past linger.

After singing a few notes of the Scots ballad, "Auld Lang Syne," we shouted, "Happy New Year!" No, they are not mere words. They are the petition of desperate prayer.

If we were offered the option of a drink from Ponce De Leon's fountain of youth or a sip of happiness, without question, we would choose the latter.

Is it possible to experience a day filled with happiness, much less a year? Although the Apostle Paul did not write a self-help book titled "Three Rules to a Happy Year," he did include a sentence in an intimate letter. It was addressed to a new church that permits us a rare peek behind the veil of Apostleship. He revealed the precepts that gave his life peace, contentment, and, dare we say it? Happiness.

He stated:

> "Beloved, I do not consider that I have made it my own, but this one thing I do: forgetting what lies behind and straining forward to what lies ahead, I press on toward the goal for the prize of the heavenly call of God in Christ Jesus." [Philippians in 3:13-14, NRSV.]

Faith Bytes

Between the parades, football games, fireworks, and servings of blackeyed peas with cornbread, take a moment to consider Paul's personal mission statement. What encouragement does it offer that a Happy New Year is possible?

___

___

___

___

January 2
The Holy Habit of Forgetting

Congratulations on remembering your New Year's resolution to prioritize your relationship with God. The most challenging day of any new lifestyle is the second. Yes, I intentionally avoided the H-word.

I have observed the stigma we attach to the term "habit." We apply it to negative behaviors such as overeating, cursing, or an addiction to be broken. Yet, we wonder, shouldn't an action be spontaneous and not a habit for it to be holy? I maintain a book in my library titled "Holy Habits" as a visual reminder that the two ideas can work together.

The Apostle Paul weighed in on some of his holy habits, which may help us experience a Happy New Year. In Philippians 3:13, he wrote: "But this one thing I do: forgetting what lies behind and straining forward to what lies ahead, I press on toward the goal for the prize of the heavenly call of God in Christ Jesus."

There we have it. Holy Habit number one. FORGETTING. Wait a minute! This isn't what we were expecting. However, with his "Forgetting what is behind," Paul wasn't speaking about letting go of something as mundane as a pair of misplaced reading glasses.

How long does it take to form a habit? One substantial study reported an average of 66 days. [How Long to Form a Habit? - PsyBlog (spring.org.uk)] How do three years sound? Did you know Paul went off the grid for three years before he began his ministry? I believe it was because he had much forgetting he needed to do, and some new habits required time. The holy habit of forgetting takes time. This is because of the tough remembering necessary before we can surrender it to God in forgetfulness.

Perhaps, as we prepare our New Year's list of resolutions, we would be wise to ask God, "What must I remember so you and I may forget it together?"

___

___

___

___

January 3
The Hard Work of Remembering to Forget

Well, did you remember to forget? Perhaps now we understand why Paul spent three years in desolate Arabia. Remembering to forget is hard work. Memory is a precious commodity. Without it, each day would place us in peril.

When purchasing a smartphone, the crucial question is, how much memory does it have? Yet Paul's formula for happiness involves "forgetting what is behind." Obviously, he did not mean we should do a hard reset and return to our original factory settings. Nor should we haphazardly delete the cache of our life experiences.

Continuing our technology metaphor, we must perform a memory sweep to identify malware crippling our operating system. When the virus is removed, the hard drive can be defragged, short for defragmentation. This process identifies unused memory sectors, reallocates information, and restores space. It makes the device more efficient by freeing and creating space for fresh memories.

What memories need to be defragged in your life? Unfortunately, some memories have been with us so long we deceive ourselves into believing they are our friends. We realize we are drowning. Instead of reaching out for a life preserver, we cling to an anchor.

How do we forget what lies behind us? I cannot count the occasions I have tried to repair an electronic device, making matters worse. Eventually, I borrow a phone and call someone who knows. It turns out Paul is a technician we need on speed dial. He is an expert on forgetting what is behind.

Memory saboteurs have names such as shame and guilt. Although we confess our failures to God, our memory fails to remind us about God's nature. Which is, "What God forgives, God forgets." Which should lead us to query, "If God is willing to forget our past, shouldn't we?"

_____
_____
_____
_____

January 4
The Encouraging and Unrelenting Coach P

Even the casual football fan lives for this time of the year. The week leading up to New Year's Day is about college bowl games. Then, to not be outdone, the National Football League playoffs take over our Saturdays and Sundays, culminating with the Super Bowl.

Having read the Apostle Paul's letters to the New Testament churches, I feel confident that if he lived today, he would tune in to the Southeastern Game of the

Faith Bytes

Week. His athletic interests are evident in his guidelines for living found in Philippians 3:13. As if by "forgetting what is behind" and leaving our failures to eat our dust, Paul has become our greatest fan. He is Coach P, standing by third base, his arm a windmill, propelling us forward as he enthusiastically shouts, "Don't let up now! Strain forward to what lies ahead." The first rule a baseball coach teaches a player running the bases is "Don't look at the ball. Strain towards the base." And then, as the baserunner sprints towards third, the coach yells, "Keep your eyes on me."

Derrick Henry of the Tennessee Titans is considered, by some, the best running back in the NFL. He puts forth every ounce of strength when running, thrusting him forward. He is constantly stretching, stiff-arming would-be tacklers to gain one more yard in his pursuit of the goal line.

Can you hear Coach P? He pushes us to put our past in the rearview mirror as we stretch our spiritual muscles to "grow in the grace and knowledge of our Lord Jesus Christ." [2 Peter 3:18]. How do we build spiritual stamina? By praying, reading the Bible, participating in a small group, and serving others. Whenever we begin a new exercise routine, it feels awkward. But, eventually, as we put in the reps, it becomes a holy habit.

Have you thought about your workout plan? How are you planning to stretch forth today?

_____
_____
_____
_____

January 5
Come Out of the Bathroom!

I quit! The urge to blurt out these words may have been as recent as this morning as you spoke sternly to the person staring at you in the bathroom mirror. Such a conversation isn't as rare as you think. Thankfully for those who depend on us, we opened the bathroom door despite our reluctance and re-entered life. We embraced Paul's appeal to "press on toward the goal."

With clipboard in hand and a whistle between his lips, [wily] Coach P preaches the game plan that guided him through some frustrating seasons. The Apostle espouses his third rule for, if not a Happy New Year, a contented one. His message? Keep on keeping on. When it comes to what truly matters, don't be a quitter. Press on towards the goal.

Was Thomas Edison exceptional because of his genius, or was it his persistence? Convinced he could find a substance small enough with high resistance to an electric current that would work as a filament for an electric lightbulb, he pressed forward. After 700 failures, an assistant advised him to abandon the project. Edison refused, offering his legendary reasoning, "We have found 700 things that don't work." Finally, the electric light was delivered by the midwife whose name was tenacity.

Coach P masterfully motivates us to keep our eye on the goal and move toward it despite any obstacles. What is the objective? Prosperity? Is happiness the banner we crave to hang from the rafters for others to envy? Paul framed the aim as "the prize of the heavenly call of God in Christ Jesus." Our goal is to be as close to God as possible. Happiness, contentment, and peace are not tangibles we attain. We experience these things as we press on in our pursuit to know Jesus.

_____

_____

_____

_____

January 6 [Epiphany]
As Vast as Space. As Timeless as Infinity!

What my dad said was a desperate attempt to squelch the "How much further?" litany originating from the backseat of the car, which also happened to be just behind his ear. He said, "Up ahead, we will cross a timeline, and the time will change." Wow! What an incredible vacation. How many kids experience time travel?

The jingle from the peanut gallery shifted slightly as I asked, "How much farther to the timeline?" Finally, dad said, "It's just up ahead. Get ready. Here it is." I held my breath. What? Hadn't that strange man on television said, "There is a fifth dimension as vast as space and as timeless as infinity?" What a disappointment. However, the day came when I baited my children with the same vision of time travel.

Perhaps you have been too preoccupied to notice we left Christmas behind and entered the Christian Season of Epiphany. Although the word suggests a eureka experience, like passing into a new time zone, it would appear to lack anything remarkable. Isn't Epiphany that magical moment when the cartoonist scribbles a lightbulb above a character's head? We soon discover that the imaginary lines that carve our world into twenty-four orange wedges do actually affect us. Sometimes, it is as subtle as adjusting our schedule for a specific television program. Maybe it is more significant, such as when I FACETIMED my daughter and grandchildren when they were living in Japan.

Epiphany becomes the spotlight that pierces the darkness to reveal the authentic Jesus. Beginning with the arrival of Kings bearing gifts, God quickly declares Jesus' sonship at His baptism. Soon, we learn about water being transformed into wine, a rope woven into a whip to remove thieves from his Father's house, culminating with the Transfiguration. Then, the lightbulb clicks on. We see that the baby we have been handed is. . .? Well, he is as vast as space and as timeless as infinity!

Faith Bytes

January 7
Sand? Gravel? Or Stones?

An expert in time management addressed a group of high-powered overachievers. First, he placed a one-gallon jar and a dozen fist-sized rocks on a table. Then, he carefully put the stones into the glass container until they reached the top. Then, speaking for the first time, he asked, "Is the jar full?" The audience responded, "Yes." Finally, the presenter asked, "Really?" Reaching beneath the table, he produced a bucket of gravel. Methodically, he dumped some gravel into the jar and shook it, causing the pebbles to work into the spaces between the big rocks. Then, once again, he asked the group, "Is the jar full?"

Catching on, there was silence until someone answered, "Probably not." "Good!" he replied as he reached under the table and brought out a bucket of sand. As he poured the sand into the jar, it entered the spaces between the rocks and the gravel. Again, he asked, "Is this jar full?" This time, the group shouted, "No!" "Good," he said. Taking a pitcher of water from the podium, he poured it into the jar to the brim. Addressing the group who had paid top dollar to hear him, he asked, "What is the point of this demonstration?" Calling on a fellow who raised his hand and answered, "No matter how full your schedule, you can always fit more into it if you try!" The speaker replied, "No. This illustration teaches that if we don't put the big rocks in first, we will never get them all in. The large rocks in our lives are time with our loved ones. They are our faith, our dreams, or mentoring someone. Remember to put these BIG ROCKS in first, or you will never get them all in."

_____
_____
_____

January 8
The Value of a Smile

It is said that beauty is in the eye of the beholder. Things considered attractive about a person primarily reflect the beholder's tastes. Some are drawn to the color or shape of the eyes or the length and texture of someone's hair. The curvature of the nose fetches the remark—she is as cute as a button.

Truthfully, I have difficulty considering someone well over five hundred years old as one of the most beautiful women ever. However, since her worth has been reported to be between 750 million and 1 billion dollars, who am I to judge? Furthermore, Wikipedia describes her as "the best known, the most visited, the most written about, the most sung about, the most parodied" woman in the world.

By now, you know I am referring to Leonardo da Vinci's masterpiece, the Mona Lisa. For most, her charm rests in her billion-dollar smile. However, on this date in 1987, medical experts released a report suggesting the twenty-four-year-old

Steven B. Angus

Florentine silk heiress Lisa Gherardini's smile may have resulted from a medical condition that causes the corner of the mouth to droop known as Bell's Palsy. It seems we have the compulsion to explain everything.

The Bible explains a smile this way: "A joyful heart brightens one's face." [Proverbs 15:13, CEB]. Another woman known for her priceless beauty said: "Every time you smile at someone, it is an action of love, a gift to that person, a beautiful thing... Peace begins with a smile." Her name? Mother Teresa. Perhaps she understood Jacob's greeting to his estranged brother when he said: "What a relief to see your friendly smile. It is like seeing the face of God!" [Genesis 33:10, NLT]

Of course, we could simply Smile and cause people to wonder what we've been up to. But, whatever your motivation, why not share yours if you see someone who has misplaced their smile?

_____

_____

_____

_____

January 9
Whose Hand Is It In?

What were you doing on January 9, 2007? I am sure my day included celebrating my oldest daughter's twentieth birthday. Before you frantically search for your retired day planner, let me tell you what one chap dressed in jeans and a black mock turtleneck was doing. Steve Jobs announced the forthcoming release of a smartphone called the iPhone. By 2020, one billion people were using the Apple invention.

Today, we cannot go anywhere without seeing heads bowed reverently gazing on our electronic devices to check the weather, watch the big game, or read the latest New York Times bestseller. You are likely holding one now. The device has changed lives, but how it has done so is determined by whose hand cradles it.

The stories about Jesus are intended to demonstrate what he can do when we place something in his hands. Perhaps you have heard the following.

> *A basketball in my hands is worth about $25.*
> *A basketball in Labron James's hands is worth about $450,000 per game.*
> *It depends on whose hands it's in.*
>
> *A baseball in my hands is worth about $8.*
> *A baseball in Mets pitcher Max Scherzer renders $10,000 per pitch.*
> *It depends on whose hands it's in.*
>
> *Two fish and five loaves in my hands are a couple of fish sandwiches.*
> *Two fish and five loaves in Jesus's hands fed thousands.*

Faith Bytes

It depends on whose hands it's in.

A pitcher of water in my hands is a pitcher of ordinary water.
Water in Jesus's hands becomes the sweetest wine.
It depends on whose hands it's in.

What will you place in HIS hands today?

_____

_____

_____

_____

January 10
Unity

[In many Christian communities, the Church is called upon to pray for Christian Unity sometime in January.]

Whenever there is a change in leadership, there is often an appeal for unity. Whether speaking of a government, a sports team, or a church, the importance of unity cannot be overemphasized. Perhaps you recall this familiar children's story highlighting the significance of working together.

A flock of doves was searching for food led by their king. Having flown a great distance, they were exhausted, but their king encouraged them to continue. Soon, the Scout dove spotted some rice scattered beneath a tree, and they landed and began to eat. Suddenly, a net fell over them, and they were trapped. A hunter approached, armed with a club. The doves desperately fluttered their wings but to no avail. But then, the king had an idea. He encouraged his subjects to fly up together because together, there was strength. Each dove picked up a portion of the net and flew off, carrying a part of it. The astonished hunter tried to follow, but they flew high over hills and valleys.

They came to a hill where there lived a mouse who was a friend of the dove king. The loud noise of their approach frightened the mouse, who went into hiding. The dove king called out to his friend, who was eager to help. He began to gnaw at the net with his sharp teeth, hoping to set the king free. However, the king insisted that his subjects be released first. With understanding, the mouse complied. He began to chew the net, and all the doves, including the dove king, were freed. They thanked the mouse and flew away together, realizing their strength was in their unity.

The hunter's net is a perfect analogy for many circumstances that entangle us. Let us remember the petition of our leader, King Jesus. Addressing the one who can break the fetters that ensnare, he said, "Father, I pray that they will all be one, just as you and I are one."

Steven B. Angus

_____

_____

January 11
Unity: Time For a Gut Check

In The Message Bible, Eugene Peterson described the first New Testament church. He wrote, "The whole congregation of believers was united as one—one heart, one mind!" [Acts 4:32]. Several other translations render it: "one heart, one soul." [NRSV] Can we find a better definition of unity than one heart, mind, and soul?

When a group has unity, it begins with a common cause. A band of soldiers is molded into a military unit by shared patriotism or the fundamental goal of survival. Political parties unite to elect a public official who reflects their interest. A parent-teacher organization develops from a mutual desire that the educational needs of children are the priority. Because of a shared mission, most of them will create a slogan or statement. By doing so, not only does it help the unaffiliated know the purpose of the group, but it can motivate the membership by reminding them why they exist.

Suppose a local church or denomination hopes to be one in heart and soul. In that case, it must remember what brought them together. The Apostle Paul communicated the basis of unity: "One Lord, one faith, one baptism, one God and Father of all." [Ephesians 4:5-6].

One Lord. The church exists to serve Jesus. When the priority shifts away from Jesus, that group may still gather and be active. However, it ceases to be a church other than in name because it has forgotten its reason for existing.

Occasionally, a local church needs to do what can only be described as—a gut check. For many, the COVID-19 pandemic was such a catalyst. The result was some congregations stopped meeting and did not reopen. Those who chose to reopen required a gut check as they asked themselves, "Are we of one heart, mind, and soul in Jesus?"

_____

_____

_____

January 12
Do They Know?

"They Will Know We are Christians," or "We Are One in the Spirit," as it is sometimes referred is one of those songs that, if it isn't in our hymnal, we certainly thought it was. It was written in 1966 by Peter Scholtes, a Catholic priest serving a parish on the South Side of Chicago. At the time, he led a youth choir

Faith Bytes

in the church's basement. He was searching for an appropriate song for which the group could sing a series of ecumenical, interracial events. When he couldn't find such a piece, he wrote "They Will Know" in one day. The song gained popularity and became the anthem of the Jesus Movement of the 1960s and '70s. It brought the guitar into the church and gave momentum to the growing contemporary worship movement. The song was based on John 13:35, where Jesus said, "By this, everyone will know that you are my disciples if you have love for one another."

Sung with gusto, the lyrics reflect a yearning that the church will be united by a love that others will recognize and want for themselves. Some of the lyrics state:

> *We are one in the Spirit*
> *We are one in the Lord [2]*
> *And we pray that all unity*
> *May one day be restored*
>
> *And they'll know we are Christians by our love, by our love.*
> *Yes, they'll know we are Christians by our love.*

Let this be our prayer that others will know we are Christians by our unity.

_____
_____
_____
_____

January 13
Prayer In the Halls of Government

The role of Chaplain to the United States Senate has a long tradition dating back to 1789. Today Ret. Rear Admiral Barry Clayton Black is the 62nd Chaplain, a position he has had since 2003. He is the first African American and Seventh-day Adventist to hold the position.

Prayer may not be something we often associate with the halls of government. However, moments after Congress affirmed President Biden's Electoral College victory, Chaplain Black delivered a prayer calling for unity and a reminder that words and actions matter. His prayer is something we each should heed. He said:

> "Lord of our lives and Sovereign of our beloved nation, we deplore the desecration of the United States Capitol building, the shedding of innocent blood, the loss of life, and the quagmire of dysfunction that threatened our democracy.
>
> "These tragedies have reminded us that words matter and the power of life and death is in the tongue. We have been warned that eternal vigilance continues to be freedom's price.
>
> "Lord, you have helped us remember that we need to see in each other a common humanity that reflects your image. You have strengthened our

resolve to protect and defend the Constitution of the United States against all enemies, domestic as well as foreign.

"Use us to bring healing and unity to our hurting and divided nation and world. Thank you for what you have pleased our lawmakers to accomplish in spite of threats to liberty. Bless and keep us. Drive far from us all the wrong desires, incline our hearts to do your will, and guide our feet on the path of peace.

"And God Bless America. We pray in Your Sovereign name. Amen."

January 14
Before It's Too Late

A farmer enlisted the aid of friends in searching for his small daughter, who was lost. Although young and quite ill, she managed to leave home and wandered away into the tall brush surrounding the farmhouse. For hours, the farmer and his neighbors searched without success. He became more anxious as the dark and cold of night began to settle. Then, a volunteer offered a suggestion. He said, "The grass and weeds are quite thick. It is easy for us to miss a lot of places and go over others several times. Why don't we join hands, mark our starting place, and go through the undergrowth like a large rake? Then we'll be sure not to skip any spot." Agreeing it was a good plan, they joined hands and walked side by side. In less than half an hour, they located the child. But it was too late. She was dead. The farmer and his wife cradled their precious daughter's body into their arms. Then, loudly, they cried—'In God's name, why didn't we join hands before?'"

The tone of the parent's voices is unmistakable. It was more than sorrow. There was regret, something each of those who searched must have felt. These past several days, we have spoken about unity's importance. Although there are always exceptions, my moments of greatest regret occurred in isolation. Agreements motivated by wrong intentions can lead to mob rule. Unity based on faith, built upon Jesus, may not always end as we hoped, but seldom is it characterized by regret. There is rarely remorse in taking someone's hand. To whom will you extend a hand today?

Faith Bytes

January 15
Rectifying Deficiencies

In 1986, the third Monday in January was designated a national holiday to honor the legacy of Dr. Martin Luther King, Jr. Less than ten years later, I began an eighteen-month adventure that influenced my life immensely as I became the pastor of an African-American congregation.

The eyes of the African and Anglo communities and denominational leadership watched to see if it could work. The congregation and I felt the stares but also recognized the significance of what we were doing. This was apparent on a Sunday afternoon before Martin Luther King, Jr. Day. The African-American churches in the community came together to celebrate the day. The sanctuary was packed as each pew held people who were shoulder to shoulder. When I entered the sanctuary, I was immediately approached and invited to join the other pastors in the chancel area. Being the only Anglo in the room may have been a clue to my identity. For the first time, I knew what it felt like to be in the minority—well, I was the minority. Few of us know how this really feels. I was treated royally, not because I was white, but because I was a pastor. However, I soon realized I was expected to join my fifteen or so colleagues and deliver a brief sermon as a pastor in the African-American community. Although I found my early experience as a Baptist preacher helpful, my comments were brief because what did I really know about Dr. King? When I left, I was determined to rectify this deficiency. I hope to share some of what I have learned in the coming days. Perhaps today would be an opportunity to ponder why Dr. King is vital to each of us, regardless of our race.

_____

_____

_____

January 16
MLK: What It Takes to Serve

I had to make some choices when diagnosed with an iron deficiency. My options were to do nothing and feel continuously sluggish, preventing me from interacting at my best with others, or follow my physician's advice. So, I try to eat healthily and take vitamins and iron supplements because I hope to rectify my deficiency. Doing so has not only enabled me to enjoy life more fully but allowed me to be a better family member and citizen. I am grateful my doctor pointed out what I did not know regarding my health. He told me how I could feel better.

Yesterday, I shared an experience that helped me recognize my deficiency in understanding why Dr. Martin Luther King, Jr. is important for all of us. Remembering and learning about the man may help us understand why he is essential for all of us.

Steven B. Angus

First and foremost, Rev. King was a Christian. Although well-known as a civil rights activist, his faith was the foundation for his commitment to achieving social justice for all. His public addresses are often referred to as speeches. However, they were actually sermons almost always rooted in Scripture.

Although Dr. King received twenty honorary doctorates, most Americans are unaware he graduated from high school at fifteen and earned his bachelor's degree at nineteen. He then attended seminary, where he was elected President of a predominantly white senior class. Eventually, he attended Boston University and earned his Ph.D. in Systematic Theology. His dissertation defended his belief that God can have a relationship with humans.

Today, consider this quote by Dr. King and how it applies to us.

"You don't have to have a college degree to serve. You don't have to make your subject and verb agree to serve. You only need a heart full of grace. A soul generated by love."

_____
_____
_____
_____

January 17
His Vision Is Jesus's Vision

Beyond the fact that there is an annual holiday in his honor, most white Americans know little about Martin Luther King, Jr. Supposing we want a meaningful relationship with our sisters and brothers of color, we must recognize why Dr. King symbolizes a vision for them. His dream for all of us is the high privilege of living in a world where Jesus' vision of the Kingdom of God is a reality. One in which society genuinely loves God with all its heart, soul, mind, and strength and loves our neighbor as ourselves.

A key component of his message was nonviolence. But unfortunately, this was a courtesy seldom extended to him. 1958, during a book signing, he was stabbed with a seven-inch letter opener, barely missing his heart. In 1974, his mother was shot and killed as she played the organ in church. The civil rights leader went to jail 29 times and was assaulted four times.

From 1957 to 1968, he served as president of the Southern Christian Leadership Conference, which worked to advance the civil rights movement in a peaceful, non-violent way. He traveled over 6 million miles during those eleven years, spoke more than 2,500 times, and wrote five books. In 1964, he received the Nobel Peace Prize. He was 35 and, at the time, the youngest to receive it.

Dr. King's faith was personal. Although imperfect, he trusted Jesus and tried to follow him no matter the cost. The night before he was murdered, he told a congregation: "Like anybody, I would like to live a long life. I've seen the Promised Land. I may not get there with you. But I want you to know tonight that we, as a people, will get to the Promised Land. And I'm happy tonight. I'm not worried about anything." Today, consider what the Promised Land will be.

_____

_____

_____

_____

January 18
Live Together as Brothers or Perish Together as Fools

If someone living in 1980 read the list of activities for the week of January 18, 2021, at the Cathedral of Saint Matthew the Apostle in Washington D.C., they almost certainly would be speechless when they read the following announcement: "Fr. John Benson shares a video message as St. Matthew proudly honors Martin Luther King Jr., a peaceful advocate for racial justice. . .In his words, 'Everybody can be great. . .because anybody can serve.' Our Social Justice Committee invites you to serve those in need." They would wonder [as do we] how a Black Baptist preacher from the South could be honored in the same Catholic Cathedral where the funerals of President John F. Kennedy and at least two Chief Justices were conducted. This sanctuary was also where Mother Teresa had worshiped, and Pope John Paul II led Mass. That same perplexed person would equally be surprised to read that Mass had been canceled for the week as the church would host the second Catholic to be elected President of the United States.

I wonder what Dr. King's thoughts would be about the future of our little experiment with democracy. Would he have reservations? I realize it is presumptuous to assume what he might think, but I believe he might be hopeful. Not because of a particular political party but for this fact. A simple invitation by the president-elect to Senators McConnell and Schumer, House Speaker Pelosi, and Minority Leader McCarthy, "Will you attend church with me?"

Indeed, Dr. King would smile when he glanced at the presiding archbishop and realized he was the first African-American Cardinal.

Dr. King said,
_____

> "We must learn to live together as brothers or perish together as fools."

_____

How are we doing with this living together as brothers and sisters vision?

_____

_____

Steven B. Angus

January 19
Prophets and "Hickory Nuts"

I have a confession that may leave you appalled. Well, appalled may be an overstatement. Surprised? Very likely. Okay. Here goes. Sometimes, when reading the Old Testament prophets, I wonder if I would be better served reading other Biblical texts. I can almost hear my seminary professors of Hebrew Scripture muttering some inappropriate remark from God's throneroom. I cannot help but wonder why most Bible reading plans assign the Prophets to be read before retiring to bed. It seems each chapter has an effect equivalent to 5 mg of Melatonin.

Yet, just when I am about to abandon the likes of Jeremiah, I stumble upon a statement that jolts me from my slumber. Fully awake, I reread the words, perhaps underlining them, as I realize why I return to these ancient voices of the Lord. They remind me of my childhood romps through the woods behind my grandparents' house. I would gather small hickory nuts, smash them with a rock, and dig out the tiny kernels. The harder I worked, the tastier the morsel. This was the "goody" I encountered in Jeremiah 9:23-24.

> *"This is what the Lord says:*
> *"Don't let the wise boast in their wisdom,*
>   *or the powerful boast in their power,*
>   *or the rich boast in their riches.*
> *But those who wish to boast*
>   *should boast in this alone:*
> *that they truly know me and understand that I am the Lord*
>   *who demonstrates unfailing love*
>   *and who brings justice and righteousness to the earth,*
> *and that I delight in these things.*
>   *I, the Lord, have spoken!"*

Before we crack it open, I want to lay it before you so you can meditate on it. What does it say to you?

_____

_____

_____

_____

January 20
Bankrupt in God's Outhouse

Did you spend some time cracking open the word of the Lord recorded in Jeremiah 9? Jeremiah wants us to know that God is speaking, not the prophet himself. So, in the first sentence, he reports, "This is what the Lord says." As the mouthpiece of God, Jeremiah reports:

Faith Bytes

> *"Don't let the wise boast in their wisdom,*
> *or the powerful boast in their power,*
> *or the rich boast in their riches."*

Although humans are often a mystery to ourselves, God knows our inclinations. From the genesis of human life in the Garden of Eden until the generation of Jeremiah, men and women have been prone to place their trust in three things above God: wisdom, strength, and riches.

Little has changed, as demonstrated by the title of Richard Foster's book, "Money, Sex and Power: The Challenge of the Disciplined Life." Just as it is today, the scholar, athlete, warrior, and financier were highly esteemed in Jeremiah's world. The danger isn't money, sex, and power per se. The peril lies in believing that by possessing them, we are invincible.

Novelist Martha Osenso wrote of one of her characters, "Edith lived in a little world bounded on the north, south, east, and west by Edith." We have visited Edith many times and in sundry places. We have observed her arrogance in the White House, the Courthouse, a warehouse, the church house, and even the Waffle House. But, unfortunately, believing everything is about us will ultimately leave us spiritually bankrupt, living in God's outhouse.

James Dobson, in his book, "The Strong-Willed Child," confessed, "Whenever I'm tempted to become self-important and authoritative, I'm reminded of what the mother whale said to her baby: 'When you get to the top and start to blow, that's when you get harpooned!'"

Consider the question, "Where does my trust reside?"

_____

_____

_____

_____

January 21
Demands a Response

In Jeremiah 9:23-24 the prophet reported:

> *This is what the Lord says:*
> *"Don't let the wise boast in their wisdom,*
> *or the powerful boast in their power,*
> *or the rich boast in their riches.*
> *But those who wish to boast*
> *should boast in this alone:*
> *that they truly know me and understand that I am the Lord*
> *who demonstrates unfailing love*
> *and who brings justice and righteousness to the earth,*
> *and that I delight in these things.*
> *I, the Lord, have spoken!* [NLT]

Steven B. Angus

Reading these words, we cannot help hearing the stern warning associated with them. Yet, the urgency of God's message is tempered only by God's gracious reminder that he delights in bringing justice and righteousness to the earth. There is no doubt that God expects—no, God demands, a response from God's people. The action is the fervent prayer that our nation, its leaders, and the church can be salt and light to our fellow citizens. Let us pray.

> "Loving God, when you began to create the heavens and the earth— the earth was without shape or form. It was dark over the deep sea. Then your breath swept over the waters and spoke light into the chaos, and you declared it good.
>
> "In our efforts to create a world in our image, we seem to be back where the darkness resides today. Yet, we realize our despair is speaking because you have blessed us. You have given us the light, and the night cannot abide in the presence of Jesus. Bless our country. Protect what you have begun. Forgive our pride. Help us trust you and honestly seek to know you so we can see that you are the Lord who demonstrates unfailing love. Replace our anguish with a hope that allows you to delight in us. In the name of Jesus, hear our prayer."

_____
_____
_____
_____

January 22
The Rooster Strut

In Jeremiah 9:23-24 the prophet reported:

> *This is what the Lord says: "Don't let the wise boast in their wisdom, or the powerful boast in their power, or the rich boast in their riches. But those who wish to boast should boast in this alone: that they truly know me and understand that I am the Lord who demonstrates unfailing love and who brings justice and righteousness to the earth, and that I delight in these things. I, the Lord, have spoken! [NLT]*

As a boy, I enjoyed visiting my grandparent's farm. However, I encountered a world vastly different from city life. Scratching in the yard around their home were my Granny's chickens. Mostly, they ignored me, but the same could not be said about me. It was well documented that if something moved, I found a way to terrorize it. My grandmother warned me not to aggravate her hens, or they might stop laying eggs. Her sternest warning was reserved for the old rooster. She said the hens were his, and he would not be happy if I bothered them. Reflecting on it a half-century later, I wonder if she said this, knowing I would take the bait and learn a lesson.

Before long, I played cowboy, and the hens were cows to be rounded up. As I gave chase, their cackling grew louder. As if he were Matt Dillion, the rooster

Faith Bytes

appeared, causing me to pull back on the reins of my stick horse. Remembering my grandmother's warning, I circled him, never breaking eye contact.

The Proverbs say four things walk with a stately stride—the lion, the male goat, a king leading his army, and a strutting rooster. I can vouch for the rooster. Like two wrestlers, we circled each other. Suddenly, he threw his shoulders back, initiated his war dance, and charged straight toward me. This prideful cowboy wasn't strutting any longer as I made my tearful retreat through the back porch screen door.

As I thought about God's message in Jeremiah 9, the lesson I learned from my dance with the rooster came to mind. I often play the same game with God. I think I can boastfully strut my stuff. Are you prone to the rooster strut? God doesn't take kindly to our boasting about anyone other than him.

_____

_____

_____

_____

January 23
Which is More Important?

Thus says the Lord: "Do not let the wise boast in their wisdom, do not let the mighty boast in their might, do not let the wealthy boast in their wealth; but let those who boast, boast in this, that they understand and know me, that I am the Lord; I act with steadfast love, justice, and righteousness in the earth, for in these things I delight, says the Lord." [Jeremiah 9:23-24, NRSVUA]

I do not understand why I feel compelled to return to this passage. Perhaps we have a consensus, as you don't understand either. And yet, "understand" may be the word in God's statement that draws me back. God is clear. We are not to boast, meaning trust in—wisdom, power, and riches. Instead, our confidence should be because his people "understand and know me." So why doesn't God just say, "Trust me?" The reason is that we will have difficulty trusting God if we do not know God. Notice God's desire is to be known and understood. The Hebrew word translated "know" is the same used in Genesis—"Adam knew Eve, and she gave birth." It implies intimacy versus intellectual knowing. Without intimacy, we cannot honestly know God. The other word God used was to understand.

In the book, "Extremely Loud & Incredibly Close" [by Jonathan Safran Foer], a father writes this letter to his son.

> *"You asked me to write you a letter, so I am writing you a letter. I do not know why I am writing you this letter or what this letter is supposed to be about. Still, I am writing it nonetheless because I love you very much and trust that you have some good purpose for having me write this letter. I hope that one day, you will have the experience of doing something you do not understand for someone you love. [signed] Your father."*

Steven B. Angus

To know God does not mean we necessarily understand God. Knowing God loves us frees us to put our trust in him. How does this affect our yearning to understand God? Although we may desire to understand it, it is enough to know he loves us.

_____
_____
_____
_____

January 24
Cringe

"Thus says the Lord: but let those who boast, boast in this, that they understand and know me, that I am the Lord; I act with steadfast love, justice, and righteousness in the earth, for in these things I delight, says the Lord." [Jeremiah 9:24, NRSV]

I cringed. However, my reaction wasn't in response to the images of a mob recklessly desecrating the "People's House." In fact, as troubling as I found the sight of a gallows, its purpose obvious, it wasn't the culprit of my reaction. When I saw it, I was horrified. Yet, my mind did not want to accept what my eyes saw. It was not the first time I had had such a response. But every time I see it displayed in an arena of violence or in the hands of those standing outside a prison applauding yet another execution, seeing it gives way to nausea.

January 6, 2021, was no different as the familiar impulse to gag gave way to another desire—to weep. I never thought I would feel shame at the sight of His name. I cringed at the name of Jesus. I wonder how Jesus feels when His name appears on a placard as a way to incite violence.

God said that "those who know me," one translation adds the word, "truly know me," understand that I act with steadfast love, justice, and righteousness in the earth, for in these things, I delight.

Love, justice, and righteousness? When I see my Savior's name used to promote hate, injustice, and evil, I wince not so much for Jesus's honor. He will have his glory and doesn't necessarily need me to defend it. Instead, I recoil, recognizing my culpability in suggesting that Jesus and those who call themselves His followers would ever condone such behavior. Whose sin is more grievous? Considering the possible answer—I cringe.

_____
_____
_____
_____

Faith Bytes

January 25
Playing Catch with God

Before the advent of video games, being an only child required I had an active imagination. Sometimes, you could play with the neighborhood kids or hang out with your cousins, but not always.

As a child, I loved sports. Fortunately, my dad spent time with me in those pursuits, something I tried to do with my own children. However, from a child's perspective, parents have the inconvenience of a job. In addition, attempting to play ball in isolation can be challenging. I could shoot hoops on the basketball goal, but attempting to catch a touchdown pass from yourself was tough, although I tried.

Baseball was my passion. I could toss a ball in the air and hit it a mile, which wasn't practical or wise when you live in a neighborhood. However, I soon learned I could play an entire baseball game using my imagination. Throwing the baseball as high and as far as I could, I would rob Willie Mayes, Johnny Bench, and Hank Aaron of a homerun. Then, I would woo the fans in the stand with a phenomenal basket catch. However, it was when I made my trademark lungeing shoetop catches that made my adoring fans cheer.

I recently read about a little boy playing in his backyard, tossing a ball in the air. A passerby, obviously unfamiliar with such youthful delights, asked the boy what he was doing. The lad replied, "I am playing a game of catch with God. I throw the ball up, and he throws it back." I wish I could say I was that boy, but I wasn't, and I doubt you were either. However, it isn't too late to see God interacting with us in whatever we do today. "It's a drive, way back. . ."

_____

_____

_____

January 26
The Chase

Jean-Baptiste Alphonse Karr (1808–1890) was a French novelist who had some success as a nineteenth-century romance novelist. As a former teacher, those who knew him stated that he loved promoting education reform and going fishing. He sounds like someone we could enjoy spending time with on the banks of a stream, casting a line, and discussing how to encourage children to read. Aside from these unremarkable details, he is credited for coining a proverb stated by many without noting the source. Indeed, you have heard and probably said, "The more things change, the more they stay the same." The next time you are inclined to make such a daring declaration, you will know to whom to assign credit.

The writer of the Letter to the Colossians advised:

> *"And now, just as you accepted Christ Jesus as your Lord, you must continue to follow him. Let your roots grow down into him, and let your lives be built on him. Then your faith will grow strong in the truth you were taught, and you will overflow with thankfulness.*
>
> *"Don't let anyone capture you with empty philosophies and high-sounding nonsense that come from human thinking and from the spiritual powers of this world rather than from Christ. [2:6-8 NLT]*

This passage affirms Karr's pronouncement, reminding us that human nature is powerful. Whether living in the year 56, 877, 1959, or 2022, we cannot help ourselves. We tend to discard what we have to chase greener grass or the novel idea. Christians and Churches are not immune. It isn't that we shouldn't learn from discoveries, but doing so shouldn't be, as they used to say, "at the cost of giving away the entire store." Perhaps you recall the story of Jacob and his older brother Esau. The elder traded his birthright for a bowl of soup. Hearing Paul's words, I wonder, are we making such a trade? Are we proving Karr correct that "the more things change, the more they stay the same?"

_____
_____
_____
_____

January 27
Worry? or Pray?

Anxiety. It is real. Someone who says otherwise is not only uninformed but lacks empathy. So, how do I handle anxiety? To be honest, not very well. When I am overwhelmed, I often read Philippians 4:4-7. I have memorized it and will often say it as a prayer—focusing on one phrase at a time as if it were a prayer that I breathe in and out. Perhaps you will want to mark these words in your Bible or write them on a notecard to refer to them instantly. Let this be our prayer—

> *"Always be full of joy in the Lord. I say it again—rejoice! Let everyone see that you are considerate in all you do. Remember, the Lord is coming soon. Don't worry about anything; instead, pray about everything. Tell God what you need, and thank him for all he has done. Then you will experience God's peace, which exceeds anything we can understand. His peace will guard your hearts and minds as you live in Christ Jesus."*

_____
_____
_____
_____

Faith Bytes

January 28
You Have God's Number

The pastor gathered the children around her for the weekly Sunday morning children's sermon. She had with her a telephone to illustrate the idea of prayer. She began, "We talk to people on the telephone, but we don't see them on the other end of the line, do we?" The children nodded their heads. "Well, talking to God is like talking on the telephone. God is on the other end, but we can't see him. However, we can be sure of one thing: He always listens." Then, one of the youngsters piped up and asked, "What's his number?"

Don't you love how children think concretely? We don't need a telephone number to get through to God. We just need to know Jesus.

One of the best-loved hymns of the church, which has been sung at many Easter Sunrise services, reminds us--

> *He speaks, and the sound of His voice*
> *Is so sweet the birds hush their singing*
> *And the melody that He gave to me*
> *Within my heart is ringing*
> *And he walks with me*
> *And he talks with me [In the Garden.]*

Why not take the next sixty seconds and just speak to him?

_____
_____
_____
_____

January 29
Choose Carefully

The one-line zinger moves the laughter gauge on the sitcom. Political debates and elections are decided by them. Even if they aren't true, we arm our children with them as a defense against the bully. Do Sticks and stones may break my bones, but words will never hurt me sound familiar?

The Proverbs would lose all credibility if they did not address the most potent instrument in society—words. They have launched wars, devastated marriages, ended friendships, destroyed business relationships, guided the stock market, split churches, and set the course of a child's life. This is power. The proper use of words dominants Proverbs. Over 150 times, it uses terms such as tongue, lips, and speech. Substantial. Here is a sampling—

> *"You have been trapped by what you said, ensnared by the words of your mouth." Proverbs 6:2 (NIV)*

Steven B. Angus

> *"Too much talk leads to sin. Be sensible and keep your mouth shut." Proverbs 10:19 (NLT)*
> *"Fools' words get them into constant quarrels." Proverbs 18:6 (NLT)*

Such statements cause us to smell, even taste, the fermentation of rotting apples. Proverbs offers tasty Apples of Gold for the wise person who draws near to God.

> *Proverbs 12:25 "An anxious heart weighs a man down, but a kind word cheers him up."*
> *Proverbs 15:4 says, "The tongue that brings healing is a tree of life."*
> *Proverbs 15:23 says, "A man finds joy in giving an apt reply, and how good is a timely word!"*
> *Proverbs 16:24 says, "Pleasant words are like a honeycomb, sweet to the soul and health to the body."*

The wise person recognizes the power of a word, as the Proverbs states: The tongue can bring death or life. Proverbs 18:21 (NLT)

The Wise person will choose their words carefully.

_____
_____
_____
_____

January 30
Your First and Greatest Care

As a gift for Christmas, I received an ancestry DNA test that promises to help chart my genetic roots. With a family tree filled with Angus and McGee, I expect the arrows on the genetic compass will point due north of England. It is interesting how people will tell me their clan affiliation by hearing the name Angus. As a proud Scot, I will not be outdone. I casually point out that the surname Angus predates the clan system. In other words, my ancestors wore plaid skirts 200 years before it was fashionable.

I mention this after coming across a statement in a letter written on this date in 1839 by a 25-year-old Church of Scotland pastor. His words will resonate with those who love the mountains and rolling hills while craving the Holy Spirit. This is what he wrote.

> *"God feeds the wildflowers on the lonely mountainside without the help of man, and they are as fresh and lovely as those that are daily watched over in our gardens. So God can feed his own planted*

ones without the help of man, by the secret falling dew of His Spirit."

Hearing Rev. Robert Murray M'Cheyne's statement crafted four years before his death, we understand how he transformed a neglected congregation into crowds of over a thousand in just a few years. Yet, our thoughts betray the intent of his words. He understood that only the Holy Spirit could change a life.

In another letter, McCheyne delivered words he must have intended for us. He wrote: "Your own soul is your first and greatest care. It is not great talents God blesses so much as great likeness to Jesus. A word spoken...[when] your heart [is] full of God's Spirit, is worth ten thousand words spoken in unbelief and sin."

January 31
Spurgeon, Not Sturgeon

A Reverend Charles Spurgeon bobblehead is staring at me from across my desk. Today, January 31, marks the death anniversary of the clergyman often referred to as "the prince of preachers." He was born in Essex, England, on June 19, 1834, the first of seventeen children.

Interestingly, I have a 75-pound puppy I named Spurgeon. One of my daughters thought it odd I called him after a fish—sturgeon. Some assume my fondness for the renowned Baptist preacher is a carryover from my upbringing in that denomination. I will always be grateful for the church that led me to Jesus, licensed me to preach at 13, and, like Charles Spurgeon, permitted me to be a pastor at 17. However, I am quick to point out that I have been a Methodist pastor for almost half a century. Whereas I was a Baptist who became a Methodist, Spurgeon [not my dog] was converted to faith in a Methodist Church and later became a Baptist.

Only recently have I come to appreciate Charles Spurgeon. Granted, we would disagree on specific doctrinal matters. Nevertheless, I admire his gifts as a preacher and prolific author. There are probably more Spurgeon books in the world than by any other preacher. He was not afraid to use his pulpit to address social concerns such as the need for childcare and workplace reform. His sermons, popular in the United States, were canceled in southern newspapers because of his outspoken comments against slavery.

However, he had his personal demons. During an era lacking an understanding of mental health issues, he suffered debilitating anxiety and depression that drove him to a darkened bedroom for months. In this regard, he has been an inspiration for me.

Spurgeon had profound insights into what it means to be a vital congregation, which I will mention in the coming days. But for today, identify your Spiritual mentors and, in addition to thanking God for them, whether they are living or deceased, write them a note of gratitude.

_____
_____
_____
_____

Steven B. Angus

FEBRUARY

February 1
To Live Again

Before he was twenty, Charles Spurgeon had preached over six hundred times. At his death, he had been the pastor of the 5,600-seat Metropolitan Tabernacle in London for thirty-eight years. During his tenure, a pastor's college was founded, an orphanage was built, and two hundred new churches were established. In addition, he personally baptized 15,000 new Christians, wrote more than 150 books, and delivered nearly 3,600 sermons. [Each can be read at no cost on The Spurgeon Center website at spurgeon.org.]

Allow me to reach into this great reservoir of material to highlight one sermon delivered on November 11, 1856. It is not listed as one of his most remarkable works, and I am uncertain what effect it had on his congregation. However, 170 years later, I believe it is relevant for the church and those longing to experience vitality in our faith. The title alone warrants our attention. It captures the hunger many are experiencing. The title is "Spiritual Revival, the Want of the Church." The scripture reference is Habakkuk 3:2, which says: "O LORD, revive Your work."

Suppose we are yearning for a life with Jesus that has vitality. In that case, we must consider the word prominent in the sermon title and scripture text: revive.

We drastically undermine its significance by associating revival with a guest speaker and potluck dinners. Instead, we must imagine Lazarus, the four-day dead Lazarus, all decked out in his mummy best. Except, it isn't Lazarus who is lying in the family crypt. Instead, it is you and me. We are spiritually dead. "Vive" means life. "Re" means again. Revive means to live again. We want this, and only the Lord can make it happen. Revival is hearing your name called with the invitation, "Come forth." Visualize what it will be like for you to live again.

Steven B. Angus

February 2
God, I want to live again!

Your desire for a vibrant relationship with Jesus led you to open this book. Habakkuk 3:2 states, "O LORD, revive Your work."

Habakkuk and Charles Spurgeon use a word that has fallen on hard times. Revival for many is associated with "fire and brimstone" sermons followed by forty-eleven stanzas of the hymn "Just As I Am" until the sweetest saint in the church comes forward to "rededicate" her life.

Revive, like resurrection, isn't a bad word. Revival is the George Bailey believer, looking across his life's turbulent waters, pleading with God—"I want to live again!" We are prone to overlook the obvious: for there to be life again, there must have been life to begin with. Revival is about Christians being resuscitated.

In his sermon, "Spiritual Revival, The Need of the Church," Charles Spurgeon said there will be "groaning times [for] the Christian who needs revival." With yearning tears, he will remember how it felt to be loved with God's everlasting love. When a Christian can remember such love, the seeds of revival are sown. According to Spurgeon, this lukewarm disciple will say:

> "Such was my experience once, but those happy days are gone. My sun has set, and those stars which once lit up my darkness are all quenched. Oh, that I might again behold my Lord! Oh, that I might once more see His face! Oh, for those sweet visits from on high!"

If we are Christian, and this is our condition, according to Spurgeon, "[we] will sit down and weep by the rivers of Babylon, [we] will mourn when [we] remember. . .when the Lord was precious to [us]. . .when He laid bare His heart and. . .fill[ed] our heart with the fullness of His love. Such times will be groaning times when you remember."

Take time to remember. Where does it lead you?

Faith Bytes

February 3
Which Five Words?

We share a malady that seems more pronounced among children and men. Perhaps the female reader quips, "Is there a difference?" As a parent, we long for the day when our children can do things for themselves. Yet, when that toddler insists, "I can do it myself," when tying her shoe, we look at the clock and realize we are late for work; we understand the adage, "Be careful what you wish for." Like my fellow cavemen, I have pounded my chest and asked, "Why pay someone? How difficult can it be?"

We tend to apply the same rationale to our spiritual selves. We recognize our need for revival, revitalization, resuscitation, renewal, resurrection--whichever R-word we choose. Still, we are determined to do it ourselves and manipulate our souls as if they were merely stubborn shoestrings.

Apparently, Charles Spurgeon understood our tendencies. Concerning Spiritual Revival, he said when we recognize our need for it, we usually say, "I intend to set to work this very afternoon…to revive my soul." He warns we will inevitably break such resolutions, making our condition worse. He compares such an effort to a wounded soldier who has lost an arm trying to repair it.

Instead of saying, "I will revive myself," do nothing until you call God for help, pleading, "O Lord, revive Your work." Here, Spurgeon understood work not as labor but as the person praying. He said, "Remember, He that first made you must keep you alive. And He that has kept you alive can alone impart more life to you! Begin, then, by humbling yourself–giving up all hope of reviving yourself as a Christian! [Instead] say, "O Lord, what I cannot do, You do! O Lord, revive Your work!"

Today, instead of saying, "I can do it myself," try this five-word prayer—O Lord, revive Your work!

_____

_____

_____

_____

February 4
The Conversation Deficiency

Charles Spurgeon is considered the best preacher of his generation. This repute earned him the title of "The Prince of Preachers." His sermon, "Spiritual Revival, The Need of the Church," was preached almost 175 years ago. Despite its nearly 7000 words, it could have been spoken as recently as this past Sunday. But, of course, this is the trait of all great preaching.

A disciple of Jesus will always long for a relationship with him that is vital and fresh. They will want to be part of a church with the same desire. Spurgeon indicates that although someone's manner may be consistent with what is

Steven B. Angus

considered Christian, there is an area that may raise serious doubts. This deficiency demonstrates that Spiritual Revival is needed.

Spurgeon fearlessly asks us to observe the conversation of some who say they are Christians. He says we could live with someone for a year and never tire of their religion by how seldom we hear about it. He concludes, "They scarcely mention the name of Jesus Christ at all. [Except] On a Sabbath afternoon, [when] all the ministers are talked over and faults discussed. Then, a conversation takes place, which they call religious because it concerns religious places and Christian people." Then he asked, do they ever —"Talk of all he [Jesus] did, and said, And suffered for us here below; The path he marked for us to tread, And what he's doing for us now?"

Borrowing a question from his Methodist rearing, Spurgeon asks, how often have we inquired of one another, "Friend, how does your soul prosper?" He concludes that our faith lacks vitality due to how little we speak about Jesus. Share your faith if you hope to experience renewed energy in your walk with Jesus.

February 5
Let Us Plead with God

The text for Charles Spurgeon's sermon, Spiritual Revival—The Need of the Church, was Habakkuk 3:2-- "Oh LORD, revive your work." The Prince of Preachers concluded his message delivered in 1856 this way.

> "Others of you frequently cry, 'The Church needs reviving.' Let me tell you, instead of grumbling at your minister, instead of finding fault with the different parts of the Church, to cry, 'Oh Lord, revive your work.'

> "One says, 'Oh, that we had another minister! Oh, that we had another kind of worship! Oh, that we had a different kind of preaching!' As if that were all, my prayer is, 'Oh, that the Lord would come into the hearts of the men [and women] you have! Oh, that he would make the forms you use full of power!' You do not need fresh ways or new machinery; you need life in those that you have. There is an engine on the railway, but the train will not move. 'Bring another engine,' one says, 'and another, and another.' The engines are brought, but the train does not move. Light the fire and get up steam. That is what you need, not more engines. We do not need new ministers, plans, or ways. . . we only need life and fire in those we have. It is not a new man [or woman] who is needed; it is the life of God in him. Do not be crying out for something new; it will no more succeed by itself than what you have. Cry, 'Oh Lord, revive your work.'"

Let us ask God for it and plead with him for it. . .May God grant it, for Christ's sake! Amen. Consider making this Prayer—"Lord, revive your work."

Faith Bytes

February 6
Good Things in the Midst of Turmoil

I received a delightful note from a friend. As she reflected on the uncertainty in our world, she wrote, "There is some good in everything, even as we doubt. Thank God for good things in the midst of this turmoil. I believe this will be a strengthening of faith." Reflecting on her hopeful words, I remembered an unexpected moment demonstrating what she meant.

Early in 2021, Craig Melvin, a television host on MSNBC, was interviewing pastor Bishop T.D. Jakes about the COVID19 crisis. Melvin abruptly posed a surprising question. He said, "For folks who [weren't] able to get to church yesterday," he paused briefly, "I've never actually done this on the air. Can you lead us in prayer for 30 seconds?" Jakes responded affirmatively and proceeded to offer the following invocation:

> "Our Father and our God, we bow our heads to you in humility, understanding that we are not competent in and of ourselves to handle this kind of global calamity. We look to you, Lord, to be the source, the strength, the help, the light that we need, strengthen our first responders, strengthen even our broadcast people, strengthen all of us whose lives have been devastated and disrupted, and give us the peace that passes all understanding. In Christ's name, we pray, Amen."

To my pen pal and those like her—I also believe seasons of turmoil are occasions when our faith can be strengthened. Perhaps Craig Melvin recognized the needed first step—a willingness to ask for prayer.

February 7
Start Unloading—Now!

A pastor was visiting a member of her congregation who had spent many years caring for her father. Shortly after he passed away, her husband became ill. Now, she cared for him in ways most could never comprehend. Most of her adult life had been devoted to caring for those sick. The pastor told her friend during their visit, "You have been a good daughter and wife. You took care of your father, and the tenderness with which you watch over your husband is truly amazing. You have done very well bearing this burden." After a moment, the woman replied, "I loved my father. And I love my husband. I never thought of it as a burden."

Love enables us to do amazing things. So why, then, do we sometimes believe that God would see meeting our needs and comforting us when we are afraid as a burden? The Psalmist sang in Psalms 55:22: "Give your burdens to the Lord, and he will take care of you. He will not permit the godly to slip and fall." In 1 Peter 5:5-7, we are encouraged to "dress ourselves in humility. . .Give God all your worries and cares, for he cares about you."

If we believe that Jesus loved us enough to die for us, how could we think he would ever consider our needs as burdensome? My suggestion? Stop the delay. Start unloading them—Now!

_____

_____

_____

February 8
The One Who Loves Us Perfectly

How are you doing? Are you okay? Could it be that you are afraid? To be frightened isn't bad. It's how we choose to respond. Only a foolish person claims never to be fearful.

Martin Niemoller was a German pastor who heroically opposed Adolf Hitler. As a young man, he was part of a group of church leaders who met with Hitler. Niemoller stood at the back of the room, watching and listening. He didn't say a word. When he went home, his wife asked him what he had learned that day. Martin replied, "I discovered that Hitler is a terribly frightened man. I believe him to be a great coward."

Days later, Niemoller contradicted the Fuehrer during a public meeting. That evening, the secret police raided his home. A few days later, a bomb exploded, setting his house on fire. Friends offered to smuggle him out of the country. He declined and eventually spent more than seven years in prison.

Fear can cause us to react in harmful, injurious ways or propel us to do what needs to be done. Niemoller stated that what guided him were these words from Joshua 1:9: "Be strong and of good courage: be not frightened, neither be dismayed. For the Lord your God is with you wherever you go."

When we are afraid, and only a fool has no fear, let us remember that perfect love casts out fear. Lean into Jesus, who loves us perfectly.

_____

_____

_____

_____

Faith Bytes

February 9
Jesus and Germs!

A pastor's son was outside playing, doing everything boys do. There wasn't a tree he had not climbed or a creek without an overturned rock in his effort to catch a crawdad. Tired of these adventures, he sat on his swing set and went as high as he could, then jumped out, hoping to catch a branch on a nearby tree. His constant companion was his loyal Border Collie, who was always up for a tussle while rolling on the well-worn lawn. Finally, his mother opened the back door and called the young explorer to dinner.

As the family gathered at the table and the blessing was about to be offered, his mother looked at him and said, "Young man, let me see your hands." There was some rubbing of his hands on his jeans before he held them up. His mother looked at them and asked, "How many times do I have to tell you that you must wash your hands before you eat? When your hands are dirty, they have germs, and you could get sick. After we say the blessing, I want you to march back into the bathroom and wash your hands." Following the prayer, the little boy headed towards the bathroom sink. Then he stopped, turned to Mom, and said, "Jesus and germs! Jesus and germs! That's all I hear around here, and I haven't seen either of them."

Who can dispute such logic, especially when it has merit? So perhaps we should just smile and keep washing our hands. As the water cleanses and refreshes, we may remember that these hands can help someone see Jesus.

_____

_____

_____

_____

February 10
The Package

Super Bowl Sunday is no longer just about a football game. It is an opportunity to get together with friends and family to enjoy hot wings and check out the television commercials. Many will tune in, uncertain of the teams playing, just to watch the ads.

Do you have a favorite Super Bowl commercial? One year, FedEx ran a commercial that spoofed the movie, "Castaway." Tom Hanks played a FedEx worker whose company plane went down, stranding him on a desert island for years. In the commercial, a FedEx employee, looking like the bedraggled Hanks in the movie, goes up to the door of a suburban home with a package. When a woman comes to the door, he explains that he survived five years on a deserted island, and during that whole time, he kept this package to deliver it to her. She gives a simple "Thank you." Curious about the package he has been protecting for years, he asks, "If I may ask, what was in that package?" She opens it and reports, "Oh, nothing, really. Just a satellite telephone, a global positioning device, a compass, a water purifier, and seeds."

Like the contents in the package, God has provided the resources to help us grow in our relationship with God. You can probably name some of them with ease. The question becomes, will we open the package?

___

February 11
Don't Forget Your Camera!

Do you recall encountering something so unique that you instinctively reached for your cell phone to snap a photograph, only to realize you left it on the kitchen table? During those occasions, we want a memento to help us relive the experience. Or, more likely, we realize what we have witnessed is so improbable we felt the need for visual proof to present to all nay-sayers. Such was the case when a young girl listened attentively as her older sister told her a bedtime story. The tale began with the expected, "Once upon a time."

Once upon a time, a beautiful princess had a beautiful golden ball. Unfortunately, one day, the golden ball fell into the well. But since this is a fairy tale, along came an ugly frog who retrieved it for her. The lovely princess was so grateful she took the toad with her to her room in the palace. During the night, the ugly frog turned into a handsome prince.

At this point in the story, the little girl begins to get a skeptical look on her face. "What is wrong," her sister asked. "Don't you believe the story?" The little girl said, "No! I don't believe it. And I don't think the princess's mother believed it either!"

Matthew 17:1-9 relates such an experience for three of Jesus's disciples who joined him on a Mountian. When something spectacular occurred, having forgotten to bring their electronic devices to capture it, Peter suggested building three monuments to commemorate the occasion. But, unfortunately, if they had difficulty believing what they had seen with their own eyes, how could they expect anyone else to do so?

The event is known as The Transfiguration. And frankly, like the little girl and the three dumbfounded disciples, we also find it hard to believe. And yet, here it is. It was such a critical moment in the life of Jesus that the church assigned an annual day to remember it called "Transfiguration Sunday."

I encourage you to read Matthew 17:1-9 and ponder—Why do you suppose this event is in the Bible? Better still, what could it possibly have to do with us? Is Jesus trying to reveal something unbelievable to you?

Faith Bytes

February 12
The Purple Book

When considering a name for our youngest daughter, it did not take long to settle on Lydia. It wasn't chosen because it was a family name; instead, it was our admiration for the significant leader in the New Testament Church mentioned in Acts 16. Lydia of Thyatira was bold in her faith. Still, she also understood how to thrive in a male-dominated world. She owned and operated a business as a seller of purple fabrics. Needless to say, purple became my favorite color. Recently, my appreciation of this color was solidified.

In a college library in Nashville, Tennessee, is a book bound in purple and gold trim. I would love to spend a few hours reading it. Perhaps you are curious why I mention a purple college library book in a city with almost 30 college and university libraries. The purple book is located at Fisk University.

The book was presented to the University with the following statement.

> *"While all others. . .are offering their tribute of respect to you, we cannot omit suitable manifestation of ours. . .Towards you, sir, our hearts will ever be warm with gratitude. We come to present to you this copy of the Holy Scriptures as a token of respect for your active participation in the furtherance of our race. The loyal colored people of this country everywhere will remember you at the Throne of Divine Grace. May the King Eternal . . . protect and keep you, and when you pass from this world to that of eternity, may you be borne to the bosom of your Savior and your God."*

The Purple Bible is one of six that belonged to President Lincoln. He is often quoted as saying the following, but the context above is seldom mentioned. The president responded: "In regard to this Great Book, I have but to say, it is the best gift God has given to man . . .All the good the Savior gave to the world was communicated through this book...All things most desirable for man's welfare, here and hereafter, are to be found portrayed in it."

It was on this date in 1809 that Abraham Lincoln was born. Let us give thanks for the man and for the Purple Book.

Steven B. Angus

February 13
An Invitation to observe a Holy Lent

The weather this time of year can be frustrating. If we have the luxury of remaining in our warm homes, the worst days aren't those when the falling fluffy flakes lay a carpet of snow. No, the worst days are the dreary, overcast ones when we look across a field, and all we see is an ashen landscape. The nasty days capture the weightiness of the Christian season of Lent.

Lent is a time when Christians look inward and acknowledge their sins. However, this does not close the matter as the individual publicly declares their intent to change. Historically, they demonstrated their penance by wearing sackcloths and pouring ashes on their heads, a practice adapted from their Jewish ancestors. Today, this practice has been altered so that ashes are applied to the forehead, marking the beginning of forty days of self-examination in preparation for Easter. This action occurs on the first day of Lent, Ash Wednesday. An Ash Wednesday Service often includes an invitation such as this:

> "Dear brothers and sisters in Christ: The early Christians observed with great devotion the days of our Lord's passion and resurrection, and it became the custom of the Church that before the Easter celebration, there should be a forty-day season of spiritual preparation.

> "It was also a time when persons who had committed serious sins and had separated themselves from the community of faith were reconciled by penitence and forgiveness and restored to participation in the life of the Church.

> "In this way, the whole congregation was reminded of the mercy and forgiveness proclaimed in the gospel of Jesus Christ and the need we all have to renew our faith."

The following invitation is given, which I now extend to you: "I invite you, therefore, in the name of the Church, to observe a holy Lent: by self-examination and repentance; by prayer, fasting, and self-denial; and by reading and meditating on God's Holy Word."

_____

_____

_____

_____

February 14
"Love, Your Valentine"

I listened intently as the anchorwoman said, "If you are uncertain how to celebrate Valentine's Day with your loved one, you may want to check out Haunted Love." Suddenly, a masked Count Dracula appeared and described a zombie high school dance room and a shop of horrors filled with clowns. Viewers

Faith Bytes

were informed that a wine bar would be available for those needing liquid courage.

I always thought love could be scary. But, before we dismiss "Haunted Love," Halloween has . . . I mean, Valentine's Day has had some eerie practices associated with this day. During the Middle Ages, on Valentine's Day Eve, one superstition required a girl of marrying age to walk alone through a cemetery. As she sang, she would scatter a handful of seeds. Then, presto! Like a Bob Ross Chia plant, her true love would appear and follow her home like a stalker. So now we know the origins of the question: "Where did you dig him up?"

The identity of St. Valentine is a bit hazy, although he is thought to have existed. The most common legends are from the third century about a priest who defied the Roman Emperor's ban on marriages, thus exempting young men from military service. He was eventually arrested. He wrote letters to his flock from his prison cell, signing them, "Love, your Valentine." This is probably folklore. What does seem likely was that the Emperor summoned the priest and demanded that he convert to paganism or die. The priest refused and, for good measure, attempted to convert the Emperor to Christianity. This was Valentine's final act of love before facing an executioner's ax.

Although we associate expressions of love with cards and flowers, the legend of St. Valentine reminds us—love is more. Above all else, love is sacrificial.

_____
_____
_____
_____

February 15
Maria, Reba, and Jesus

We have heard, "Love isn't love until you give it away." The words rolled off our lips as if quoting a Hallmark card. Many music enthusiasts attribute the line to Oscar Hammerstein from the original stage version of "The Sound of Music." Although, the lyrics did not make it into the movie that starred Julie Andrews. The most memorable stanza went:

A bell's not a bell 'til you ring it –
A song's not a song 'til you sing it –
Love in your heart wasn't put there to stay –
Love isn't love 'til you give it away!"

Some years later, Reba McEntire recorded a song written by Timmy Tappan and Don Roth. The chorus stated:

Love isn't love till you give it away
Love isn't love till it's free
The love in your heart
Wasn't put there to stay

Steven B. Angus

Oh love isn't love till you give it away
Cause love can't survive
When it's hidden inside
And love was meant to be shared.

Whether sung by Hammerstein's Maria or Country's Reba, the words are accurate. However, long before either sang about love, Jesus said: "I give you a new commandment: Love each other. Just as I have loved you, so you also must love each other. This is how everyone will know that you are my disciples, when you love each other." [John 13:34-35, CEB]

We don't have to wait until Valentine's Day to share the love of Christ. So, how will you give it away today?

_____

_____

_____

_____

February 16
Thirty-five Valentines

Chad was a shy, quiet young fella. His mother was surprised when he came home from school, saying he would like to make a Valentine for everyone in his class. Her heart also sank. She had seen the neighborhood children as they walked home from school. As they laughed and talked, Chad lagged behind and was never included. Nevertheless, she decided to go along with her son. She purchased the paper, glue, and crayons and watched for three nights as Chad painstakingly made thirty-five valentines.

When Valentine's Day arrived, Chad carefully stacked the homemade cards, put them in a bag, and bolted out the door. As his mom nervously waited for him to get home from school, she decided to bake his favorite cookies and serve them warm with a cool glass of milk. She knew he would be disappointed, and maybe that would ease the pain a little. It hurt her to think he wouldn't get many valentines- perhaps none.

Just as she placed the cookies and milk on the table, she heard the children outside and looked out the window. Sure enough, they came, laughing and having the best time. And, as always, there was Chad in the rear. He walked a little faster than usual. She fully expected him to burst into tears when he got inside. His arms were empty, and she choked back the tears. She quickly said, "I have some warm cookies and milk for you." But Chad hardly heard her words. He just marched right on by, and all he could say was: "Not a one. Not a one." Her heart sank. And then, with face aglow, he added, "I didn't forget a one, not a single one!"

So, it is when God controls a servant's mind. As never before, we realize life's greatest joy is giving God's love away. Love is a gift given freely, without any

Faith Bytes

expectation of return. God demonstrated that kind of Love when he gave the world Jesus. Let us love the way that God loved us!

February 17
A Prayer for Lent

*O God, grant that we may be sensitive to Your presence in our lives;
by taking time to pause for reflection and remembrance.*

*Lord Jesus, may we use the freedom You have given us;
to liberate those with burdens too heavy to bear.*

*During this Lenten season, O God,
You enlighten us to walk in truth and in love;
lead us to share the blessings we receive from You.*

*Creator God, enkindle within our hearts;
a cheerfulness of spirit as we approach each day.*

*O Christ, Lent is the season to renew our lives;
may Your Spirit help and guide us.*

*Lord Jesus, You count as done to You all that we do for others;
help us to love others as You love them.*

*Christ Jesus, You are the Way, the Truth, and the Life;
come to the aid of those searching for meaning in life.*

*God of mercy,
as we journey through this season of Lent,
opening ourselves to Your grace,
we ask that You will guide us into a true change of heart
and reorientation of our lives.
We ask this in the name of Jesus, our Brother and Savior,
who showed us how to live and to love. Amen.*

— posted on A Prayer During Lent, on the Christian Brothers of the Midwest website. http://www.cbmidwest.org/

Steven B. Angus

February 18
You Must First Go Down

The appeal of the yo-yo seems to go up and down. I vividly recall playing with one during my childhood when it was a national fad. I remember going to the mall and purchasing an authentic Sisler yo-yo signed by the "world champion," who happened to be the salesman. And he was good! I marveled at the way he "walked the dog," "rocked the baby," and took the slender yo-yo on a "trip around the world." With practice, I finally mastered some of his tricks and razzle-dazzled my classmates. Eventually, I proudly added my autographed yo-yo to the treasures stored in my cigar box. I truly wanted to become a yo-yo champion. However, I soon learned that before I could do any of the fantastic tricks, I had to master the basic up and down motion.

Have you noticed that when it comes to faith, it can seem like a yo-yo? It's up and down, up and down, and then it gets tangled like the string on a yo-yo. Perhaps this is why the Bible is an entire Who's Who of those who encountered tangles, and then, as we watch, they turned into knots. The good news is that many of them turned out okay. Those knots worked their way out.

May your days have more ups than downs! However, remember this. To come up, you must first go down.

_____

_____

_____

_____

February 19
A Prayer for Our President

Early on January 26, 1949, the Presbyterian minister and Chaplain of the United States Senate, Peter Marshall, died at forty-six. He had been Chaplain only two years. His widow, Catherine, told his story in the book "A Man Called Peter," which eventually was made into a movie. She reported that his longest prayer before the Senate lasted two minutes. His briefest thirty-six words. Still, legislators would arrive early to hear them. His first prayer before the Senate began:

> "O Lord our God, even at this moment [as] we come blundering into Thy presence...haunted by memories of duties unperformed, promptings disobeyed, and beckonings ignored. Opportunities to be kind knocked on the door of our hearts and went weeping away." [January 4, 1947]

The third Monday in February is a federal holiday in honor of those who have served as President of the United States. Dr. Marshall offered this prayer for then-President Harry Truman during his tenure as Senate Chaplain. It can be a model as we pray for our current President and all elected to civil service.

Faith Bytes

"We pray, Lord Jesus, for our President. We are deeply concerned that he may know the will of God and that he may have the spiritual courage and grace to follow it. Deliver him, we pray, from all selfish considerations. Lift him above the claims of politics. Fill him with the Spirit of God that shall make him fearless to seek, to know, to do the right. Save him from the friends who, in the name of politics or even friendship, would persuade him from that holy path.

"Strengthen and empower his advisers. Bring them, too, to their knees in prayer.

May their example and influence spread that we, in these United States, may yet have a government of men who know Thee, the Almighty God, as their Friend and who place Thy will first in their lives as well in their prayers . . . through Jesus Christ, our Lord. Amen."

_____
_____
_____
_____

February 20
Sing a Song, Any Song to Jesus

There's within my heart a melody
Jesus whispers sweet and low,
"Fear not I am with thee,
Peace, be still In all of life's ebb and flow."
Jesus, Jesus, Jesus,
Sweetest name I know
Fills my every longing,
Keeps me singing as I go.

When you feel discouraged to the point that you cannot pray, what do you do? When I am disheartened, I have found that singing is the best medicine. When we recall the most meaningful hymns, they generally share this trait: they were born out of hardship, even tragedy. The African-American spirituals provided encouragement to those who struggled to be hopeful. Although unplanned, it isn't surprising that the Book of Psalms is located in the middle of the Bible, suggesting that singing is central to faith and hopefulness.

The hymn "There's Within My Heart a Melody" is seldom sung without the singer feeling encouraged. The lyrics and tune were written by Luther B. Bridgers shortly after his wife and three boys died in a house fire. Are you feeling a little discouraged? Then, sing a song, any song, to Jesus.

Steven B. Angus

Jesus, Jesus, Jesus,
Sweetest name I know
Fills my every longing,
Keeps me singing as I go.

February 21
When We See Only Trouble and Sorrow

Got trouble? How about sorrow? If these words describe how you feel, then Psalm 116:3-5 are intended for you. The hymn writer sang,

"I saw only trouble and sorrow.
Then I called on the name of the Lord:
Please, Lord, save me!

How kind the Lord is! How good he is!
So merciful, this God of ours!" [Psalm 116:3b-5, NLT]

When I read the Psalmist's prayer, "Please, Lord, save me!" I remember an experience that occurred when I was seventeen. I was returning home from a preaching engagement. I came upon a curve, probably going faster than I should. My vehicle went into the gravel, and suddenly I was airborne. My '73 Nova spun as fast as a bullet fired from a revolver. My body felt like a slow-motion scene from The Matrix as my hands gripped the stirring wheel tightly. I prayed an abbreviated form of the Psalmist prayer, saying, "Lord, save me!" My car was totaled; however, I walked away without a bruise. I can relate to John Wesley's analogy of being "a brand plucked from the fire." Sometimes, our prayers must be to the point.

Got troubles? Don't be afraid to shoot those bullet prayers to God. God is eager to affirm his kindness, goodness, and mercy!

Faith Bytes

February 22
Overcoming Flabby Faith

God said, "Unless your faith is firm, I cannot make you stand firm." [Isaiah 7:9] Would you describe your faith as firm or flabby? What are you doing to make it stronger—healthier? Like unused muscles, a dormant faith will weaken and eventually lose its tone. Unless faith is exercised, it will cease being firm and become flabby.

Sometimes, flabby faith can pass itself off as firm faith. It can be like an out-of-shape football player who can play a few downs but quickly folds. It can be like the boxer, who can go one or two rounds, and then it's knockout time.

How do we strengthen and maintain a firm faith? How do we shed the flab for the fabulous? As a Rocky Balboa fan, I recall when Apollo Creed explained to Rocky why he had experienced a devastating defeat. He said, "You forgot where you came from. You got to go back and remember where you came from—It's the eye of the Tiger, Rock."

God said, "Unless your faith is firm, I cannot make you stand firm." God desires that we have faith in Him. God wants us to place our trust in Him. It is up to us to exercise it.

_____

_____

_____

_____

February 23
A Rendezvous with God

It is called "the graveyard shift" for a reason. While attending college and serving as a part-time pastor, there were occasions when I found it necessary to work while others slept. The nights can seem long. Your mind and body scream, "Take me to bed, you silly man!" Then came the sunrise, and you could hear the birds singing as if they were celestial midwives promising the birth of a new day. Even with heavy eyes, the toil of blackness slowly fades to be replaced by the fresh and vibrant.

I do not know if the Prophet Hosea ever worked the graveyard shift, but he did grasp the concept of newness that comes in the presence of God. In Hosea 6:2-3, he said:

> "In just a short time, he will restore us so that we may live in his presence.
> Oh, that we might know the Lord! Let us press on to know him.
> He will respond to us as surely as the arrival of dawn or the coming of rains in early spring."

For Hosea, for Christians, this newness is "knowing God." When we enter the presence of God, it is like the arrival of dawn. What can you do today that will

Steven B. Angus

bring you into the presence of God? Perhaps a walk at dusk to review the day. Or maybe you can get up earlier tomorrow morning and meet God as a new day dawns. Wherever or however you choose to rendezvous with God, take your Bible, read Hosea 6:2-3, and ask God for restoration.

___

February 24
"My soul is now opened by you to meet you."

His parishioners affectionately called him The Doctor. The Reverend Robert Hawker (1753–1827) was an 18th-century Anglican priest. His contemporaries referred to him as the "Star of the West" because of the popularity of his preaching. His pastoral concern for his congregants and why his words touched their hearts is evident in his prayers on their behalf. However, his petition to God was not only for those in his care but for himself. Consider this prayer as offered for you.

> *Gracious Lord! Nothing can reconcile us to you better than to humbly and patiently learn obedience in the school of suffering. We learn by knowing that Jesus, though you are the Son of God, in the eternity of your nature, you were pleased in your human nature to [you] learn obedience by the things which you suffered.*

> *Precious Jesus! To your love and your grace, be all praise and glory. Under your banner of love alone, we are more than conquerors. Come then, blessed Lord, in all your fullness. I desire only you. With my soul have I desired you in the night. And now, with the first dawn of day, I seek you early.*

> *Surely, when you come, as I know you will come, you will in deed and in truth be the tree of life. My soul is now opened by you to meet you. So Lord, show me your person, glory, grace, and love, and fill every portion of my heart. As I wait for your coming, I pray that my view of your grace and sense of my unworthiness may melt my whole soul before you and your presence.*

> *And how refreshing it is to know that "Since the children share in flesh and blood, you yourself likewise partook of the same things. So when my poor heart is afflicted, when Satan storms or the world frowns, when I suffer sickness, or when all your waves and storms seem to go over me, what relief it is to know that you, Jesus, see me. And that you care!*

> *So help me, Lord, to look to you and remember you. And oh! That blessed Scripture: In all their affliction he was afflicted, and the angel of his presence saved them; in his love and in his pity he redeemed them; he lifted them up and carried them all the days of old. Amen.*

Faith Bytes

February 25
"So that we might know the Lord"

Were you able to take that walk at dusk yesterday? How was your early morning rendezvous with God as you greeted the dawn together? Did meditating on Hosea 6:2-3 reveal something about your relationship with God? Clearly, the Prophet made some daring statements. He said:

> *"In just a short time [God] will restore us, so that we may live in [God's] presence. Oh, that we might know the Lord! Let us press on to know him. He will respond to us as surely as the arrival of dawn or the coming of rains in early spring."*

As our part of the Earth broke its fast of light with the arrival of dawn, did you experience God melting away the heaviness of spirit symbolized by the darkness? Hosea assures us this occurs so "that we might know the Lord."

It is easy to relate the dawn as a part of a continuous cycle—sunrise, midday, sunset, darkness, repeat. How marvelous to know that the dark night of the soul will come to an end. However, Hosea hopes we can break the belief that God can only be understood in the dawn of day.

It is true. God's restoration can be compared to the dawn. However, the goal is to live in God's presence. The rhythm of life is constant. Yet, when we "live in the presence of God," we realize how God dwells with us during the darkness of night, the toil of the midday heat, and the breaking of dawn.

Where are you in the cycle of life? Whether your circumstance can be characterized as darkness, scorching heat, or sunset, look for God. Live in his presence. Press on. Don't give up in your pursuit to know him. The more we know him, the less life will appear dark.

February 26
Knowing Where to Look

How about a smile? It does the body and the soul some good!

A substitute Sunday School teacher couldn't open the combination lock on the supply cabinet. So, she went to the pastor for help. The pastor started turning the dial of the combination lock, stopped after the first two numbers, and looked up serenely toward heaven. Then, he moved his lips silently, turned to the final number, and opened the lock. The teacher gasped, "I'm in awe of your faith, pastor." "Really," he said, "it's nothing. The number is on a piece of tape on the ceiling."

I wish the answers to life's problems were on a piece of tape on the ceiling, don't you? Then, when we hit a difficult time in life, all we would have to do is look up. It doesn't work that way, but the Psalmist encouraged us to lift our eyes. He said:

> "I lift up my eyes to the hills—from where will my help come?
> My help comes from the Lord, who made heaven and earth." [Psalm 121:1-2]

Isn't it nice to know where to look when life becomes complicated? Look up!

February 27
The God Who Sings!

The Prophet Zephaniah said:

> "Cheer up, Zion! Don't be afraid! For the Lord your God is living among you. He is a mighty savior. He will take delight in you with gladness. With his love, he will calm all your fears. He will rejoice over you with joyful songs." [Zephaniah 3:16-17, NLT]

Wow! How encouraging these words are! Did you notice the various ways God relates to us?

First, God sees and acknowledges our fear and sadness not once but twice. Then, notice what God is doing or will do for us. "He is living among us." "He is a mighty savior." "He takes delight in us with gladness." "He calms our fears with his love."

And this is my favorite: "He rejoices over us with joyful songs." Has anyone ever mentioned to you that our God is a singing God? If not, let me be the first, but this is the thrilling part—the songs are about us! Go ahead and sing. You have reason to do so!

> "I sing because I'm happy.
> I sing because I'm free,
> For His eye is on the sparrow,
> And I know He watches me."

Faith Bytes

February 28
Praise God...

Early one morning, a fellow got into his car and started driving through the mountains, hoping to leave some of the stresses in his life behind. No one was on the road as the hills were quietly beginning a new day. The beautiful colors of autumn were splashed all over the trees. It was a magnificent sight as the early morning sun glistened upon the wonders of the mountains and the valleys below.

And then it happened. The man saw one of the most beautiful things he had ever witnessed. Right at the edge of that incredible mountain peak and facing the gorgeous valley below stood a young man with a trumpet pressed to his lips as his lungs expanded fully, releasing all the energy in his soul. He listened, hoping to recognize the tune. What he heard made all the sense in the world.

"Praise God from whom all blessings flow
Praise Him, all creatures here below
Praise Him above ye heavenly host
Praise, Father, Son and Holy Ghost!"

Hearing the Doxology and saying the words reminded him how much he had to be grateful. And yet, there was something more. It was not enough to escape or even endure stress. Instead, it is the realization that God is present in the midst of it, and his grandeur surrounds us if we only look and listen.

Feeling stressed? Why not hum a few bars? Praise God from...

_____

_____

_____

_____

February 29
Here a little, There a little

Are you patient? If your ability to wait is anything like mine, the answer is "not very." Americans are motivated by speed. We are intrigued by fast cars, horses, and our computers' start-up time. So we approach the checkout lines in the supermarket, trying to gauge which checker can scan the barcode with the most fluid motion while quickly calculating the number of items in each customer's shopping basket. Then, having made our best guess, we make our move and slide into line just ahead of Mayberry's Aunt Bea. We want it now, if not sooner. We want an instant relationship, so we speed date, or hoping to cut to the chase, we opt for Christianmingle.com. We long to achieve instant sainthood garnished with some microwavable Jesus on the side.

Steven B. Angus

Simply, wanting to know God and the things of God doesn't make it so. In Isaiah 28:9, the Prophet asked, "Whom will [God] teach knowledge, and to whom will [God] explain the message?"

Then, answering his own question, he stated: "For it is precept upon precept, precept upon precept, line upon line, line upon line, here a little, there a little."

If the COVID pandemic revealed anything about ourselves, it is how frustrated we become when waiting. I frequently heard that the pandemic demonstrated how little faith Christians have in God. It is difficult to disagree. It seemed to take all the faith I could muster to wait and not rush back into doing things as I preferred them in the past. But, the wisdom of the Prophet, who understood the importance of patience, said, "The things of God are taught precept upon precept, line upon line, here a little, there a little."

What precept is God attempting to teach you as you wait?

_____
_____
_____
_____

Steven B. Angus

MARCH

March 1
Communion Cups, Chalices, and Children

Many churches designate the first Sunday of the month as Communion Sunday. When we take communion in my congregation, the people usually come forward to the Chancel to receive it. One of the reasons I enjoy this method is how it allows me to see each person's face. I especially love to watch children take communion. By the time they arrive, some of their angelic faces have that sleepy look, and I know that Mom awakened them from their sermon nap. Others hide behind their dad's leg, still uncertain about all that blood and body stuff. However, most are very deliberate, respectful, and attentive.

Intinction is another way churches receive Communion. This is done when a piece of bread is placed in the person's hand, and they dip it into the Communion Chalice. On occasions when I present a child with a small communion cup that looks like a shot glass, I can tell when they have been accustomed to taking the Lord's Supper by intinction. They will often place the tiny cup on the chancel rail and proceed to manipulate the bread into the miniature Chalice. Precious.

I have some unforgettable memories of Holy Communion. Such as the time during a Christmas Eve service, a visitor wrestled the Chalice from a server and took a massive gulp from it. I quickly recognized my youngest son's voice, seated in the second pew, as he let out a window-rattling, "Gross!"

Communion means so many things. Indeed, it is a sacred time, but amid its holiness, there is room for laughter, especially for children. Communion is an opportunity to gather around the table where Jesus is the host and know that all God's children are welcome.

Steven B. Angus

March 2
Onion Juice

I could do a segment for America's Funniest Videos called "Pastor Steven's Greatest Communion Bloopers." Some I would omit, like the fellow who dropped his bread in the cup and went finger-dipping to retrieve it. Nor would I mention the dear lady who, realizing she forgot to dip her bread, said, "Oops," as she removed it from her mouth and then dipped it. I was so thankful there was another chalice on the communion table. I have presided at the Lord's Supper, which used saltine crackers, grape Kool-Aid, and grape soda. A most memorable occasion in Jerusalem was when I purchased what I thought was grape juice at a corner market to discover it was onion juice. That was the only time I served communion and omitted the juice.

I read about a pastor who uncovered the elements and discovered that the grape juice in the communion cup was entirely covered in mold. Thankfully, the pastor had learned to think on his feet. He asked the congregation to pray, and as he led them in prayer, he scooped out the mold with his hand and hid it in the cloth. When everyone said "Amen," they lifted their heads and opened their eyes. No one was the wiser.

It turns out that the preparers set everything up earlier in the week before going on vacation. So perhaps the message I hope to convey is this—When it is time to have the Lord's Supper, don't wait until the last minute to prepare [yourself] for it.

_____
_____
_____
_____

March 3
Are You a Cat-Person?

Did you know that cats can't taste the flavor of sweetness? That's right. David Biello, a contributing editor at Scientific American, says felines cannot taste sweet. It's like their tongues are color-blind to sugar. They can taste sour, bitter, saltiness, and meatiness, but not sweet.

Are you a cat person? Not a cat owner but a cat person? You can taste everything but sweetness. So maybe you should get a dog in your life. Possibly, when dogs are barking at cats, they're just trying to cheer them up! So, if you're a dog person, use your bark to cheer up a cat. And if you're a cat who struggles to taste the sweetness of life, find a dog to be your friend. I know dogs can be annoying. They will eat almost anything, including cat food, but they're good for your soul. So, if you are feeling somewhat down today, ask God to bring a tail-chasing cat person or a yelping dog person into your path.

Faith Bytes

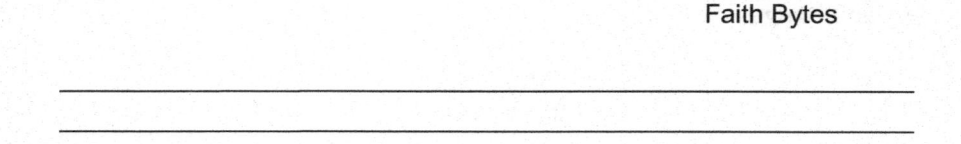

March 4
Jesus the Resilient

In his book, "Belief: What It Means To Believe And Why Our Convictions Are So Compelling," James E. Alcock discusses the combined effect of belief and stress on the body. For decades, psychological research has shown that life's adversities and pressures can cause harm to the human body. Intuitively, this may make sense, but Alcock says that the data shows that it may not be stress itself but the belief that stress is bad for you that harms health.

He refers to a study conducted on executives experiencing high work-related stress levels. It found that those who interpreted the stress as a challenge rather than a threat experienced few negative consequences. They were resilient. In metallurgy, resilience refers to a material's ability to bend but not break under physical stress. The author argues resilient people are those who "bend but do not break" under psychological pressure.

As Christians, we can go a step further. In Isaiah 42, God points to Jesus, saying:
"Look at my servant, whom I strengthen. He is my chosen one, who pleases me." Jesus never buckled under stress. Of Jesus, Isaiah 4:3 wrote: "A bruised reed he will not break, and a dimly burning wick he will not quench."

This means that in our pain and weakness, we come to him and trust him with our deepest hurts and bruises. We find resilience not in our own strength but in his. Feeling stressed? Remind yourself—Jesus has got this!

March 5
It's All About *the Cast*

As many as seven of Jesus' twelve disciples were likely fishermen. Although it may not have been their full-time occupation, living in an area where fishing was the primary industry would suggest they understood the basic rudiments of the trade. In fact, its influence was such that when Jesus began assembling his team with the invitation, "Follow me, and I will show you how to fish for people."

Steven B. Angus

The traits associated with the professional fisherman served Jesus and his disciples well. In fact, many of the skills and tools related to the trade can help us become fishers for Jesus. In the days ahead, we will discuss some of these and see how they can help us become effective fishers for Jesus. To do this, we must set aside our image of the fisherman with his pole dangling an earthworm. The fishing net was the tool the New Testament fishermen relied on.

The skill that could make or break a fisherman was his ability to cast a net. Even if they used the smaller and simpler circular net, it required practice, strength, and patience to perfect. It is all about the cast.

Cast is a verb that means to throw (something) forcefully in a specified direction. Synonyms include toss, fling, pitch, hurl, launch, let fly, propel, chuck, and heave, to name a few. Two thoughts we need to note. First, cast removes from one's presence. Second, the definition of cast included doing this action forcefully in a specified direction. Heaving something in the wrong direction renders the effort futile.

It is interesting how often the word cast occurs in the New Testament. So, over the next few days, I want you to consider the question: Is there something I need to cast, hurl, or chuck from my life, and am I sending it in the specified direction appropriate as a Christian?

This is a skill we may need some practice. In the meantime, Cast. Cast. Cast.

___

March 6
Cast, Cast, Cast means to Pray, Pray, Pray

For several years, I lived on a road that led to a public boat ramp. During that time, I learned there is often a correlation between the type of water vessels headed to the ramp and the time of day. It was usually mid-morning if it was a pontoon boat with a middle-aged couple. If there were children or youth, it was lunch or later. On the occasions when I was heading to the church office at 5 a.m., and I met a truck, it would be towing a fishing boat. In fact, at 5 a.m., I often saw trucks with fishing boats leaving the lake. Most fishermen have discovered that casting a line in the early morning produces more satisfying results.

One day, the disciples tried to heal a sick child. When they couldn't, Jesus stepped in and helped. Afterward, they asked him, "Why couldn't we cast out that evil spirit?" Jesus replied, "This kind can be cast out only by prayer."

Is there something you are trying to cast, toss, fling, propel, chuck, or heave from your life? Perhaps we can learn from those who understand the art of the cast: fishermen and Jesus. They knew the best time to cast was early in the morning. Jesus routinely began his day with prayer. If we wonder why some things stick to us like two-sided masking tape, it's because "this kind can be cast out only by prayer."

Maybe today our prayer should begin—Lord, you said, _____ (fill in the blank) can be cast out only by prayer, so I'm asking.

Cast, Cast, Cast means to Pray, Pray, Pray.

_____
_____
_____
_____

March 7
Cast, Cast, Cast Your Anxiety

Are you ready for another day of casting? Take a deep breath as we set ourselves to toss, fling, pitch, hurl, launch, let fly, propel, chuck, and heave something in the direction of Jesus. In scripture, we are encouraged to "Cast all your anxiety on him because he cares for you." [1 Peter 5:7]

Perhaps you are like me and seldom go to the lake and cast a fishing lure into the water. When I do, it isn't uncommon for me to overdo it and wake up with stiff and sore muscles the following day. Casting is not passive. Most fishermen cast using an athletic stance and forcefully launch the line into the deep.

This is helpful when it comes to casting our anxiety. Whatever causes us to worry wants to stick to us. We may feel it is futile to try at all. We will need to muster all our spiritual strength to claim this verse and hoist that which makes us anxious in the direction of Jesus. The marvelous thing is that we will be less sore tomorrow than today. The subsequent day, stiffness subsides. Eventually, we discover this casting stuff isn't so bad. In fact, it will soon become joyfully natural.

So, Cast, Cast, Cast your anxiety on him. Remember, He cares for you.

_____
_____
_____
_____

Steven B. Angus

March 8
Love is Anti-fear

Did you find time to do some early morning casting? Did you hurl some anxiety toward Jesus, realizing he cares about you? Letting go of the familiar can be frightening. So, this next New Testament "casting" text is a fantastic addition to our spiritual tackle box. In 1 John 4:18, we are told that "perfect love casts out fear." If you are alone, why not say it aloud—"Perfect love casts out fear."

Consider what this means. Love is anti-fear. "Anti" can be good. When we have a sore muscle, we are prescribed an anti-inflammatory. When the Spring causes our allergies to bloom, we take an anti-histamine. We use an anti-perspirant to avoid BO. If we have an upset stomach, we take Pepto as an anti-dia... You get the idea.

In her book, "Fearless: Free in Christ in an Age of Anxiety," Rachel Starr Thomson states, "Love is a fundamentally different orientation to life than fear. Fear is about ourselves. It filters everything through the questions 'How will this affect me?' and 'Is this safe?' Love filters everything through the questions 'How will this affect others?' and 'Is this good?' Love shapes our character in a fundamentally different way from the way fear shapes it. Love trusts. Fear distrusts. Love gives. Fear hoards. Love believes. Fear will not go out on a limb. Love seeks unity. Fear builds walls."

Do you need to cast out some fear? Ask Jesus to make His perfect love real in you. Why not do the most loving thing you can do for yourself, be loving towards another?

So Cast, Cast, Cast. Love, love, love!

_____
_____
_____

March 9
The Prayers of Old Saints

We have yet to breathe the breath of dawn when we do not need to pray. However, some days beg us to do so, and we find ourselves lost, searching for the words to say. This is when the prayers of old saints can bless us. Vicar Robert Hawker, a priest in the Church of England, recorded such a prayer in his popular "The Poor Man's Morning and Evening Portion," published in 1829.

> "Dearest Lord, I blush to think how slender, at times, my faith is! When I read of the acts of those heroes in the gospel, who 'through faith conquered kingdoms, performed acts of righteousness, obtained promises, stopped the mouths of lions,' and the like, I am ashamed of my unbelieving heart.

"Did Joshua bid the sun and moon to stand still? Did Peter call Tabitha from the dead by faith in Jesus? And am I so much at a loss, at times, to fear that I will one day perish at the hand of the enemy? I beg You, Lord, strengthen my soul in this grace, that I may never more question Your divine faithfulness.

"Blessed Jesus, pour in Your resources upon my poor, forgetful, and unbelieving heart when doubts, fears, and misgivings arise. Help me to see that in all my journey past, You have brought me through difficulties and dangers. Help me to see that Your strength is made perfect in my weakness.

"What is difficulty when Jesus steps in for His people? The challenge, be what it may, is more for the display of Your glory and the exercise of my faith. Help me then, Lord, to look to You — and not to the difficulty because I have nothing to do with it. It is enough for me that my God has promised.

"You can, God, and You will. How will You do it, Jesus? That is Your concern, not mine. You are faithful. You have promised. And that is enough for me. There is no doubt. Yes, Lord! I know Your hand is not weak and that all You have said must come to pass. Because 'He who calls you is faithful, and He will surely do it!' Amen."

— **Robert Hawker**

_____
_____
_____
_____

March 10
The Perfect Plant

Caelie Wilkes, a California stay-at-home mom, received the plant as a gift and worked hard to nurture and protect it, ensuring it received enough water and sunshine. Succulents don't need much water. She would carefully wash the spongy leaves and become defensive if someone else tried to water it.

Admittedly, her plant didn't grow much over the two years, but Wilkes seemed to have a green thumb otherwise. It never developed blackened tips or discolored leaves. Instead, she said, "It was the perfect houseplant." Finally, it came time to transplant the little fellow from its original container, and Caelie picked out the cutest vase. Expecting to find a ball of roots in the container, she was shocked to find styrofoam with sand glued to the top. Instead, it turned out that her cherished plant was plastic. She thought, "I put so much love into this plant, and it's completely plastic! How did I not know?" I've seen photos, and it does look real.

God has a way of getting our attention, and when He does, we discover that many things we thought were real and significant aren't. We would be wise to ask God to help us recognize those things in our lives that truly matter and to be intentional about watering them.

Steven B. Angus

What are some of the plastic plants consuming your time? Are there relationships that are wilting from inattention?

March 11
Welcome to Your Dramedy

Each morning, when I fire up my computer and check my email, like you, I am greeted by an assortment of information. Some are thoughtful reflections from a parishioner or colleague. I also receive several "On This Day" emails and various devotional thoughts from teachers I respect. Hoping to improve my vocabulary, I subscribe to wordgenius.com, which suggests a word of the day. Although this often introduces me to unfamiliar terms, I am reminded of words I seldom use. Recently, I read an expression that seemed perfect for our generation.

The word is "dramedy." The concept is so new my spell checker highlighted it and failed to offer a synonym. The website identifies it as a noun with the following definition: "A movie, play, or broadcast program that combines elements of drama and comedy, adding, in a dramedy, you might have humorous actors playing out serious situations — or absurd realities with significant consequences."

I wonder if this is what our parents meant when they said, "Some days are such that if I didn't laugh, I would cry?" The truth is our present reality often seems absurd. We couldn't make it up if we tried. We keep hoping it is a dream, but we awaken, and it is still as it was when we went to sleep.

Dramedy. Aren't you glad this dramedy we call Life isn't a Steven Spielberg or Spike Lee production? If they were, there is no telling how things would turn out. However, as Christians, we believe that although much of what happens in our lives results from our sinful choices, as the director, Jesus continues to steer life into what is ultimately best for us.

Where in your life do you see a dramedy? Actually, a dramedy can be fun when we remember we are in God's story, and He knows how it ends.

March 12
A Shapeless, Chaotic Mass

The sun was just breaking the eastern horizon. Although I could not see it, I knew it was there despite the clouds. I wish I had the gift of a poet to describe the beauty of what I saw. Dark, black, and grayish clouds were present, as expected

Faith Bytes

when the weather forecast calls for rain. Yet, somehow, they mingled in such a way as to form a picture frame that only nature can construct. In the center was a canvas so alive with an aurora of bursting pink that not even the master of light, Thomas Kinkade, could have adequately captured it. What I saw was vibrant and fluid. I realized that it would never be that precise moment again, even if I pulled to the shoulder of the highway and attempted to capture it with the camera on my phone.

The crimson cotton candy tones of cherry blossoms emerging from the darkness propelled my mind to the opening words of Genesis[1:2]. One Bible translation says, "The earth was a shapeless, chaotic mass, with the Spirit of God brooding over the dark vapors.[TLB]" Another, "Earth was a soup of nothingness, a bottomless emptiness, an inky blackness. God's Spirit brooded like a bird above the watery abyss.[MSG]"

Out of chaos, God delivered wonder. Chaotic, inky blackness seems to describe society right now. It appears to hover over our heads like a demonic drone. The writers of the creation story want us to know that nothing is too tumultuous for our God to handle. In fact, turbulence can usher into our lives something incredible provided we allow ourselves to trust the hand of the artist.

_____
_____
_____
_____

March 13
An Entire Cupboard

One day, Carl was driving home when he saw a group of young children selling Kool-Aid on a corner in his neighborhood. They had posted the typical hand-scrawled sign over their stand: "Kool-Aid, 10 cents." Carl, who worked in sales, was intrigued. So he pulled over to the curb. A young boy approached and asked if he would like strawberry or grape Kool-Aid. Carl placed his order and handed the boy a quarter. After much deliberation, the children determined he had some change coming and rifled through the cigar box until they finally found the correct amount. The boy returned with the change and then stood by the side of the car. Finally, he asked Carl if he was finished drinking. "Just about," said Carl. "Why?" The boy responded, "Well, that's the only cup we have, and we need it to stay in business."

Operating a Kool-Aid business is difficult if you only have one cup. Unfortunately, we sometimes make that mistake in the Church. Yet, the content never changes: A God of love has reached out to the world. We must offer this message in as many ways [cups] as possible. By the way, the Church is an entire cupboard of cups. You are one, and so am I. How will you offer God's love today?

_____
_____

Steven B. Angus

March 14
What Does Your Sermon Look Like?

When we hear the name Saint Francis, our first thought is to identify him as the patron Saint of animals and pets. However, many stories about the kindly thirteenth-century monk do not include animals. One goes something like this.

One day, Francis informed his brethren that he planned a preaching mission in a nearby village. He invited a novice monk to go along. On their way, they passed an injured man, and Francis promptly stopped, saw to the poor fellow's needs, and arranged medical care for him. They went on and soon passed a homeless man who was near starvation. Again, Francis stopped his journey and ministered to the hungry, homeless man. So, it went through the day: people in need, Francis lovingly caring for them as best he could until the sun was low in the sky. Finally, he told his novice friend that it was time for them to return to the monastery for evening prayers. But the young man said, "Father, you said we were coming to town to preach to the people." With a smile, Francis said, "My friend, that's what we've been doing all day."

Here is a challenge for you—How many sermons can you preach from this moment until you lay your head on your pillow tonight?

_____
_____
_____
_____

March 15
Amen to Your Amen.

Thomas Brooks lived in the early seventeenth century. He was an influential preacher, often speaking in the House of Commons. Charles Spurgeon said, "Brooks scatters stars with both hands, with an eagle eye of faith as well as the eagle eye of imagination." This was equally true of his prayers, such as this one titled, "My Amen to your Amen."

> "Lord! Lay whatever burden you will upon me. Only let your everlasting arms be under me. Strike, Lord, and do not spare me. I lay down in your will. I have learned to say Amen to your Amen. You have a greater interest in me than I have in myself, and therefore, I give myself up to you. I am willing to be at your disposal, and I'm ready to receive whatever impression you want to stamp upon me. Blessed Lord, again and again, you have said to me, as once the king of Israel said to the king of Syria, 'I am yours, and all that I have.' [First Kings 20:4] I am yours!

> "Your mercy is mine to pardon me. Your blood is mine to cleanse me. Your merits are mine to justify me. Your righteousness is mine to clothe me. Your spirit is mine to lead me. Your grace is mine to enrich me. Your glory is mine to reward me.

Faith Bytes

"Therefore, my soul cannot help but resign myself to you. Lord! Here I am; do with me as seems good in your own eyes. I know the best way to have my own will is to resign myself to your will and to say Amen to your Amen."

Is there a part of yourself you have yet to yield to Jesus? If so, what is preventing you?

_____
_____
_____
_____

March 16
Smore of God

Martin is a cute blond-headed Estonian boy who, when you take one look at him, you find yourself wanting to adopt him. Martin is about ten years old and about four feet tall. It quickly became evident to those on the trip to Estonia that Martin was the Eastern Europe equivalent to Dennis the Mennis. He could not keep his hands to himself and was constantly picking at everyone. His favorite pastime was climbing. One minute, he would turn a handrail into a balance beam; the next, he would have figured out how to get on top of a building. When the children went swimming in the Baltic Sea, he would come up with a handful of seaweed and start a seaweed fight. He was constantly pushing the limits, doing something that would get him in trouble with the staff, and he would miss out on some special treat. Most of the mission team members had a tender heart towards Martin. Even though he was mischievous, he was never malicious. He never did anything terrible but could not stay out of trouble.

On our last night, we had a bonfire with sodas and all the makings for smores. Every child received a brown bag with two small Hershey bars, two marshmallows, and two graham crackers. You would have thought we had passed out a sack of money. Martin was standing next to another boy who had just roasted his marshmallow. As the boy put it on his graham cracker, it slipped off and landed on the ground, all gooey. Martin looked at this other boy, saw the disappointment, then reached into his sack and gave him one of his marshmallows.

I saw God in that moment.

_____
_____
_____
_____

Steven B. Angus

March 17
He Chose

If you are wearing something green, you probably know Saint Patrick's Day is today. Although he is the patron saint of Ireland, Patrick was not Irish. He was born in Scotland around 385. As a boy of sixteen, he was captured during a raid and taken to Ireland as a slave and given the job of a shepherd. For six years, he cared for his master's flock alone on the hills. During his captivity, he learned the language and practices of the Irish people. Although he was not raised as a Christian, he turned to God. Those desolate hills were conducive to prayer. He wrote:

> "The love of God and his fear grew in me more and more, as did the faith, and my soul was roused, so that, in a single day, I have said as many as a hundred prayers, and in the night, nearly the same. I prayed in the woods and on the mountain, even before dawn. I felt no hurt from the snow or ice or rain."

Patrick's captivity lasted until he was twenty-two. Then, believing God wanted him to return to Scotland, he walked 200 miles to the coast and found a ship preparing to sail. The journey was difficult, and often he had no food. His companions mocked his Christianity and asked why his God didn't help him. Patrick replied that the Lord would help all of them. It wasn't long until they came upon a herd of wild pigs and enjoyed a two-day feast.

Sometime after he returned to his family, Patrick dreamed of the people of Ireland weeping as they pleaded with him to return. So, he began his studies for the priesthood. Then, after ordination, he returned to Ireland and preached the Gospel for forty years.

Patrick could have written off the entire nation because of how cruelly they treated him. But instead, he chose to reject bitterness and trust God with his life. So perhaps the significant phrase in the previous sentence you and I should focus on is—"He chose." You and I may not control what may happen in our lives, but we have a choice in how we react and whether or not we will trust God. Have you chosen bitterness? Or trust?

_____

_____

_____

March 18
A Different Path

Soon after Richard Allen, an African American slave, became a Christian, he convinced Freeborn Garrettson, a circuit rider and former slaveholder, to preach at his master's house. Garrettson's sermon text was—"Thou art weighed in the balance, and art found wanting." If we were the slaveholder, how would we have reacted? Would we have responded in anger, or would we, like this man, have

Faith Bytes

been convicted of our sin and changed? This slaveholder chose a different path and allowed for Richard's and his brother's freedom.

Now a free man, Allen's only thought was to preach and would awake from his sleep, preaching and praying. He became a licensed Methodist preacher but was more of a circuit walker than a circuit rider. Sometimes, his feet became so sore and blistered that he scarcely could put them to the ground. However, this did not prevent him from traveling through Delaware, New Jersey, Pennsylvania, Maryland, and perhaps as far south as Virginia and the Carolinas. Later, he was invited by Bishop Francis Asbury to travel with him to the slave states. However, Allen declined for a variety of reasons. Richard Allen was the first Christian bishop of African descent in North America, founding the African Methodist Episcopal (AME) Church.

We live in a culture where being unkind to anyone different is acceptable. However, remembering Bishop Allen's legacy allows us to ask the hard questions—Have I been found wanting, and what will I do differently today?

March 19
Weep to Laugh

We've all heard the saying—"I must laugh to keep from crying." We say it as if tears are the enemy to be resisted at all costs. This is far from the truth. Our tear ducts can be considered pressure valves that allow our pain, fear, and anxieties to escape and restore balance. We may need to speak with a mental health professional or pastor if we are continuously weeping. However, tears are a gift God has given, and to my knowledge, they are unique to humans. So precious are our tears that we are told that God records each in a book and collects them in a bottle [Psalm 56:8].

Days before Palm Sunday, John the Gospel writer tells us that "Jesus wept." Perhaps it wasn't his teachings or his miracles but his tears that proved we have a God who truly understands what it means to be human.

Maybe we should rethink what we have previously thought about tears. It could be that we have it backward. Instead of laughing to keep from crying, we must weep to truly appreciate the laughter. Laughter and tears are tools to help us cope during troublesome times. Does the insight that Jesus wept change your perception of Him? How? Why?

Steven B. Angus

March 20
Joyful Tears

According to those who know about such things, women do this an average of five times a month, whereas men only do it once. The Bible teaches that Jesus did it on several occasions. One of those times occurred days before he entered Jerusalem on Palm Sunday. What am I referring to? The shedding of tears.

When we speak of tears, we may sing, "Big boys, don't cry," embracing the popular notion that they are a sign of weakness, that only "sissies "cry. The last thing most of us would ever do is refer to Jesus as a sissy.

Life is filled with an assortment of tears. One of the most beautiful weddings I conducted was overshadowed by tears. I considered loaning the groom the sleeve of my robe as he alternated between smiling, weeping, and turning green. Obviously, they were tears of joy. Research has indicated that one in five tears we shed is a tear of happiness. When did you last allow yourself to appreciate a moment so profoundly that you cried? Was it the good news—"It's a healthy baby girl?" Perhaps it was a sunset. A field of wildflowers. The assuring words, "the tests were negative." So, you have permission to count your blessings and shed a joyful tear—or several.

_____

_____

_____

_____

March 21
Marinated In Tears

Tears have been described as "agony in solution" or just "liquid pain." According to Minnesota's Dry Eye and Tear Research Center, 60% of our tears can be attributed to sadness, anxiety, or fear. Sometimes, life's hurts and disappointments build inside us to the point that they can no longer be suppressed. The only recourse is for our bodies to squeeze this grief out of the tear ducts of our eyes. Once the floodgates have been raised, we weep until the tears dry. Life can quickly become a baptism of tears!

The first reference to tears in the Bible is in Genesis 23:2. The great patriarch Abraham is found to be weeping at the death of his wife, Sarah. Theirs was one of the longest marriages recorded in scripture. Together, they left their home and moved to a foreign land just because God told them to do so. Then, they struggled all those years to have a child. All in all, God was faithful, and they had a good marriage. Death hurts and brings tears.

Then there is the story of Job. His story is in the book bearing his name, but it could easily be called "The Book of Pain." Job wept and did so often. Compared to Job's hardships, a Greek tragedy would be a short story. Job's children died,

Faith Bytes

he lost everything he owned, his friends turned their backs on him, and finally, his body was covered with sores. What did he do? Among other things, he wept.

Tears. Are you acquainted with Loss? Rejection? Physical pain? Injustice? Hopelessness? Job described his plight: "My friends scorn me, but I pour out my tears to God." [Job 16:20] His agony became marinated with saline and flowed from his eyes. You have permission to name your tears as you pour them before God.

_____

_____

_____

_____

March 22
The Need for a Good Cry

Tears! Tears! And more tears! The Psalmist expressed how numerous they are; "I am weary with my groaning; All night I make my bed swim; I drench my couch with my tears." [Psalm 6:6]

You and I may forget how to do many things in life, but one thing we will never forget is how to cry. For this reason, the story of Jesus at the tomb of Lazarus is significant. Although we shed tears, we have a God who understands what it means to weep. Word came to Jesus that his friend Lazarus had died. He had spent many evenings in the home of Lazarus and his sisters, Mary and Martha. When Jesus arrived, Lazarus had already been dead for four days. He is first greeted by Martha and then by Mary.

The Gospel writer reported, "Then, when Mary came where Jesus was, and saw Him, she fell down at His feet, saying to Him, "Lord, if You had been here, my brother would not have died." Therefore, when Jesus saw her weeping, and the Jews who came with her weeping, He groaned in the spirit and was troubled. And He said, "Where have you laid him?" They said to Him, "Lord, come and see." Jesus wept. Then the Jews said, "See how He loved him!" [John 11:32-36]

Several translations record verse 35 simply, "Jesus wept." It is considered the shortest verse in the Bible. One question often asked is, "Why was Jesus moved to tears?" Some suggest it was Mary and Martha's lack of faith or the remorse he felt in calling Lazarus back from a far better place. Who really knows for sure?

Perhaps there is another reason, one that is much simpler. Maybe Jesus just needed a good cry. In this story, we see a God who recognizes human pain and, through Jesus, experiences it for himself. God remembers what they represent. Maybe the writer of the Letter of Hebrews had our tears in mind when he said of Jesus: "For we do not have a High Priest who cannot sympathize with our weaknesses." [Hebrews 4:15]. When Jesus wept at the tomb of his friend Lazarus, He demonstrated his bond with you! How does this make you feel?

_____

_____

_____

March 23
Resuscitate a Life

"Jesus wept." These two words construct a bridge unlike any other. Suddenly, each one of the millions of tears we shed over a lifetime became genuinely priceless. In Psalm 56:8, David said: "You keep track of all my sorrows. You have collected all my tears in your bottle. You have recorded each one in your book." [NLT] So, the Shepherd King sketches the portrait of a God so connected to His people that every tear is recognized and recorded. However, not even this is enough. Our tears are so precious that the Lord God Almighty personally captures them in a bottle for safekeeping. Just Imagine! When we weep at the loss of a loved one, God captures those tears. When the pillow that cradles our heads at night becomes damp with the tears shed because of the pain we feel in our bodies, God has taken notice and captured them. When we sob over the pain our children are experiencing from poor choices, God is there to record that agony.

The raising of Lazarus teaches us many things about our God. Still, perhaps the realization that God can weep right along with us is so dear. However, tucked into this remarkable story is a lesson we must not overlook. It is this—Jesus demonstrates how we should try to relate to others.

Perhaps you are thinking, "Sure, Jesus could cry, but he was also God. So, therefore, he could bring Lazarus back to life, which is something we cannot do." Although accurate, we can never resurrect; perhaps when we recognize the tears of those around us, we can help "resuscitate" a life. I think of those brave paramedics who refuse to give up on someone whose heart has stopped beating. Instead, they continue to give CPR and occasionally restore the remaining life. I am thankful they do not give up.

Sometimes, we are too quick to give up on people, believing there is no hope for life. We cannot give life, but sometimes, we can help to resuscitate life. How might you do this?

_____

_____

_____

Faith Bytes

March 24
Francis and Fanny

The date March 24 is significant for all Christians, particularly those from the Wesleyan-Methodist tradition. On this date, 1816, Bishop Francis Asbury preached his last sermon before his death. He was so weak that he spoke while lying on a table. However, he still managed to preach for an hour. Four years later, in 1820, the blind hymn writer Fanny Crosby was born. During her lifetime, she wrote more than 9000 hymns. These two remarkable people helped shape the course of Christianity in America.

What is your favorite Fanny Crosby hymn? Perhaps it is one of these: To God be the Glory; Pass Me Not; O Gentle Savior; Close to Thee; I am Thine, O Lord; or Rescue the Perishing. However, as we are in the Season of Lent, these lyrics from "Jesus, Keep Me Near the Cross" have profound meaning for us today.

Near the cross, a trembling soul,
love and mercy found me;
there the bright and morning star
sheds its beams around me.

Chorus:
In the cross, in the cross, be my glory ever;
'til my raptured soul shall find, rest beyond the river.

Steven B. Angus

HOLY WEEK

March 25
Monday of Holy Week

The journey of Holy Week began on a Sunday as Jesus rode a borrowed donkey into Jerusalem. He was greeted by a palm-waving crowd pleading their case—"Hosanna! Blessed is he who comes in the name of the lord."

In all likelihood, Jesus spent Sunday night in the village of Bethany in the home of Mary and Martha and their brother Lazarus. Near the hamlet was a garden called the Mount of Olives. The following day, Jesus returned to Jerusalem and thus began what is traditionally called Holy Monday. The events of the day can be read in Matthew 21:12-22.

As Jesus made this short trip from Bethany, he passed a fig tree that had produced leaves out of season. Their presence suggested the presence of fruit. When Jesus did not find any, he cursed the tree. When Jesus and the disciples passed the tree the following day, his followers pointed out that it had withered entirely.

Jesus continued his journey with a specific destination in mind: The Temple. Entering the House of God, He was appalled by what He saw. This holy place had been reduced to a shopping mall. In anger, Jesus overturned the merchants' tables, fashioned a whip from a rope, and drove them into the streets. The crowd, as well as the Disciples, were perplexed by his behavior. Explaining his actions, he said, "It is written, 'My house shall be called a house of prayer,' but you have made it a 'den of thieves.'" [Matthew 21:13]

As mysterious as these two events seem, they compel us to ask two significant questions. First, am I bearing fruit? Second, if my heart is the temple of God, is there something present that I need to allow Jesus to overturn and sweep away? So do not rush through your Monday. Allow it to be holy to God. Consider how you can make this prayer your own.

> "Almighty God, show me how to honor you today by bearing fruit. Cleanse me, sweep away those things that hinder my heart from being your house. May I walk with you through this Holy Week and beyond. In the name of Jesus, Amen."

Faith Bytes

March 26
Tuesday of Holy Week

If our work week began on Sunday, then today would be "Hump Day." For Jesus, it was Teaching Tuesday as He demonstrated why he was often called Teacher. First, on the day's syllabus was an object lesson based on the now withered fig tree. This was followed by a debate between "The Teacher" and some religious studies professors. Finally, the day culminated with a private seminar with his disciples, often called the Parables on the Mount of Olives. The day had the emotional tension of an all-night cram session preparing for a final exam.

Jesus, the teacher, saw the red light on the dashboard accompanied by the warning ding and realized the situation was critical. Matthew 26:1-2 states that when Jesus finished his lecture, he summarized for his pupils, "You know that after two days is the Passover, and the Son of Man will be delivered up to be crucified." Can't you hear the soundbite: "Danger Will Robinson!?"

What is our lesson on this Teaching Tuesday, the hump day of Holy Week? It turns out to be good news for us. Jesus was already preparing His followers for what lay ahead. The disciples did not know what would occur but could rest assured that Jesus was on it.

We will always have more questions than we have answers. Take hope. When the crucial moment arrives, Jesus is already present. We will find the courage we did not know we possessed. We have an advantage the Disciples did not yet grasp. We know we will be met with understanding and compassion when we stumble and fail. Such knowledge is good news on hump day!

Consider making this prayer your own.

> "Almighty God, you sent Jesus to be our rescuer. All wisdom, strength, and glory are found in him. He is our shelter in the storm. In you, I place my trust. So allow me to walk confidently, knowing Jesus goes before me to light my path. Amen."

_____
_____
_____
_____

March 27
Wednesday of Holy Week

The Bible refers to two events associated with this day. First, it has been called "Spy Wednesday" because it is believed to be the day Judas conspired with local authorities to betray Jesus for thirty pieces of silver.

However, something occurred before striking this deal with the enemy that may have pushed Judas to the dark side. Jesus was in the home of a fellow known as Simon, the leper. As they were enjoying a respite from a trying week, a woman

Steven B. Angus

entered the room with an expensive jar of perfume. Without saying a word, she poured the fragrant ointment over Jesus's head. This upset the disciples, causing them to say, "Why this waste? It could have been sold to help the poor." Knowing their thoughts, Jesus said, "Leave her alone. She has done a good thing, preparing my body for burial."

We encounter two individuals who spent time with Jesus but took very different paths. Although we may never know their true motivations, we know this: How we perceive Jesus will dictate our actions.

The lesson for me is unsettling. Some days, I am this nameless woman ready to pour everything out for my Lord. But, on other days, I will likely sell him out and never blink an eye. When I play the part of the spy, I am thankful it's just Wednesday, and Friday is almost here! If I can just make it to Friday! Then—well, as all of us spies know—Easter is just around the corner.

I can hardly wait!

_____
_____
_____
_____

March 28
Thursday of Holy Week

The Thursday of Holy Week is referred to as Maundy Thursday. It is associated with the Upper Room, where Jesus washed his disciples' feet and observed the Passover Seder. "Maundy" is a Latin word meaning "commandment." So, when we say Maundy Thursday, we call it Commandment Thursday. It is an appropriate designation because it was when Jesus gave his followers what he called a new commandment. On a night when he assumed the role of a servant, washed their feet, offered them broken bread and a drink of wine, and said, "I give you a new commandment that you should love one another as I have loved you." What a challenge! To love as Jesus loved.

Andy Wade has written a prayer that embodies Jesus' new commandment to love as He loves. This is part of that prayer.

> *We have chosen to fast*
> *Not with ashes but with actions*
> *Not with sackcloth but in sharing*
> *Not in thoughts but in deeds*
>
> *We will give up our abundance*
> *To share our food with the hungry*
> *We will give up our comfort*
> *To provide homes for the destitute*
> *We will give up our fashions*
> *To see the naked clothed*

Faith Bytes

Then God's light will break out on us. . .
We will be like a well-watered garden
We will be called repairers of broken walls
Together, we will feast at God's banquet table

_____
_____
_____
_____

March 29
Friday of Holy Week

This is not a typical Friday. The Bible tells us around the sixth hour [noon], darkness came over the land, and the sun stopped shining for three hours.

12:01. Darkness.

The time frame of Good Friday is uncertain. Did the darkness occur when Jesus called out from the cross, "Father, into your hands I commit my spirit," or was it the prelude to his death three hours later? If so, his death would have meant a restoration of Light.

I find comfort in believing Jesus' suffering occurred under the veil of darkness. This would have meant a grieving Father was spared from watching a Son die while simultaneously preventing the lurking eyes of bloodthirsty assassins from taking satisfaction in their hideous deed.

Wouldn't you agree there is something wonderfully poignant if, at the moment Jesus gave up His spirit, Light pierced the darkness? "The Earth was without form and void; darkness was on the face of the deep. Then God said, "Let there be light, and there was Light." No. This was not a typical Friday. It is Good Friday and the dawning of a new creation.

Consider lighting a candle as you invite the Light of the world to overcome the darkness in your life.

_____
_____
_____
_____

Steven B. Angus

March 30
Saturday of Holy Week

Ask someone who has lost a loved one, and they will tell you the most challenging time isn't the day of visitation or the funeral. Instead, it is when the house becomes silent as family and friends return to their lives of routine. Alone, they feel the need to do something yet are at a loss as to what that would be. So they are left to wait and wonder what the new normal will be.

Such is Holy Saturday. As Good Friday ended, Jesus' friends had to act quickly before the Sabbath began at sunset. So they hastily deposited His body in a donated tomb and rushed away. Their Saturday consisted of hopeless waiting. Without a clue as to what would occur next, they put their lives on hold until the first light on a Sunday that had yet to be christened as Easter.

Having postponed portions of their grief, when there was just enough light to see one step ahead, a group of women rushed to the tomb, uncertain what they would find. However, they soon discover that the wait has been worth it.

Some Christians observe the Saturday night before Easter as a Vigil. They remain awake, waiting for the first light of dawn, similar to the women of so long ago. Like these women, they hope to rush and see with fresh eyes the wonderment of what Easter will reveal. Sisters and brothers, the Christian season of Lent is nearing its end. Let us make good use of these final hours of waiting. Easter is almost here when the words "It is finished" will take on new meaning and give way to "He is risen!"

_____
_____
_____

March 31
Resurrection Sunday

When Resurrection Sunday occurred, the world entered unchartered waters. Although the Bible chronicles a few occasions when an individual had been summoned back from the grave [for example, Lazarus], no one had ever decided to get up, take the time to fold their burial garments and walk out free—free as a canary who managed to open the door of its own cage.

When Neil Armstrong took those momentous first steps on the moon and said, "That's one small step for a man, one giant leap for mankind," they were televised to Earth and heard by millions. However, no cameras clicked in the garden tomb to record the movements of the one who had boldly gone where no human had before.

The paparazzi had not been tipped off, so there was no boom mic. The only evidence presented was the testimony of the only person who could report it— the individual who had desperately been searching for Him with tear-clouded

Faith Bytes

eyes. Jesus approached her and asked not one but two questions. Although addressed to her, they seemed intended for anyone willing to listen. He queried, "Why are you weeping? Who are you looking for?" followed by her name, "Mary."

Jesus accomplished what was needed by the entire world but wasn't so preoccupied that He could not recognize the tears of one searching for him. As you participate in this day's busyness, look for the living Jesus. Listen in anticipation for Him to call your name. Make the time to see and hear.

_____
_____
_____
_____

Steven B. Angus

APRIL

April 1
April Hoaxes and Belly Laughs

Is it appropriate to say, "Happy April Fools' Day?" Don't worry; I am not going to prank you. It may be my imagination, but there seems to be a decline in attempted hoaxes and pranks. Unfortunately, this may signal that we take ourselves too seriously and don't want to laugh. Perhaps as we reflect on our present circumstance, we have concluded we are trapped in a loop of endless April Fool's days. We must restrain ourselves from screaming—"Enough already!"

And yet, we would be the first to admit we could benefit from a good "Belly Laugh." Laughter is a fantastic gift that God has given to us. Laughter helps us cope with sadness and the frustrations of life. The Bible gives examples of when and when not to laugh. Laughter is often referred to as the best medicine, which doesn't go unnoticed in the Bible. Consider these statements.

> *"A merry heart does good, like medicine." Proverbs 17:22*
> *"A merry heart makes a cheerful countenance." Proverbs 15:13*

Joy is one of the fruits of the Holy Spirit, and what better way is there to express it than through laughter?

> *"He will yet fill your mouth with laughing, and your lips with rejoicing." Job 8:21*
> *"Then our mouth was filled with laughter, and our tongue with singing. Then they said among the nations, 'The Lord has done great things for them.'" Psalm 126:2*

Go ahead and laugh. We are more likely to do so if we give ourselves permission. By the way, have you heard the one about. . .?

_____
_____
_____
_____

Faith Bytes

April 2
The Best of All

Westminster Abbey is one of the most famous religious buildings in the world, and it has served an essential role in British society for more than 1,000 years. The facility still hosts important religious activities and has been the site of forty royal coronations and thirty-nine monarchs crowned since 1066. The most recent was King Charles III in May 2023.

The church has over 600 wall tablets and monuments, and over 3,000 people have been buried there. These include Chaucer, Newton, Handel, Kipling, Hawking, Shakespeare, and Dickens, to name a few.

On March 30, 1876, a white marble memorial to the Methodists John and Charles Wesley was unveiled. It includes profile portraits of the brothers and an image of John preaching from his father's tombstone. On the monument are three quotes, usually attributed to John. One is, "GOD BURIES HIS WORKMEN BUT CARRIES ON HIS WORK." Also included are the words reported to be his last before dying. According to those who witnessed his death, John Wesley raised his arms upward from his bed and said, "THE BEST OF ALL IS GOD IS WITH US."

For Wesley, this was the best news. It is the hope that exists during those in-between times. Whether it is a day of unrest or a season of calm, "THE BEST OF ALL IS, GOD IS WITH US." When and where have you recently recognized God was with you?

_____
_____
_____
_____

April 3
Great Expectations?

One of the most famous theologians of the twentieth century was Karl Barth. One day, as he was seated on a streetcar in Basel, Switzerland, where he lived and lectured, a tourist boarded and sat beside him. The two began chatting, and Barth asked, "Are you new to the city?" "Yes," said the tourist. "Is there anything you would like to see in this city?" asked Barth. "Yes," he said, "I'd love to meet the famous theologian Karl Barth. Do you know him?" Barth replied, "Well, as a matter of fact, I do. I give him a shave every morning." The tourist got off the streetcar, delighted. He returned to his hotel, saying to himself, "I met Karl Barth's barber today."

Whether the story is true or not, I do not know, but I like it. The tourist was in the presence of the person he most wanted to meet. Unfortunately, he never realized he was talking with the great man himself.

Steven B. Angus

When we reflect on the events of Easter, it seems those who encountered the risen Lord had a similar experience. Mary in the garden, the travelers of the road to Emmaus, and even the disciples locked in the Upper Room failed to recognize him. Granted, why should they? The evidence pointed to another conclusion.

We typically will not see what we aren't expecting to encounter. So, throughout this day, why not look for a Jesus sighting? Although we are unlikely to see nail-scarred hands, we may observe His greatness in other ways.

April 4
Hey Siri, I'm Frustrated!

Listening to the tone of the voices that fill the airways, something is amiss. The words and the accompanying body language we encounter in the workplace, grocery store, post office, and sometimes in church reveal annoyance. It seems we are in a constant state of frustration that has us snapping at our spouse, sending our children to their room, yelling at Siri, and contemplating hurling the Alexa device against the wall. Our patience is wearing thin. We are frustrated by our frustration.

Reminding ourselves that we are not the first to encounter such emotions is comforting. In fact, some of those who expressed such sentiments had the same first name—Saint. The following prayer was offered almost 1700 years ago by St. Augustine. So, if you are feeling discouraged, consider this prayer and find hope that things will get better.

> *"God of our life, there are days when the burdens we carry chafe our shoulders and weigh us down; when the road seems dreary and endless, the skies grey and threatening; when our lives have no music in them, and our hearts are lonely, and our souls have lost their courage. Flood the path with light, run our eyes to where the skies are full of promise; tune our hearts to brave music; give us the sense of comradeship with heroes and saints of every age, and so quicken our spirits that we may be able to encourage the souls of all who journey with us on the road of life, to Your honor and glory. Amen."*

(From Prayers of the Saints: An Inspired Collection of Holy Wisdom, ed. Woodeene Koenig-Bricker – San Francisco: Harper Collins, 1996)

Faith Bytes

April 5
No Problems. Just Opportunities. Really?

Problems. We all have them. I have a friend whose favorite statement is, "There are no problems, just opportunities." Honestly, his never-ceasing optimism can grate on his companions' nerves, causing a look that says, "Hear we go again." In fairness, his comments should guide us to some sincere self-evaluation as we ask, "How do we handle the problems (the opportunities) that come our way?"

I heard about a middle school that was facing a unique problem. It involved some girls who were beginning to use lipstick. Since they were not allowed to apply it before leaving home, they would go to the school's restroom and do so. That was fine, but after they put on their lipstick, they would press their lips to the mirrors, leaving dozens of little lip prints. Finally, the principal decided that something had to be done. Accompanied by the school custodian, she called all the girls to the bathroom. She explained that all these lip prints were causing additional work for the custodian, who had to clean the mirrors daily. To demonstrate how difficult it was to clean the mirrors, she asked the custodian to clean one of the mirrors. He removed a long-handled brush, dipped it into the nearest toilet, and scrubbed the mirror. The report stated there have been no lip prints on the mirror since then.

I would call that "creative problem-solving." Sometimes, the best approach to dealing with a difficulty is to present the advantages of a particular choice and leave the rest to the imagination. Allow me to suggest a resource to help us solve some of the challenges that confront us. This tool is not "creative" because it is new. The creative part comes in our actually using it. The tool is prayer. When we talk to God about our problems, regardless of how mundane we might think they are, God has a way of helping us see the situation positively. Like my friend, instead of a problem, we have an opportunity to allow God's grace to work through us.

_____

_____

_____

_____

April 6
Roses, Tomatoes, and a Dish of Okra!

Are you planning to put out a vegetable garden? How about a flower bed? My wife, Cheri, and I enjoy working in our yard. Cheri has planted dozens of flowers and shrubs in the past few days. I have worked up a plot of ground, hoping to set out some tomatoes, peppers, and okra.

I marvel at the dedication and perhaps even love that some gardeners lavish on their plants. The long hours involved in preparing the ground, planting, fertilizing, and tilling inspire most of us to go to the Farmers' Market or order an arrangement from the florist. However, the labor doesn't seem to matter for the true gardener. They find enjoyment in seeing these things grow and mature.

Steven B. Angus

Interestingly, most gardeners give the produce away after all the hard work. Why? Perhaps they are attempting to offer a little beauty into a sometimes borderline ugly world.

As you work in your yard or notice the neighbor pulling weeds from the flowerbed, you may want to consider John 15:1-8. In verse 1, Jesus said, "I am the true vine, and my Father is the gardener (NIV)." Hmm. . .God is a gardener. This metaphor can teach us volumes about our God. As a gardener, God births us, nurtures us, prunes us, and provides countless other things, and for what purpose? To help us grow into something beautiful so He can share us with someone else. As you go about this day, remember that "The Master Gardener" has placed you in this world to help bring beauty into someone's life. How will you do so?

___

April 7
The Domino Effect

As a child visiting my grandparents, I enjoyed playing with dominoes. Eventually, I learned how to play the game, but my first recollection of those dotted rectangles was using them to build skyscrapers. Sometimes, I would use my tiny cowboys and Indians to construct a fort for a grand battle.

One day, two of my cousins and I came up with several sets of dominoes. We stood the dominoes, placing them about an inch apart, creating a long line. When we had them strategically placed, we would tap the first one. It would fall into the next one, setting off a chain reaction. Sometimes, we would set up multiple lines and have races.

Since then, I have seen exhibitions where millions of dominoes were used. The Guinness World Records reports thirteen categories for world records in domino toppling. The current record stands at over 4.5 million dominoes, when toppled, took over two hours to complete. It began because of the action of one domino.

In the gospel of Luke 24:13-35, two disciples encountered the risen Jesus on the Emmaus Road. They immediately returned to Jerusalem and told the others what they had experienced. They had no way of knowing the chain reaction they helped to start. When the disciples recognized Him, Jesus told them to share the story with every nation. How was this to occur? One person telling one person, who told another, and so forth. Jesus's plan has not changed. We can build towers, hoping people will come. However, it returns to the domino effect—one person telling another. Whom are we telling?

Faith Bytes

April 8
"When We Know Our Place"

The Jewish Rabbi Hanokh told a parable about a man who had a problem. When he got up in the morning, he could not get dressed because he could not find his clothes. It was so bad he found it challenging to sleep thinking about the trouble he would have on waking. Then he had an idea. As he undressed, he took paper and pencil and noted precisely where he placed each item.

The following day, he was pleased with himself. He took the slip of paper and read: "cap" -- there it was, he set it on his head; "pants'! -- there they lay, he put them on, and so it went until he was fully dressed. "That's all very well, but now, where am I?" he asked in great consternation. "Where in the world am I?" He searched in vain but could not find himself. "And that is how it is with us," said the rabbi.

Do you know where you are? I acknowledge this is an odd question if we mean our geographic location. However, if we are speaking about our relationship with Jesus, it suddenly isn't a silly question. It is often said that the most critical detail regarding a business's success is location, location, and location. The same can be said about the effectiveness of a Christian—it is location, location, and location. Do you know where you are? I invite you to consider this as you read Matthew 5:1-12. When We Know Our Place as Christians, our perception of our life and the world changes.

_____

_____

_____

April 9
Learning to Trust

"I can do it myself." If the words sound familiar, it may suggest we have had a lot of practice saying them. They have been a staple since we began combining words to articulate a complete thought. Sooner, more so than later, we discovered, saying it didn't necessarily make it so. Whether we are speaking about an individual, a nation, a marriage, or a church, each will confront some obstacle that will render the boast null and void. What then?

A child attempting their first steps is surprised when she loses her balance and realizes her diaper-encased bottom has found the floor. Immediately, she looks to her parent, who will pick her up, dust off the seat of her pants, and then help her to stand again. Soon, she will learn to trust the promise of this loving presence in her life. What is remarkable about this promise is it has never been articulated in a way the child can understand. It simply occurred. Soon, the "I can do it myself" will be accompanied by a quick glance over the shoulder just to be satisfied. Before long, the need to look is no longer necessary.

Steven B. Angus

The Apostle Paul faced countless obstacles yet never wavered. He was equipped with trust much like that of the before-mentioned child. Paul would not be deterred because experience had taught him that Jesus was watching over him. He didn't need to look over his shoulder for confirmation. He just knew. He did reframe "I can do it myself" to accurately express his confidence. He said, "I can do all things through Christ who strengthens me." [Philippians 4:13].

During the coming days, we will visit some of the Philippians 4:13esk passages in the Bible. Today, I ask you to write Philippians 4:13, no, not under your eye, like Tim Tebow. Instead, I challenge you to memorize it, writing it upon your heart. You will not regret the effort. "I can do all things through Christ who strengthens me."

_____

_____

_____

_____

April 10
Called, Servant, and Chosen

The words of Isaiah 41:9-10 were initially spoken to the nation of Israel. However, because of Jesus, they became a promise made to all those called by God. They are extended to you as a follower of Jesus. Long before the Apostle Paul wrote the words of Philippians 4:13, the Prophet Isaiah described who we are in God's eyes. See if you can identify some of God's promises that can give us the courage to walk the way of a Disciple.

> "I have called you back from the ends of the earth, saying, 'You are my servant.' For I have chosen you and will not throw you away. Don't be afraid, for I am with you. Don't be discouraged, for I am your God. I will strengthen you and help you. I will hold you up with my victorious right hand."
> [Isaiah 41:9-10, NLT]

Did you hear how God identifies us? God said: "I have called you." "You are my servant." "I have chosen you." Called, servant, chosen—that is you.

Did you hear God's promises? God said:

> I have chosen you—*I will not throw you away.*
> Don't be afraid—*I am with you.*
> Don't be discouraged—*I am your God.*
> I will strengthen you and help you.
> I will hold you up—how? *With my victorious right hand.*

Faith Bytes

What more could we hope or ask? Make Isaiah 41:9-10 one of your "go-to" passages when you need a faith boost.

April 11
Jesus! Prime My Pump!

I find myself wishing I were in the mountains. I yearn to hear the crashing sound of a waterfall plunging freefall onto boulders rendered smooth over time. No, what I genuinely believe would refresh my soul isn't the violent torrents of water attacking stone but the unmistakable trickling rhythm of a steady spring feeding a continuously thirsty mountain stream. Just thinking about it tempts me to abandon my chores, mount my motorcycle, and head to higher ground.

Are you looking for a passage to help you focus as you prepare your day's agenda? How about these words that Jesus said in John 7:37-38? "Let anyone who is thirsty [Did your hand dart upward?] Let them come to me, and let the one who believes in me drink." [7:37-38, NRSVUE].

I hope you noticed Jesus' words included the person who is already a believer. Believers always need more to drink. Then he says, "Out of the believer's heart shall flow rivers of living water."

Are you familiar with the expression "priming the pump?" I remember the wellhouse next to my grandparents' home. Occasionally, the pump stopped delivering the water. Inside the small building was a bucket of water for such emergencies. Water was poured into the pump to prime it so the water would flow again.

This is your verse for today: "Out of the believer's heart [my heart] shall flow rivers of living water."

Can you say—"Jesus! Prime my pump?" Trickle. Trickle. Trickle. Ahhh!

Steven B. Angus

April 12
"I Will Let You Find Me" —God

The late Dr. Ellsworth Kalas, a scholar, author, and preacher, often referred to Luke 15 as God's "Lost and Found Department." A woman lost a coin, a shepherd, a lamb, and a father, his son. Each did what was necessary to find what they cherished, even if it meant looking under furniture, roaming the cul-de-sacs of the Judean hills, or waiting patiently for a child to come to their senses and return home. We correctly read these stories as portraying God unrelentingly searching for us.

But what if there is another side to these stories? Could these parables express our longing to deepen our relationship with God once He has found us? Are we willing to do the spiritual house cleaning, abandon the security of the sheepfold for a time, or just be still, knowing that by doing so, we find God?

Let me phrase it this way. "Is it your desire to find God?" Not to be redeemed, but as the redeemed seeking a relationship with our Redeemer God? Lest you think I am taking liberties, listen to this promise of God found in Jeremiah 29:13-14. God said: "When you search for me, you will find me; if you seek me with all your heart, I will let you find me." [NRSVUE].

Gene Edwards has described our relationship with God as "The Divine Romance." In other words, God wants to be the center of our desire and takes joy in being sought. If you are struggling today, why not search and seek God? Thankfully, God does not play hard to get. Instead, he tenders the promise: "I will let you find me."

_____

_____

_____

_____

April 13
Sing a Different Tune

As I read Psalm 70, I found myself on YouTube searching for a weekly segment on the television show *"Hee Haw."* It is the one where Buck Owens and Roy Clark sang:

Gloom, despair, and agony on me
Deep, dark depression, excessive misery
If it weren't for bad luck, I'd have no luck at all
Gloom, despair, and agony on me

Psalm 70 was one of David's "Gloom and Despair" songs. He sincerely believed he had reached the end of his rope. He felt alone, as if he was being attacked on every side, and truthfully, he wasn't mistaken. Desperation was the state of his heart, mind, and soul. Are you feeling overwhelmed? David chose to be brutally

Faith Bytes

vulnerable with himself and with God. This is how Eugene Petersen stated it in The Message.

God! Please hurry to my rescue!
God, come quickly to my side!
Let all who love your saving way say over and over, "God is mighty!"
But I've lost it. I'm wasted. God—quickly, quickly!
Quick to my side, quick to my rescue! God, don't lose a minute. [Selected]

When we feel gloomy and desperate, it seems we have two choices. We can sing along with Buck and Roy or join David and sing a different tune to God.

April 14
Review

As a student, I was always grateful when the instructor said, "Today, we will review for the exam." I could look back over my notes and refresh my memory so that I could be ready. This week, we have mentioned five promises in Scripture that can help us when our faith is tested. Are you up for a review?

Philippians 4:13 is a favorite of many: "I can do all things through Jesus who strengthens me."

Isaiah 41:9-10 [NLT] speaking through the prophet, God says: "You are my servant. For I have chosen you and will not throw you away. Don't be afraid, for I am with you. Don't be discouraged, for I am your God. I will strengthen you and help you."

In John 7:37-39,[NIV] Jesus said: "Let anyone who is thirsty, let them come to me, and let the one who believes in me drink. Out of the believer's heart shall flow rivers of living water."

In the voice of Jeremiah 29:13-14, [NRSVUE]. God said: "When you search for me, you will find me; if you seek me with all your heart, I will let you find me."

And then we have the earnest plea of David in Psalm 70 MSG, Selected]:

"God! Please hurry to my rescue! God, come quickly to my side!
But I've lost it. I'm wasted. God—quickly, quickly!
Quick to my side, quick to my rescue! God, don't lose a minute."

Steven B. Angus

When we signed up for the course, we knew testing would come. These are five promises that, if written in our hearts, will help us to be ready.

_____
_____
_____
_____

April 15
The Righteous Gentile

The ten Boom family were Dutch Christians who helped many Jews escape the Nazi Holocaust of WWII. However, the entire family was imprisoned when their home was raided after an informant tipped off the Nazis of their activities. Corrie and her sister were sent to a notorious Nazi concentration camp. She was miraculously released from prison just days after her sister had died there. Many have read the book or seen the movie, "The Hiding Place." Among Jews, she has been called a "righteous gentile," considered the highest of compliments.

Today, April 15, marks the birthday of this remarkable woman of faith, Corrie ten Boom. At 91, on this date in 1983, she entered the Father's House. According to Jewish belief, having the same day for one's birth and death is a unique sign of an extraordinary individual. Many would agree Corrie was such a person.

Corrie was known for her many one-liners of faith. Here are a few to encourage us today:

> "Don't bother to give God instructions; just report for duty."
> "You can never learn that Christ is all you need until Christ is all you have."
> "God takes our sins – the past, present, and future, and dumps them in the sea and puts up a sign that says NO FISHING ALLOWED."
> "What wings are to a bird and sails to a ship, so is prayer to the soul."
> "Worry is like a rocking chair: it keeps you moving but doesn't get you anywhere."
> "Never be afraid to trust an unknown future to a known God."

Thank you, Corrie ten Boom!

_____
_____
_____
_____

Faith Bytes

April 16
Here I Stand

On April 16, 1521, Martin Luther arrived at the Diet of Worms. He went believing he was attending a hearing he had requested to discuss the abuse of indulgences and his essay referred to as the "95 Theses." Instead, he faced a judicial hearing. Twenty-five books were laid before him, and he was asked two questions: "Are these books yours?" And "Will you recant them?" Luthur's response was, "Here I stand. I can do no other. God help me! Amen."

Luther was condemned and allowed twenty-one days to return to his home in Wittenberg. After that time, he would be treated as an obstinate heretic, which most likely meant execution. Along the way, friends snatched him and delivered him safely at the Wartburg Castle. He would use those ten months of isolation to translate the New Testament into a readable document for the German people. He continued his efforts in what became known as the Protestant Reformation.

Whether Protestant or Catholic, being a Christian is about Reformation. It is about personal renovation, where we become more like Christ. To do so means we offer a little hope to others. Where? Luther said it—"Here. Not somewhere else. Here. Where we stand." Luther was correct. "We can do no other." So let our prayer also be—"God help us. Amen."

_____

_____

_____

_____

April 17
I Bake

Perhaps you have heard the story of a religious man living in Glasgow, Scotland. He taught Sunday School, preached in outdoor meetings, and served the church in many other ways. He was a baker by trade. While traveling on a train, he was confronted by a zealous passenger who asked him if he was a Christian. When he said yes, she asked what work he did for the Master. Instead of mentioning his Sunday School Class or his popularity as a preacher, he said, "I bake." She said, "I did not ask you about your occupation, but what kind of service do you give to the Savior?" With a smile, he said, "Madam, I bake." She persisted. "What I mean is, how are you seeking to spread his gospel?" Again, his only reply was, "I bake."

Although this event supposedly occurred in another century, it remains relevant. It reminds us that our primary witness for Jesus isn't what we do inside the church. It is what we do outside it that speaks the loudest. How we reach people for Jesus has changed significantly. No longer can we wait for people to come to us. We must go where the people are. Our culture has experienced a mega-shift regarding institutions and their representatives. Suspicion is the operative word, as most people believe organizations want something, usually their money. This includes the church. Those who attend are seen as company cronies instead of Jesus' followers. We can only correct this stigma by leaving the comfort of our sanctuary and being with our neighbors. Jesus intended this as He did most of his work away from Houses of Worship. The Apostle Paul worked as a tent maker to be with those Jesus came to save. It has been reported that Martin Luther did more for the kingdom over a beer stein at the pub than inside churches. Finding opportunities to listen and to laugh with a neighbor has a way of bringing down walls of suspicion. Such occasions can demonstrate who we are in Christ to those unfamiliar with Jesus and His followers. In addition, it may encourage someone disheartened by organized religion to give Jesus another chance. What do you do to serve Jesus?

_____

_____

_____

_____

April 18
In the beginning, God Created.....Relationships!

I would be hard-pressed to identify my favorite book in the Bible. Although I have never assembled a top ten list, I am confident the book of Genesis would be on it. I simply love this grand document, but this is not true for everyone. On occasion, it seems some Christians find it embarrassing. If they happen to reference it, they do so with a wink of the eye, suggesting to their audience, "Of course, we don't take this part of the Bible as relevant to our scientific world."

Perhaps we are perplexed by its stories because we have attempted to make them applicable to secondary themes or force them to answer questions that aren't being asked. Yet, I firmly believe that without a firm grasp of Genesis, we will always have difficulty understanding the depth of Jesus's message.

For example, one foundational tenet of Genesis is "relationship." Genesis is more concerned with the "why" of creation than the "how." The why is relationship. God longed for it and formed humans with a need for it. Thus, Adam craved it so passionately that it hurt in a place just behind his rib. Recognizing this human need, God took steps to satisfy it. All was good until the relational creature became enticed by selfishness—and well, the following sixty-five documents of the Bible demonstrate what became of us and what God did to restore it.

I ask you to consider the relationships in your life. Are they what you hoped they would be? Like Adam and Eve's various relationships, have we allowed ours to be tarnished by our less-than-honorable selves? Have we adequately prioritized our relationships?

Perhaps the words of the Apostle Paul to the Church in Rome are helpful. He said, "So now we can rejoice in our wonderful new relationship with God because our Lord Jesus Christ has made us friends of God." [Romans 5:11, NLT].

Faith Bytes

April 19
Do They Know?

In 1966, a Roman Catholic priest, Peter Scholtes (1938–2009), served a parish in South Chicago. Although he would marry and leave the priesthood, he gifted a hymn that lives on in Catholic and Protestant hymnody. According to music historian Joshua Taylor, the song "They Will Know We Are Christians" has become essential in the church's efforts to sing a theology of active participation and discipleship in and for the world. Its accessible melody and folk-guitar accompaniment include stanzas that reflect "what" the church's life together should demonstrate to our world. These include such images as "walking hand in hand, working together, and praising together." In addition, the stanzas are anchored by the repeated refrain, "Yes, they will know we are Christians by our love."

There is seldom a day when we do not have the opportunity to demonstrate to our world who we are in Christ. Our love for one another and our neighbors becomes concrete in our walking, working, and praising God as one. But, unfortunately, our world cannot see through rock, mortar, and steel walls. This leaves us with one option: to come out of gathering places and allow others to see someone in Jesus Christ. "They will know. . ." But do they know?

April 20
If Moses Had Been a Woman

Araminta Ross was born into slavery, perhaps in March 1822. Her parents called her "Minty." About 1844, she married John Tubman, a free black. Five years later, she heard a rumor that she was about to be sold. She became a runaway and fled to Philadelphia, leaving behind her husband, parents, and siblings. In December 1850, she went to Baltimore, Maryland, where she led her sister and two children to freedom. This was the first of some 19 forays into the South. Over the next decade, she helped to lead upward of 300 fugitive slaves along what was known as the Underground Railroad.

In the movie "Harriet," there is a moving scene. The free Araminta has the opportunity to replace her slave name with one of her own choosing. She chose her mother's name, Harriet, and her husband's Tubman.

Steven B. Angus

On April 20, 1853, Harriet Tubman became a conductor on the Underground Railroad. To her generation, she was known as "Grandma Moses," which infuriated slaveholders who posted a $40,000 reward for her capture, which never occurred. Harriet's friends and fellow abolitionists claimed that her strength came from her Methodist faith in God as a deliverer and protector of the weak. She said, "I always tole God I'm *gwine* [going] to hole stiddy on you, an' you've got to see me through."

Can there be a better prayer for us? Why not make it yours today?

April 21
Choose Wisely

The Holy Grail refers to the cup used by Jesus at the Last Supper. According to one legend, Joseph of Arimathea used it to receive Christ's blood at the Cross. There have been many stories written about the search for it.

Do you have a favorite story about this search? We certainly are not lacking choices ranging from Lord Tennyson, Dan Brown, and Monty Python. Mine is the movie "Indiana Jones and the Last Crusade." My fondness for actors Sean Connery and Harrison Ford may have more to do with it than the storyline. Towards the film's end, the ancient protector of the Holy Grail presents several possible cups to the treasure hunters but warns, "Choose wisely, for while the true Grail will bring you life, the false Grail will take it from you." The Nazi villain goes first, selects the most beautiful vessel, and dies drinking from it. The ancient one simply said: "He chose poorly." Indiana Jones then chooses the simple wooden chalice, obviously the one fit for a carpenter. The Knight of Grail said to Indie, "You chose wisely!"

I like this scene because it illustrates the importance of wisdom. Wisdom for a follower of Jesus often appears different from what logic suggests. In the New Testament letter of James, the author states that wisdom is understanding God's ways. He says:

> "But the wisdom that is from above is first pure, then peaceable, gentle, willing to yield, full of mercy and good fruits, without partiality and without hypocrisy. Now the fruit of righteousness is sown in peace by those who make peace." [James 3:17-18]

If we apply these traits to our daily living, it is likely to be said of us, "You chose wisely."

Faith Bytes

April 22
Being Ready

We never know when an opportunity will present itself, and it may do so only once. Ask Tom Brady or Aaron Rodgers, two of the National Football League's greatest quarterbacks. Their accomplishments occurred when they were sent into a game off the bench. Perhaps Brady and Rodgers borrowed a play from one of our nation's greatest field generals who said, "I will prepare, and someday my chance will come." His name was Abraham Lincoln. [Abraham Lincoln Quotes. BrainyQuote.com, BrainyMedia Inc, 2020.]

How do we prepare ourselves for an opportunity, or on the flip side, how do we plan for disappointment, illness, or family conflict? Truthfully, those minions are as apt to show up as unexpectedly. I am sure Brett Favre, who was replaced by Aaron Rodgers, and Drew Bledsoe, who lost his job to Tom Brady, would testify to this.

This is why Nehemiah should be our mentor in such things. So much about him made him a great and godly leader. Many of his people were being held as slaves in Babylon. He wept, fasted, and prayed for days when he heard how bad things were back home. He was the "Wine tester" for the King, which meant he tasted it first to ensure it wasn't poisoned. One day, the King saw how sad he was and inquired why, and he told the King about his people's suffering. In Nehemiah 2:4, the King asked: "What can I do?" This was Nehemiah's opportunity. What did he do? Like a good quarterback, Nehemiah called an audible that not even Bill Belichick could have seen coming. In Nehemiah 2:4, we read, "So I prayed to the God of heaven. Then I said…" Nehemiah learned the importance of "the breath prayer." He had about 5 seconds, but it was time enough.

When opportunity or trial comes knocking, part of our readiness is remembering the power of "the breath prayer" and our immediate access to God.

_____
_____
_____
_____

April 23
The Birth of a Church

"Happy Birthday to you. Happy Birthday to you. Happy birthday, dear. . ."

Before I give the name of whose birthday we celebrate, you may wish to prepare a cake. However, leave room for many candles. Imagine the flicker of the flame as representing miniature torches. Although we celebrate today as a birthday, the wedding anniversary image is equally appropriate. Ok. I will stop teasing.

Steven B. Angus

On April 23, 1968, Bishop Reuben H. Mueller of The Evangelical United Brethren Church and Bishop Lloyd C. Wicke of The Methodist Church joined hands at the General Conference in Dallas, Texas. They declared, "Lord of the Church, we are united in Thee, in Thy Church, and now in The United Methodist Church."

A new denomination was born with the logo of a cross-linked by a single flame with dual tongues of fire. The image demonstrated how this near denomination was yoked to Christ, symbolized by the cross. Also, the flame of fire portrays the Holy Spirit's work. The word United also represents a coming together of black Methodists and white Methodists in the same conference, with the same preachers and bishops, as opposed to segregated conferences.

No one knows what the future holds for the United Methodist marriage. However, this day allows us to thank God for the great things He has done through this part of His Church. Instead of blowing out the candles and making a wish—a prayer of gratitude and guidance is appropriate.

_____
_____
_____
_____

April 24
Drink a Beer, Sing a song. . .?

It has been said that we often entertain angels unaware. What about prophets? Sometimes, I wonder if they wander among us disguised as Country Music songwriters. They can be "earthy" in their composition yet prophetic in meaning. Take, for example, the Kenny Chesney song "Get Along," written by Shane Mcanally, Ross Copperman, and Josh Osborne. Visualize John the Baptist before a surprised congregation delivering a sermon similar to these lyrics.

> "We find out when you die, the keys to heaven can't be bought
> We still don't know what love is but we sure know what it's not
> Sometimes you got
>
> "To get along
> Down the road
> We've got a long, long way to go
> Scared to live, scared to die
> We ain't perfect, but we try
> Get along while we can
> Always give love the upper hand
> Paint a wall, learn to dance
> Call your mom, buy a boat
> Drink a beer, sing a song
> Make a friend, can't we all get along?"

Truthfully, the church could benefit from Martin Luther's example and enjoy a gathering at the local pub to discuss Jesus. Likewise, congregations could profit if we "give love the upper hand." The Apostle Paul offered wisdom on Church folk getting along. He wrote: "Bear with one another and, if anyone has a complaint against another, forgive each other. . . Above all, clothe yourselves with love, which binds everything together in perfect harmony." [Colossians 3:13-15]

Take a moment to re-read Paul's words through the eyes of a Country Music prophet. Then consider, "What must change to get along with others, particularly my sisters and brothers at church?"

_____

_____

_____

_____

April 25
Does Your 'Floogie Bird' Fly?

John 4:5-42 is the story of a nameless Samaritan woman who, from her vantage point, had a chance encounter with a Jewish teacher. She had chosen the hottest time of the day to walk two miles to draw water from a well. As the hot sun bore down on her, she probably pondered retracing those two miles back home with the added burden of a water-filled jar. However, the truth is soon revealed that she was already carrying a weight far exceeding that of a water pitcher. Her problem wasn't unique. We recognize it in the disciples, the residents of her village, and, frankly, ourselves. What is the load we humans struggle with? The past.

The author, Margaret Storm Jameson is unfamiliar to most of us. However, we have likely read a sampling of her work without realizing it. By the early 1950s, "Storm" was such a respected author she was asked to write the introduction to the haunting thoughts recorded in a red and plaid diary by a young Jewish girl. The book was "The Diary of Anne Frank." Storm expressed that we spend too much time living in the past, feeling regret for lost joys or shame for poorly done things. She stated, "The only way to live is to accept each minute as an unrepeatable miracle. [Therefore, we should] Work at your work. Play at your play. Shed your tears. Enjoy your laughter. Now is the time of your life."

The individuals in John 4 [and we] could have benefited from Storm's advice. But instead, they seemed focused on everything except the "unrepeatable miracle of the now."

Harry S. Truman, our 33rd president, was known for his no-nonsense approach to doing his job. He was reported to have said, "Men who live in the past remind me of a...small wooden [toy of a] bird called the 'Floogie Bird.' Around [its] neck [was] a label reading, 'I fly backwards; I don't care where I'm going. I just want to see where I've been.'" Of course, the Floogie Bird doesn't exist, but those who live looking to the past certainly do, and truthfully, it is a terrible weight. Read John 4 and imagine life if you relinquish the past to Jesus.

Steven B. Angus

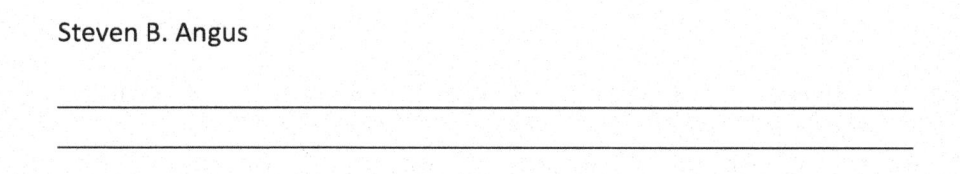

April 26
Sing!

A group of humans listened as the animals and birds in the forest debated who was the loudest and the greatest of all the animals. Initially, everyone thought of the lion, elephant, tiger, or rhinoceros. However, when all the talk had died down, only the elephant remained unchallenged as Africa's loudest and most feared animal. The elephant said he could trumpet the loudest, and his voice would carry further than any other animal. The only creature who challenged the elephant was a small canary bird. All the people laughed at the canary, and they suggested a contest between the elephant and the canary.

On the day of the contest, the elephant was chosen to go first. All the people held their ears as the elephant trumpeted his loudest trumpet. Then, a runner was sent out to see how far away the elephant's trumpet was heard. After three days, the runner returned and gave his report. The people were amazed.

When it was the canary's turn, the humans laughed as the canary began to sing his sweetest song. But soon, everyone quieted down because they wanted to hear the beautiful sound. Suddenly, other canaries started singing the same beautiful music in the distance. In fact, the canaries in the next village began to sing and continued from village to village. Finally, a runner was sent to see how far the canary's song could be heard. The runner never returned.

The people learned a great lesson that day. They discovered it is not how loud you speak but how much love you share that changes the hearts of those who listen. This exemplifies what a life or church surrendered to Jesus can do. It is not about our size or how loud we speak. It is about the beauty and hopes we demonstrate through our love. Why not sing to someone a song of Jesus' love?

April 27
Such a Small Price

In March of 1736, John Wesley, who would become the father of the movement called Methodism, began his ministry in the Colony known as Georgia. For this journey of more than 4,000 miles, John had a copy of a book by his favorite poet. A decade later, Wesley arranged for copies of this book to be available in the

Faith Bytes

small libraries he was starting throughout Great Britain. The Methodist Conference of 1746 ruled that all preachers should read this book.

The blind author had dictated his work and, needing money, on this day, April 27, 1667, signed an agreement that would pay him 10 pounds, the equivalent of $2000, for the rights to his book. The poet was John Milton, and the book was "Paradise Lost." Historians say the work influenced English thought nearly as much as the King James Version of the Bible. Following his death, his widow sold the perpetual copyrights for eight pounds. It's hard to imagine selling something so valuable for so little.

Today, as we celebrate John Milton's wonderful gift, perhaps we should ask ourselves if we are exchanging something of great value for something of little significance. Jesus framed it this way: "What can anyone give in exchange for their soul?" The book "Paradise Lost" describes how such a trade can be costly. How are we bartering the 1440 minutes of this day? Is it worth it? At the very least, we should give it some thought.

April 28
The Power to Change Lives

I always thought "Mutiny on the Bounty" was nothing more than a movie that helped to make Marlon Brando, Trevor Howard, and Richard Harris into Hollywood stars. The film tells a fictionalized story of the actual mutiny led by Fletcher Christian against Captain William Bligh.

On April 28, 1789, a band of hedonistic sailors staged the famous mutiny in the South Pacific. The mutineers sailed to uninhabited Pitcairn Island, where they soon fell into drinking, fighting, and murder. Their fate was unknown until twenty years later when the American sailing ship Topaz rediscovered the Island. By then, only one man and several women (taken earlier as slaves) and children survived. John Adams, who had changed his name to Alexander Smith, discovered the ship's neglected Bible, repented, and transformed the community by teaching the women and children to read and write using the Bible. The islanders also converted to Christianity. Adams was eventually granted amnesty.

Today, around forty people live on the Island, almost all descendants of the Bounty mutineers. The capital is Adamstown, named for John Adams. The Bible is still on display in a local church. Let this be a reminder that the message of the Bible can change lives.

Steven B. Angus

April 29
"You're One Sweet Rat."

Research has demonstrated that the human brain will remain healthy when challenged. For example, lab rats were given food in one experiment. In contrast, another group had obstacles placed in front of their dishes. The fewer problems a rat experiences, the faster its brain deteriorates.

Twelve rats were then placed in a cage and given challenges. Their brains developed better than those facing the same obstacles in isolation. When researchers ran the same experiment with rats that were 600 days or older (the equivalent of 60 human years), they lived to be 800 days old.

Then, researchers decided to show them some love. The rodents had the same challenges as before, but afterward, they were picked up, held, petted, and told something like, "You're one sweet rat." Not only did they break the 800-day barrier, but at 904 days, they continued to thrive.

The lesson? You and I need God-given challenges, people to love and love us, and meaningful communication to thrive. The Apostle Paul understood this without the assistance of rodents. In the Message, 1 Thessalonians 5:11 states: "So speak encouraging words to one another. Build up hope so you'll all be together in this, no one left out, no one left behind."

We must intentionally challenge ourselves and reach out to one another in loving ways. We could always begin a conversation by saying, "You may be a rat, but you're sweet, and I love you anyway." On second thought, maybe not!

_____
_____
_____
_____

April 30
Accepting Your Forgiveness

For some, Ernest Hemingway's writing ability was unparalleled, demonstrated by his receiving the Nobel Prize in Literature. For others, he represented a lifestyle that would cause some to blush and others to imitate.

Hemingway grew up in a Christian home yet never experienced kindness nor was introduced to a God of grace and forgiveness. Unlike the bad boy prodigal of the New Testament, a parent wasn't waiting for him at the end of the driveway to welcome him home. Some believe this contributed to his struggle with depression. His short story "The Capital of the World" revolved around one of his favorite subjects, bullfighting. It may hint at what Hemingway was searching for—grace and forgiveness.

The tale is set in Spain and is about a father and son who had a falling out. As a result, the son Francesco, nicknamed Paco, ran away from home, although why

Faith Bytes

he left is not revealed. Paco found himself wandering the streets of Madrid, hoping to enter into a profession that would most likely get him killed, that of a matador. Paco's recollections of his mistakes and guilt over what happened blindly drove him to this one-way street to suicide.

His father was also experiencing regret, which led him to an act of desperation. Realizing there was little chance he would find Paco by wandering the streets of Madrid, he placed an ad in the local newspaper. The advertisement read, "Paco, meet me at the Hotel Montana at noon on Tuesday. All is forgiven! Love, Papa."

When the father arrived at the hotel, he was shocked. Because Paco was an ordinary name in Spain, 800 young men were waiting to be reconciled with their fathers. Some have discussed why such an overwhelming response. Was it because Paco was a common name or the more profound need for forgiveness?

The name Poco is interchangeable with Steven, Susan, Ann, Bob, and your name. The heart and soul of the Christian faith is forgiveness. To be a disciple of Jesus is to accept forgiveness.

_____

_____

_____

_____

Steven B. Angus

MAY

May 1
Give Us This Day Forgiveness

Take a moment to pray this prayer.

> "Our Father, which art in heaven, Hallowed be thy Name. Thy Kingdom come. Thy will be done in earth, As it is in heaven. Give us this day our daily bread. And forgive us our trespasses, As we forgive them that trespass against us. And lead us not into temptation, But deliver us from evil. For thine is the kingdom, The power, and the glory, Forever and ever. Amen."

What a wonderful gift is the Lord's Prayer? Jesus has given us a way to address the needs He knew we would have. When we pray, "Give us this day," we typically associate them with the following phrase: "Our daily bread." However, they apply to each following petition, for example—"Give us this day forgiveness of our trespasses."

Forgiveness. Jesus realized that even disciples would need it--daily. Furthermore, we will likely have multiple reasons to extend forgiveness—daily, if not hourly. Each day, we must accept forgiveness and render it to another. Forgiveness is a need in all areas of life: at work, in our family relationships, and even with other Christians. For most of us, it isn't so much that we have a sin problem as it is a forgiveness problem. As Christians, we need guidance in accepting our own forgiveness and how we give it.

The first thing we need to understand about forgiveness is it already exists. We do not have to create it. Forgiveness has a twin sister, and her name is Grace.

Faith Bytes

Each already is and can be received and given. Take time today to accept it and to extend it.

_____
_____
_____
_____

May 2
A Spare Tire Named Forgiveness

Answering the phone, I heard the frantic voice of my youngest daughter, who was away at college. Lydia and her roommate had gone to the store, and when they returned to her car, she was confronted with a flat tire. When she was learning to drive, I taught her how to change a tire, but she had never needed to do so. With Mom and Dad on the phone, she opened the trunk, saw the floor mat, and thought— "I don't have a spare!" Perhaps you can relate. It is a horrible, vulnerable feeling.

When needing forgiveness, it is easy to experience a spiritual panic attack. The good news is we do not have to reinvent the wheel. Forgiveness has already been secured and is waiting for us. What does this mean? Jesus has already died on the cross. He has already arisen from the grave. Jesus has thought of absolutely everything. Forgiveness already exists.

After we calmed our daughter down and guided her to lift the flooring in the trunk, she breathed a sigh of relief. There was indeed a spare. If you are worried about the availability of forgiveness, I have good news! It doesn't matter how you got your "flat," whether it was something small like a nail or a loud and total blowout—you have a spare. When receiving God's forgiveness, we must understand we cannot create it. It is a gift that can only be accepted.

When Lydia looked in the trunk, she found a spare tire and a jack. Everything she needed was available, but she was uncertain what to do with them. Lo and behold, a kind man saw their need and changed the tire for them.

Perhaps you are feeling the same way about forgiveness. Okay, it's available, but how do I accept it? Ponder this thought and its meaning for you—Accepting forgiveness begins with realizing we need it.

_____
_____
_____
_____

Steven B. Angus

May 3
Even Now, Return to Me

Accepting forgiveness begins with realizing we need it. Although this seems obvious, the longer we have been a Christian, the more likely we must be reminded of our need for it. Jesus told a story about a father and two sons. Although we tend to focus on the prodigal son who left home, he had an older brother who needed a reminder of forgiveness.

Have you said, "I wish I didn't feel guilty about. . .?" Don't be too quick with that wish, as remorse can be a friend to a Christian. The Holy Spirit can use it to help us see a need for forgiveness in an area we hadn't noticed. If we do not experience guilt for our sins, the Bible refers to this as having our conscience seared. It suggests that we have wandered so far from God's plan that we have become hardened to sin.

For most of us, admitting we have done wrong is not difficult. However, accepting forgiveness does not conclude with our acknowledgment that we need it any more than our stomach will stop growling when we say, "Humm. I am hungry."

Accepting forgiveness begins with repentance. Consider this passage: Notice this passage from.

> "'Even now,' declares the Lord, 'return to me with all your heart, with fasting and weeping and mourning. Rend your heart and not your garments. Return to the Lord your God, for he is gracious and compassionate, slow to anger and abounding in love, and he relents from sending calamity.'"
> [Joel 2:12-13, NIV]

We see a correlation between repentance and forgiveness. Repentance is more than regret. Regret says, "I am sorry I got caught." God says in the text from Joel, "rend your hearts." Repentance begins in the heart. We mourn the fact that our action or inaction has hurt someone else.

Notice how Joel's text states, "Even now," declares the Lord, "return to me with all your heart." God says, "Don't wait until everything is okay before you come to me. Don't try and put all the pieces of your life back together before you return. Come as you are. I can help you."

Faith Bytes

May 4
May the Fourth Be with You!

If you have not been appropriately greeted, allow me to be the first to say, "May the fourth be with you!" The appropriate liturgical response would be—"And also, with you." Perhaps you are thinking… "Holy Sith! Why is he saying that?"

"May the Fourth be with you" is a standard phrase sci-fi fans use on what has become known as Star Wars Day. The date was chosen as a pun on the catchphrase "May the force be with you," made famous by the Skywalkers, the Resistance, and the Great Jedi Master, Yoda. The slogan was first coined in a newspaper advertisement on May 4, 1979, to commemorate the day Margaret Thatcher took office as the United Kingdom's Prime Minister.

I confess to being a Star Wars junkie. Every few years, I will spend several evenings watching each movie and, if possible, any of the spin-off series. I have no trouble saying, "May the fourth be with you" and enjoying the day because each time I say it, in my mind, I also hear, "May the peace of Christ be with you," and offer a prayer of gratitude, that "The Force," the Holy Spirit is always with me.

So, go ahead and say it in your best impersonation of your favorite Star Wars character, and give thanks that the Lord's great love and compassion are new every morning.

_____

_____

_____

_____

May 5
God is Smiling at You!

If you are unfamiliar with the New Testament book of First John, let me introduce you. It has five chapters, and I invite you to read one daily for the next five days. The author almost immediately states that his purpose for writing is that "Our joy may be complete." Joy. The ink barely has time to dry when he launches into a discourse on how life's "light" and "dark" events affect us. Frankly, we wonder what this can possibly have to do with Joy. We have all heard the phrase, "He or she has a smile that lights up the room." We recognize that it applies to that person with a smile so magnificently vivid we wish we could dive into it and swim around as we soak up its warmth. We find it to be a blessing, providing us enjoyment.

One of the great benedictions in the Bible states, "May God be gracious to us and bless us and make his face shine upon us." Our joy is made complete when we realize God is smiling upon us. Let these words wash over your spirit—"God is smiling at you!"

Steven B. Angus

A smile tends to multiply itself. Those who experienced the COVID-19 pandemic realize how it affected our language. One statement I used frequently was, "I know you can't see it, but I'm smiling behind my mask." Introducing "The Mask" into our culture helped me appreciate how important a smile is.

We all know what they say about the person who speaks to themself. I cannot help but wonder what they would say about someone who smiles at themself? Actor Andy Rooney said, "If you smile when you are alone, then you really mean it." Perhaps this is what the writer of First John had in mind. When we realize Jesus is smiling at us, we must trust that He really means it. So contagious is His smile that we must explain to our neighbor, "Behind this mask, I'm smiling!"

May 6
Something Old, Something New.

"Something old, something new, Something borrowed, something Blue, A silver sixpence in her shoe." This poem from seventeenth-century Scotland is so woven into the fabric of society that Prince William and Catherine Middleton observed it during their 2011 Royal Wedding. It is a custom intended to bring lightness to a high-stress event while bridging the generations. I thought of this custom as I read:

> "I am not writing a new commandment for you; rather, it is an old one you have had from the very beginning. This old commandment—to love one another—is the same message you heard before. Yet it is also new." [1 John 2:7-8, NLT]

Perhaps you understand why I thought of "something old, something new." We hear the text from 1 John 2 and wonder—Isn't love always love? How can something old simultaneously be new? Subtly, the author has drawn us in. Although he uses the word love more frequently than any New Testament book except for the Gospel of John, he does not use it until he has written a fourth of the letter. It seems his original audience had become so acquainted with love that it was considered a dated word, which is another way of saying it was an old word.

John wants his audience to know that love is neither old nor outdated. Instead, it is always new. Love was present in the Old Testament law, but it wasn't a person. The love that is in Christ is continuously new. How can that be? Perhaps

Faith Bytes

the Message translation can help: "Love is new, freshly minted as it is in both Christ and you."

Some would say marriage is always marriage. But is it? Isn't each one new and unique based on its partners? First John reminds us that Jesus's love is afresh each morning as it is lived out daily in each disciple.

As you read 1 John 2, how will you be the love of Jesus to the world today?

_____
_____
_____
_____

May 7
How Are You Feeling Today?

About this time of the year in 1977, with my high school diploma in my back pocket and plans to begin my college career, I felt pretty good about life. As a seventeen-year-old, those feelings were subject to change. Add to the mix young love, and things could become confusing. Thankfully, a song was floating across the radio waves to remind me that I wasn't alone in all these—these feelings.

> *"Feelings, nothing more than feelings*
> *Trying to forget my feelings of love*
> *Teardrops rolling down on my face*
> *Trying to forget my feelings of love."*

The song's title isn't surprising as it is repeated twenty-three times in the lyrics, "Feelings." We place great value on them. As casually as if we were asking someone to pass the salt, we ask, "How are you feeling?" Feelings are powerful and can bring about good or destruction. We are prone to say, "I can't help how I feel," as if that makes everything okay.

In 1 John 3:20, one translation has the author saying, "Even if we feel guilty, God is greater than our feelings, and he knows everything." [NLT] We are reminded that the God who spoke the world into existence and calmed a storm at sea is larger than our emotions. God can help us get in touch with them and sort through those that are true and those that are self-lies. It begins when we trust God enough to say, "God, you already know this, but this is how I feel. By your grace, help me to process them."

"How are you feeling today?" That is God asking, not me.

_____
_____
_____
_____

Steven B. Angus

May 8
A Different Kind of Boxed Chocolates

First John 4 can be described as a box of white chocolate, raspberry-filled sea stars. Allow me to explain.

I have had the opportunity to be the pastor of various churches ranging from rural, county seat, and metropolitan. Each comes with its unique challenges and opportunities. One perk I enjoyed about living in a large city was being within walking distance of a prominent mall. This meant I never had to guess when selecting a gift for my late wife. I would walk to the Godiva Chocolate Boutique and purchase some white chocolate raspberry-filled starfish. I did not mind the cost because of how she savored them. She did not eat them all at once but treated each one the way someone would nurture a glass of exquisite wine. She never rushed the experience and usually encouraged me or one of our children to bite off a tentacle of the helpless starfish. When we objected, she would say they are better when you share them.

Which of 1 John 4's white chocolate raspberry starfish would you like to sample? Here are some options.

> "Greater is he that is in you than he that is in the world." [v.4]
> "Let us love one another: for love is of God." [v.7]
> "This is real love—not that we loved God, but that he loved us and sent his Son as a sacrifice to take away our sins." [v.10]
> "No one has ever seen God. But if we love each other, God lives in us, and his love is brought to full expression in us." [v.12]
> "There is no fear in love, but perfect love casts out fear." [v.18]
> "We love because he first loved us." [v.19]
> "The commandment we have from him is this: those who love God must love their brothers and sisters also." [v.21]

Don't rush! Instead, take one and savor it. Remember, it is always better when you share.

___

May 9
Chasing Fluffy White Rabbits

We sometimes wonder if the letters ADHD are more prevalent in our society than perhaps BS, MA, and Ph.D. combined. Parents and educators recognize the letters as an acronym for Attention Deficit Hyperactivity Disorder. For most of my life, I have struggled with ADHD. However, I usually compensate with medication, prayer, well-hidden tics, and coffee by the pot. In adults, it does present differently. Some are surprised to learn those with the disorder are often

Faith Bytes

overachievers [codename for workaholics] in their professions and excel in higher education. It can also explain why a sermon or a chapter in a book is continuously refined.

It can be exciting when two ADHD folks have a conversation. The number of rabbits my fellow ADHD coworkers and I have chased in staff meetings is incredible. Our colleagues suppress laughter on those occasions when we actually catch that jackrabbit.

Although it may seem I am chasing the preverbal rabbit presently, I don't believe so. Although the writer of First John 5 wasn't familiar with ADHD, he did recognize how Christians, like Alice, are prone to chase those attractive fluffy white rabbits down a hole, hoping to discover a Wonderland.

In verses 4-5, he advised: "Everyone born of God overcomes the world. This is the victory that has overcome the world, even our faith. Who is it that overcomes the world? Only the one who believes that Jesus is the Son of God." [NIV] John specifically points out how we overcome the harmful things in our world by keeping the main thing, the main thing. What is the main thing? Our faith in Jesus.

Are you unclear about a matter? Why not try John's insight? Take a moment and breathe in our faith's essence, "Jesus Christ is Lord."

_____

_____

_____

May 10
The Danger of Nifty Slogans

Young Jimmy sat on the kitchen floor, playing with his cars and trucks. He seemed lost in a land of make-believe, utterly unaware of his mother working in the kitchen. Out of the blue, he looked up to his mother and asked: "Mommy? Do you love me?" His mother was startled at the sudden question but responded, "Yes, Jimmy. I love you." Satisfied, he continued pushing his dump truck. A few moments passed, and again, he asked, "Mommy? Do you love me?" "Yes, Jimmy, I love you so much." He returned his attention to his toys. Once more, Jimmy looked up to his mom, this time setting his bulldozer aside; he asked, "Mommy, do you really love me?" Somewhat annoyed by his persistence, she said, "Yes, Jimmy, I really love you!" This time, he did not return to his favorite toys. Instead, he looked into his mother's eyes and asked, "Show me." Putting her work aside, his mother knelt, held him close, and said, "Jimmy, I really do love you!"

Sometimes, we speak of God's love so casually that those around us find it easy to tune us out. As you have read 1 John, I trust you noticed the theme of love. John was in touch with his world and recognized the danger of phrases such as "I love you" and "God loves you" becoming nifty slogans or empty platitudes.

Steven B. Angus

Nestled almost in the center of his letter, in 1 John 3:18, he reminds the followers of Jesus: "Little children, let us love, not in word or speech, but in truth and action." [NRSV]

Who is Jimmy in your circle of influence? How will you respond to their "If you love me, show me?"

_____

_____

_____

May 11
Hefty! Hefty! Hefty!

A familiar commercial asks, "What would you rather rely on? Something wimpy or something hefty?" The scene changes to a trash bag tearing as garbage scatters. The spokesman continues. "Wimpy bags are fine for wimpy jobs, but don't send one to do a hefty job when the pressure is on." Then comes the catchy cadence, "Wimpy, wimpy, wimpy! Hefty, hefty, hefty!" The jingle is a reminder being a Christian isn't for wimps! We want to believe we are flexible and tear-resistant, but sometimes we aren't.

The story of Esther is a fine example of the wimpy versus hefty factor. A young, beautiful Jewish girl suddenly became a queen with all the perks one would expect if she kept her ethnicity a secret. However, an occasion arose if she were to help her people; she would have to approach the King uninvited, which carried a death sentence. Adding to the drama, she would have to reveal that she was a Jew, which could be equally detrimental. The choice was crystal clear--maintain her personal security with her silence or be obedient to God and possibly risk everything.

Esther demonstrates those occasions when our identity as Christians will require us to take risks, which requires faith. Following Jesus isn't for the wimpy. It requires us to place our security in Him and not our surroundings. Most of us want to prevent risk by avoiding choices. However, we do not realize our avoidance has the chance of something more tragic. We may not see or experience something that can only be God's doing. What is God prompting you to do today that seems frightening or out of your comfort zone? Don't risk missing a blessing.

_____

_____

_____

_____

Faith Bytes

May 12
A Mother's Day Surprise

The late Reverend Billy Graham reported that one of his favorite stories is about a husband who was not very attentive to his wife. One day, he thought about it for some unknown reason and felt guilty. He decided he needed to change and shouldn't put it off. So, on his way home from work, he stopped and bought a box of candy and some flowers to surprise his wife.

He approached the door and decided to ring the doorbell instead of waltzing in. When his wife opened it, he stood there with candy in one hand and flowers in the other. In a moment of inspiration, he begins singing, "I love you truly, truly, Dear." He believes he has hit the romantic home run. Suddenly, she starts crying, as big tears gush from her eyes. She sobs, "Oh, Harry! Everything went wrong today. We had a leak in the plumbing. The kids were terrible. The house is a wreck. And now you come home drunk!"

Ladies, we love you! And allow me to be among the first to say Happy Mother's Day.

_____
_____
_____
_____

May 13
Right Beside Us

Not long after I began preaching, I visited a church whose pastor was one of my mentors. I had preached for him many times when he had been the pastor of another congregation. When it was time for the sermon, he took a few moments to introduce me to his folks and then did something that caught this sixteen-year-old entirely off guard. He said, "And now Brother Angus will come and bring today's message." He wasn't kidding. He beckoned me forward, and I had about thirty seconds, the time it took me to walk from the pew to the pulpit, to decide what my text would be. Well, I did it, and I chose my favorite passage, John 14.

In Acts 2, we have Peter preaching his first sermon, which apparently was an impromptu message. He wisely relies on his personal relationship with Jesus and what I believe were his favorite scriptures. One such text was from Psalm 16:8-11.

Although he used it to speak of Jesus's resurrection, I believe the Holy Spirit brought it to Peter's memory because he found himself out of his comfort zone. But isn't that where we spend much of our time as Christians? We tend to find ourselves at odds with what is occurring around us. Quoting King David, Peter said: "I see that the Lord is always with me. I will not be shaken, for he is right beside me."

Steven B. Angus

When facing a daunting situation, this passage may help us, as it did Peter. If we can visualize Jesus standing beside us in an overwhelming circumstance, we, too, can be unshaken. The good news is He really is beside us.

May 14
Industrial Strength Prayer

During my first year of college, I pastored a church part-time. I also worked what is typically called" the graveyard shift" in a large industrial factory. Years later, I still recall the hours of my shift. Each night, I clocked in at 11:36 and punched out at 7:12 in the morning. It was considered the first shift because ours was the first crew to go to work on Sunday night. Walking into such a large facility with all the enormous machines sitting idle was spooky. It had a deafening silence about it. Suddenly, the workers began pushing buttons and turning keys. The quiet machinery would come to life, transforming chunks of steel into bearings.

These images often come to mind when I think about Pentecost. The disciples had quietly remained behind closed doors, praying for wisdom and guidance as they moved forward in uncertain times. Although Pentecost occurred 2000 years ago, prayer remains the button, the starter key, that invites the Holy Spirit to come and bring life into each of us and to the church. As we move to Pentecost Sunday, why not ask the Holy Spirit to jumpstart your life and your passion for him. Pray. In the quiet moments of this day, invite the Holy Spirit to come as wind and fire into your world!

May 15
One-Liners

Poetry is an acquired taste some never attain. I try samples on occasion and usually find myself better because of it. More often than not, I prefer a good one-liner. Do you, by chance, know which famous poet said the following?

> "The soul should always stand ajar, ready to welcome the ecstatic experience."
> "Saying nothing... sometimes says the most."
> "Dogs are better than human beings because they know but do not tell."

Faith Bytes

"Forever is composed of nows."
"That it will never come again is what makes life sweet."
"Morning without you is a dwindled dawn."
"Fame is a fickle food upon a shifting plate."
"Where thou art, that is home."
"A wounded deer leaps the highest."
"Death is a Dialogue between the Spirit and the Dust."

If you guessed Emily Dickinson, you are correct. She was an American poet who wrote many poems about death, eternity, God, and the afterlife. It was on this day in 1886 that she died. She wrote some 1,775 poems. Unfortunately, it felt like we were required to read most of them in High School or college. Notably, of her 1,775 poems, only seven had been published before her death. This offers me hope that someday, the things I have written may be discovered and appreciated by some. But more than that, I am reminded that what we do today in Jesus's name may impact us or someone else deeply.

_____
_____
_____
_____

May 16
More Things Are Wrought by Prayer

The English poet Lord Alfred Tennyson wrote in "The Passing of Arthur," the familiar: "Pray for my soul. More things are wrought by prayer Than this world dreams of." The Church's birth during Pentecost believed this to be true. Before taking any action, they would pray. It may be more accurate to say having prayed, they acted. We tend to forget that the book we casually call Acts was "The Acts of the Apostles."

Huddled in the Jurusalem Upper Room, the disciples prayed and selected a replacement for Judas. Following a season of prayer, the Holy Spirit showed up at Pentecost. As the Church prayed in a member's home, the locked door of Peter's prison cell miraculously swung open. Why did the Holy Spirit do so much through the Apostles and the early church? I tried identifying references to prayer in the book of Acts. I found at least forty references to prayer in a book with 28 chapters. Prayer and the Holy Spirit, each is fuel for the other.

Tennyson's often overlooked thoughts on prayer continue with a request and a question we should ponder.

"Wherefore, let thy voice
Rise like a fountain for me night and day.
For what are men better than sheep or goats
That nourish a blind life within the brain,
If knowing God, they lift not hands of prayer
Both for themselves and those who call them friend."

Steven B. Angus

_____

_____

May 17
Superstar

If you enjoy trivia, here is a question for you. What popular Broadway Musical began as a master's thesis project at Carnegie Mellon University? Not ringing any bells for you? Then you have permission to look it up on your electronic device as you hum your version of Jeopardy music.

Still baffled? Here is another clue. This Musical opened on this date in 1971 at the Cherry Lane Theater in New York City. More thinking music. Well? Ok, I know I didn't play fair. And the question is, "What is the rock musical "Godspell," based on Matthew's Gospel?"

One of the most memorable tunes is Superstar, which introduced Judas as he asked Jesus questions that many have asked. The one who betrays Jesus Christ queried:

> "Did you mean to die like that? Was that a mistake, or
> Did you know your messy death would be a record-breaker?
> Don't you get me wrong?
> I only want to know.
> "Jesus Christ, Jesus Christ,
> Who are you? What have you sacrificed?
> Jesus Christ Superstar,
> Do you think you're what they say you are?
> "Jesus Christ, Jesus Christ,
> Who are you? What have you sacrificed?"

The questions remain pertinent: "Jesus Christ, Who are you?" How do you respond?

_____

_____

_____

_____

May 18
Get Ready For a Party!

I cannot recall attending a birthday party that did not have some sense of happiness. We greet the guest of honor with "Happy Birthday," after all.

We are in the season when Christians celebrate a Happy Birthday day! We call it Pentecost. Christians celebrate the church's birth and recall how Jesus provided

Faith Bytes

the gift—the Holy Spirit. As you contemplate ways to prepare for a Birthday experience, you may wish to consider these suggestions.

Red is the color associated with Pentecost, representing the Holy Spirit coming like tongues of fire. So make as many things red as possible. Prepare a red birthday cake with white icing. Why not a strawberry shortcake? Let me vote for strawberry or cherry ice cream dished up in a red bowl. We could take a page from the Irish celebration of Saint Patrick's Day and pinch anyone who isn't wearing something red.

How about doing something that involves the wind. When the Holy Spirit came, it did so as a rushing wind. Therefore, it is a perfect occasion to invite the kids to join you in flying a kite. Take a walk by the lake and count the waves. Turn on a fan and feel the breeze, perhaps making paper airplanes and having a contest. Locate items that jingle and design a Pentecost wind chime, and then sit back and listen to the rhythm.

Read the story of Pentecost in Acts 2, then sing Happy Birthday to the church. Allow yourself a day to celebrate God's good gifts. After all, you are the church, so enjoy your birthday!

_____

_____

_____

_____

May 19
Restoring Normalcy

Pentecost is an important day for the Church and those participating. We often refer to it as the Church's birthday as the Holy Spirit came upon those who loved the Lord Jesus, transforming them into the body of Christ. What a magnificent gift the Holy Spirit is to all Christians. When we read about life in the early Church, the enthusiasm and spiritual power they demonstrated was beyond the imagination of humans. Reading the book of Acts, it seems every few verses, we have a movie trailer drawing us into another incredible epic event that characterized Christians.

The believers who made up the early Church were filled with joy, never doubting that Jesus was the source of this happiness. It was simply too good to keep to themselves. Those in society who observed the followers of "The Way," as the Christians were called in those days, levied this charge against them: "They turned the world upside down." As we continue the countdown to Pentecost, what are you doing to turn our world upside down for Jesus? Consider this. If we turn society upside down from its present state, are we not restoring it to God's normalcy?

_____

_____

Steven B. Angus

May 20
Becoming the Face

In the sports world, certain players are described as the face of the franchise. In advertising, executives are forever looking for someone to carry the banner of the company's brand. Would NIKE be where they are without Michael Jordan and the Air Jordan shoe? What would the Tonight Show be without Jimmy Fallon?

Of course, talent is essential. Personality and image have a place, but the sport, the product, and the company are more than one person. The quarterback can only become the "face" if the unfamiliar guard or tackle gives adequate protection and the trainer understands when to apply heat or cold to a particular muscle. Do we actually believe those late-night talk show personalities write the jokes? We see the person out front and forget they stand on the shoulders of others.

When we speak about Pentecost, we forget that Peter was not alone. The blessing of the Holy Spirit and the accompanying gifts are not limited to the face of the franchise. The Holy Spirit is for all believers. On the day of Pentecost, the lives of 119 other disciples were changed. They also received the Holy Spirit and, in a sense, became the face of Jesus and the Church to the person they spoke to.

Although we celebrate Pentecost, it has already occurred. The Holy Spirit is with us. The Holy Spirit is for you, not just Peter or a pastor. Consider this. Invite the Spirit to make you the face of Jesus to the people you meet.

_____

_____

_____

_____

May 21
Yes. You.

My youngest daughter has been schooling me in the competitive and grueling sport of table tennis. I use the title table tennis as it sounds more harrowing than—ping pong. As I came to terms with the results of our heated contests, I was reminded of a story about an out-of-shape, overweight man who decided to take up tennis. He took lessons from an instructor and read self-help books that advised him to "think positively" and "develop a winning attitude."

A friend asked him how his tennis was going. With a positive, winning attitude in his voice, the man replied, "When my opponent hits the ball to me, my brain immediately barks out a command to my body: 'Race up to the net.' Then, it says, 'Slam a blistering shot to a far corner of the court. Then immediately jump back into position and return the next volley to the other far corner of the court.' And then my body says, 'Who, me?'" [Billy D. Strayhorn, "Go!"]

Faith Bytes

Jesus gave some outlandish instructions, such as, "Love your neighbor as yourself," "Love one another as I have loved you," and "Go into the world." Knowing something about human nature, you can see a perplexed look on the disciples' faces as they ask, "Who? Me?" Frankly, the question crosses my mind daily. How about you? Jesus answers, "Pentecost has occurred. You have the Holy Spirit. So, Yes. You!"

_____
_____
_____
_____

May 22
Jagged Stones Worn Smooth

The first holiday of the summer is upon us—Memorial Day. It is a day when we think of great military heroes and battles. The truth is some of us feel as if we are in a great fight every day as we go one-on-one with a combatant who has us at a disadvantage. One of the greatest and most familiar battles of all time involved an undersized youth named David battling with a giant of a man named Goliath. You can read about it in 1 Samuel 17:32-49.

David carefully chose five smooth stones from a stream when he prepared to face Goliath. He realized that a jagged rock thrown from his sling would seldom go in the direction he intended. Neither would it go as far as a smooth one, and the rough stone would miss the mark. Jagged rocks become smooth because the harsh elements of nature have come against them, and the water flows over them repeatedly!

In the coming days, we will reflect on five smooth stones that fill the Christian's pouch. Today, however, think about your battles. How is it going? Have you carefully chosen the best stones?

_____
_____
_____
_____

May 23
The Stone That is a Sword

Young David, a shepherd, declined a warrior's armor, choosing instead five smooth stones that had stood the test of time. Once obtained, he placed them in his pouch. God has given us many smooth stones, not just five. One that has turned away many giants determined to destroy faith is the Bible.

Steven B. Angus

In his Letter to the Ephesians, Paul reminded the church that God had given it a warrior's armor forged by God. Along with this armor is the sword of the Spirit, which is the scriptures. Quoting the Prophet Isaiah, Peter wrote: "All flesh is as grass and all the glory of man as the flower of the grass. The grass withers and its flower falls away, but the word of the Lord endures forever." [1 Peter 1:24-25]

When facing temptation in the wilderness, Jesus prevailed by relying on scripture. He knew the wisdom of the sacred text was smooth and powerful, capable of confronting any adversary. Are you well equipped? Is your pouch stocked? Do you have certain Bible verses you rely on? Which ones are you going to memorize?

_____

_____

_____

_____

May 24
Strangely Warmed

Acts 9 reports the transformation of a ruthless persecutor of Christians named Saul. While traveling to Damascus, he encountered the resurrected Jesus. As a result, he became the missionary and preacher known as The Apostle Paul. It isn't uncommon when someone dramatically becomes a Christian to call it a "Damascus road experience." On this day, in 1738, John Wesley had a similar transformation. Instead of a road, Wesley's conversion became known as his Aldersgate Experience, receiving its name from a street in London. Wesley described what happened in his Journal:

> "In the evening, I went very unwillingly to a society in Aldersgate Street, where one was reading Luther's preface to the Epistle to the Romans. About a quarter before nine, while he was describing the change which God works in the heart through faith in Christ, I felt my heart strangely warmed. I felt I did trust in Christ, Christ alone, for salvation; and an assurance was given me that He had taken away my sins, even mine, and saved me from the law of sin and death."

To appreciate the significance of Wesley's statement, we need only read his account of a meeting he had in Georgia with a slave girl from Barbados as he was trying to book passage on a ship back to London. In his Journal, he records what he said to her as he attempted to explain what it means to be a Christian. He wrote:

> "[God] made you to live with himself above the sky. And so you will, in a little time — if you are good. If you are good, when your body dies, your soul will go up and want nothing, and have whatever you can desire. The next day she remembered all, readily answered every question; and said she would ask Him that made her, to show her how to be good." [Wesley's Journal, Saturday, April 23, 1737.]

Faith Bytes

Wesley's Aldersgate experience moved him from a "being good" religion to a "Christ alone" trust. When John Wesley experienced the freeing of his heart from having to earn salvation to accepting it, his heart was warmed, and he could joyfully share it with others. Today can be our Aldersgate Experience if we trust Christ alone.

_____
_____
_____
_____

May 25
The Buzzard, Bat, and Bumble Bee

Like the shepherd boy David, are you ready to add another smooth stone to the pouch you carry into your world of giants? The second stone we have in our bag is prayer. Someone shared this interesting analogy.

If you put a Buzzard in a pen that is six feet by eight feet and open at the top, the bird will be an absolute prisoner despite its ability to fly. It will not even attempt to escape because it requires ten to twelve feet for its running takeoff. The ordinary Bat that flies around at night cannot take off from a level place. If it is on a flat surface, it will shuffle about helplessly. If dropped into an open tumbler, a Bumble Bee will be there until it dies unless removed. It never sees the means of escape above it but persists in trying to find some way out where one does not exist.

We are like the Buzzard, the Bat, and the Bumble Bee in many ways. We struggle with our problems and frustrations, never realizing that all we have to do is look up. Prayer is our way of looking up! Don't let prayer be the "last resort" in your life.

_____
_____
_____
_____

May 26
The Name

We love to root for the Cinderella team. Instinctively, we want to see the Goliaths go down because they seem to have all the advantages—size, equipment, financial backing, to name a few. However, David saw things differently. When the two combatants approached each other on the battlefield, David said to the nine-footer, "You come to me with a sword, spear, and javelin, but I come to you in the name of the Lord."

Steven B. Angus

God has given us the name that is above every name. Before the one who bears this name, "Every knee shall bow, and every tongue will confess." The name is Jesus. We believe that "Whoever calls upon the name of Jesus will be saved." We believe "We can do everything through Jesus, who strengthens us."

Do we, like David, carry in our spiritual fanny pack the name of Jesus? Not only has God given us the precious name, but God has also named us. We have an identity that serves as one of our stones. The name? Christian.

When my children left home for an outing, I usually told them what my dad had said to me when I was their age. It has a tone reminiscent of those spoken by David—"Remember who you are." Our smooth stone is a name. Are you feeling a trifle overwhelmed? Remember who you are and in whose name you are sent.

May 27
The Source of Confidence

When David volunteered to face Goliath, his brothers believed he was showing off, and King Saul thought he was nuts. When the King looked at David, it was all he could do to keep from laughing in the boy's face. However, the confidence in David's voice persuaded Saul to sign off on the mission.

David said, "The Lord, who delivered me from the paw of the lion and from the paw of the bear, He will deliver me from the hand of this Philistine." [1 Samuel 17:37] David was determined to face Goliath because he believed God would be with him!

The stone I present to you is Jesus's promise to his followers moments before he ascended into heaven. He said,

> "Teach these new disciples to obey all the commands I have given you. And be sure of this: I am with you always, even to the end of the age." [Matthew 28:20, NLT]

Goliath comes in many shapes and sizes. He arrives as trouble, disappointment, and as evil. In our pouch is a smooth stone you will want to reach in and touch many times daily. It is the confidence that accompanies the promise—"I am with you always."

Faith Bytes

May 28
Bravery Isn't the Absence of Fear

According to the Medal of Honor Historical Society of the United States, the first Medal of Honor was awarded to Private Jacob Parrott on March 25, 1863, for his part in the "The Great Locomotive Chase," ending just outside Chattanooga. Forty percent of the 3,527 Medals awarded were for actions during the Civil War.

Nineteen service members have been awarded the Medal of Honor twice. The first was Thomas Custer, brother of George Armstrong Custer. The only woman awarded was Mary Edwards Walker, a civilian Army surgeon during the Civil War. Theodore Roosevelt is the only U.S. president to have received the Medal. Technically, the youngest recipient was William Johnston, a drummer who refused to abandon his drum at age eleven. However, President Lincoln heard about his courage and presented him with the Medal posthumously when he would have been thirteen.

One recipient was the late Lt. Col. Joe Jackson, who passed away in January 2019. He served during WWII, the Korean War, and the Vietnam Conflict. When asked about his actions during the Vietnam conflict leading to the Medal of Honor, he said, "I've never thought of myself as brave so much as I've thought of myself as scared. If scared is a criterion, then I've been brave lots of times."

Like most people of valor, Jackson was humble about his bravery. Bravery isn't the absence of fear. It is doing the right thing even when you are afraid. These are good words every Christian should remember.

_____
_____
_____

May 29
Keeping the Stones Ready

During the days surrounding Memorial Day, we have thought about one of the famous military battles reported in the Bible. The shepherd boy David would become a great warrior, leading the masses to sing, "Saul has slain his thousands, and David his ten thousand." Even so, his finest hour and most significant victory would always be the day he defeated Goliath.

In American Sign Language, the sign for "rock" or "stone" is a clutched right hand. The symbol for the Church is the clutched hand, with the left hand forming a C and placing it on the fist. It represents the Church that is built on the rock, who is Jesus. The Church has a solid foundation.

Steven B. Angus

I hope we will remember how important the Church is in helping us prepare to face our giants. Five smooth stones: Scripture, prayer, a promise, a name, and the Church have each stood the test of time.

One concluding thought, a question, actually. Where did David keep his weapons?

We are told he placed the stones in his pouch. He did this so he could have immediate access to them. What are you doing to keep these spiritual stones close at hand? Are you taking them out and checking them? Are you teaching your children and grandchildren how to use them? We must never underestimate Goliath; therefore, we must remain ready.

_____
_____
_____
_____

May 30
Feeling the Love

I recently had a satisfying phone conversation about a project that honors our county's deceased veterans. I thought of the joy this could bring to the families and friends of these heroes. As I ended the conversation, a family member came in from outside, carrying a vase of stunning flowers in various colors. More attractive than the flowers was the glowing smile they had brought to her face. She said, "Aren't they beautiful," and proceeded to share their conversation. Learning we had just acquired some Kayaks, our friend invited us to put them into the creek behind her home.

Reflecting on these acts of kindness and the various emails, texts, and cards that have come my way recently, I felt the love. The songwriter said, "Love is a many splendid thing." This is true. However, knowing we are loved isn't necessarily the same as "feeling" loved.

One of the tools I recommend when discussing relationships is a simple yet profound book titled "The Five Love Languages." Although Gary Smalley's is a worthwhile read, it is unnecessary to rush out and purchase it. You can go to the website 5lovelanguages.com. There, you can discover your love language and, more significantly, the love language of those in your life.

Do you remember young Jimmy who appealed to his mother from the kitchen floor, "If you love me, show me?" He was asking her to speak his love language. You and I are Jimmy, but we are also the mom. Let's brush up on the language Jesus spoke—the language of love.

Today, your mission, should you choose to accept it, is to visit the website 5lovelanguages.com. Look around and use some of the free resources.

_____
_____

Faith Bytes

May 31
Speaking a Different Language

Am I the only one who hears the Radiologists say, "Now don't move," and immediately develop an itch demanding to be scratched? This urge may be the younger sibling to the dreaded *Imp* known as temptation. Hundreds of times throughout the day, the mindless process repeats—itch, scratch, satisfaction.

We tend to approach love as if it were an itch to be scratched. We treat it as if it can be satisfied as easily as a craving for ice cream that can be curbed by cruising into the Dairy Queen. Love should work as efficiently as our longing for light is satisfied in the tenth of a second it takes the eye to blink. We realize our sense of sight will involve an occasional adjustment requiring eyeglasses or a more drastic cataract removal and implant. We expect some changes when it comes to love, yet we often say love isn't supposed to be this difficult. We act as if love is the sixth sense.

Love is a language. Learning to speak a language is never as natural as it seems. Love is work, not mindless, but the type continually requiring us to learn new skills. Have you invested in love by visiting the website 5lovelanguages.com? Is your love language "Words of Affirmation, Acts of Service, Receiving Gifts, Quality Time," or "Physical Touch?" You may have discovered that your spouse, child, parent, or co-worker speaks a love language different from yours. You may realize you have been discussing love but not communicating it.

The Apostle Paul wrote: "Though I speak with the tongues of men and of angels, but have not love, I have become sounding brass or a clanging cymbal." [1 Corinthians 13:1] These familiar words were likely included in the wedding ceremony if you are married. Take some time to reread 1 Corinthians 13. Consider how its message relates to the language of love in your other relationships.

_____
_____
_____
_____

Steven B. Angus

JUNE

June 1
Provide the Subtitles

I typically avoid movies requiring subtitles. However, the French series sounded intriguing, and I was hooked after one episode. Because it was an unfamiliar language, not only were the subtitles necessary, but attention to body language and voice inflections were necessary. Without the captions, I would have been lost. Love Languages do not come with subtitles. We must learn the language and hope our partner will recognize our sincerity and help teach it.

Someone whose love language is "Words of Affirmation" will feel safest when they hear how we think of them. "I love you" may warm the heart, but hearing why we love them truly hits the mark. Listening to a coworker say, "I appreciate you," is pleasant. Still, the extra step of stating what is appreciated gives the affirmation its merit. Conversely, words that are delivered harshly can injure.

We tend to speak our own love language when addressing others. If "words of affirmation" help us feel appreciated, we tend to affirm others. If affirmation isn't that individuals love language, we might as well be throwing pebbles at a stop sign. They will never hear us, much less feel it.

If I had not risked watching a program in French, I would have missed a rewarding experience. I had to overcome my laziness and, if I am brutely honest, my arrogance. Who do you know whose love language is Words of Affirmation? Perhaps you need to provide the subtitles.

Faith Bytes

June 2
Nothing Says I Love You Like a Sugar-free Mocha

Actions speak louder than words. Those who spend their lives as wordsmiths, such as preachers, teachers, and politicians, place great value on them. However, for many, experiencing and expressing love isn't about the talk, but can you walk the walk? For them, actions aren't just loud. They shout!

The cross and the empty tomb are the ultimate act of love by Jesus. He also recognized our need to see love. He called upon his followers to share expressions of love through Holy Communion and washing one another's feet. The significance of Jesus' taking a towel, a pitcher of water, and a bowl and bathing his disciples' tired, dirty feet cannot be overstated. This gesture affected the disciples deeply because it exceeded their expectations. The Passover meal was on the program, but washing their feet was a spontaneous act of caring.

Those whose love language is "Acts of Service" are keenly aware of deeds that make their lives easier. Likewise, they often express their love by doing for others. A co-worker brings you a sugar-free mocha just the way you like it, or a friend delivers a vase of flowers from her garden. Each is an expression of love. If our love language isn't acts of service, we may overlook these gestures. However, by doing so, we fail to recognize that individuals "I love and appreciate you."

How can you speak love and appreciation to someone whose love language is Acts of Service? Who could use a pick-me-up? Make someone's day by acknowledging actions that make your life pleasant.

_____
_____
_____
_____

June 3
Five Love Jeopardy

Welcome to this special edition of "The Five Love Languages Jeopardy!" I am your host—Steven B. Angus. I will provide you with the answer, and you will give the correct question. Let's play "Five Love Jeopardy!"

And the answer is—To maintain eye contact when your spouse, friend, or coworker is speaking. **The correct response:** What is spending meaningful quality time with someone?

And the answer is—Not listening to your spouse and doing something else simultaneously. **The correct response:** What is an example of not spending meaningful time with someone?

And the answer is—I can tell you are feeling discouraged, perhaps angry. **The correct response:** What is quality time listens for emotions?

Steven B. Angus

And now for the Five Love Languages Final Jeopardy answer: "Can you hold that thought?" "Let me watch this replay." "I must interrupt you there." **And the correct response is:** What are ways that say, "I don't care what you're saying. Listen to me instead."

And today's winner is—Those whose love language is Quality Time.

Today's sponsor has been Gary Chapman, who wrote:

> *"Quality time is giving someone your undivided attention. I don't mean sitting on the couch watching television. I mean sitting on the couch with the TV off, looking at each other and talking, and giving each other your undivided attention."*

_____

_____

_____

_____

June 4
Gift Giving and Receiving

Are you uncomfortable acknowledging that your love language is gift-giving and receiving? If so, you will be pleased to hear that each love language originates in God. Can you imagine life if God wasn't a gift-giver? Most Christians enjoy quoting the familiar, "For God so loved the world that he gave his only son." We are reminded that God delights in our gifts of praise and worship.

I know a man married to someone whose love language is gift-giving. She is the sort who has yet to pass a donation pail without dropping something into it. And as far as receiving is concerned, it's not the big-ticket item that appeals to her. But one that reflects the giver's understanding of her interests. As their wedding anniversary approached, he invested five dollars and purchased a perpetual daily flip calendar. He took time to handwrite a message specific to his wife until each day was complete. Some days, it was a trait he appreciated about her or an acknowledgment of what she did for him and the family. On other days, he wrote a sentence prayer for and about her. In an effort towards romance, he wrote such things as, "remember this as the day we first met," "first date," or "first kiss."

When he presented the gift, she melted. She placed the calendar on her work desk and began each day with a new gift for several years. One of their daughters recently came across the calendar, quizzed her mother about it, and asked to borrow it. This simple act of speaking someone's love language extended to the generations.

Who can you bless with a heartfelt gift? I would add, help a cheerful giver out by being a grateful receiver.

_____
_____
_____
_____

June 5
An Apple a Day

Legend has it that a young Isaac Newton was struck on the head by a falling apple, providing a 17th-century "aha moment" that led to the formation of the Apple Corporation. Well, not exactly. However Newton's law of gravity did not entirely unfold as tradition stated.

In reality, had it not been for an outbreak of the bubonic plague, forcing the closure of Cambridge, and Newton's return home to witness an apple drop in the family orchard, who knows what the state of science would be today. The apple falling straight to the ground inspired the principle that every entity in the universe is attracted to every other body, etcetera. Stephen Hawking stated, "Newton's theory will never be outmoded. He is a colossus without parallel in the history of science."

Not until Newton's nonscientific writings were auctioned in 1936 did the world realize he spent more time on theology than science. He wrote about 1.3 million words on biblical subjects. Listen to Newton's words:

> "This most beautiful system of the sun, planets, and comets could only proceed from the counsel and dominion of an intelligent and powerful Being. . .This Being governs all things, not as the soul of the world, but as Lord over all; and on account of his dominion, he is wont to be called Lord God. . .The true God is a living, intelligent, and powerful Being. . .He governs all things and knows all things that are or can be done."

On this day in 661, Issac Newton was admitted to Trinity College, Cambridge. What leads you to acknowledge God as Lord over all creation as you observe the world around you?

_____
_____
_____
_____

June 6
The Need for Some Skin

Touch ranks right up there with sugar-sweet, iced tea and fried okra as an expression of Southern hospitality. During the COVID-19 pandemic, it was said that some of us wore garments with pockets just to have something to do with our hands as a reminder not to extend them for a shake. Southerners are huggers.

If your love language is physical touch, you can relate to the little girl who heard a loud clap of thunder, jumped out of bed, ran into her parent's room, and launched herself between her parents. Trying to calm her fears, her father said, "Don't worry, Honey. We've got you, and the Lord will protect you." Snuggling closer to her parents, she said, "I know that, Daddy, but right now, I need someone with some skin on!"

We know God loves us, but like this little girl, there are occasions when we need to feel the touch of another person. For those with this love language, nothing is more significant than the physical touch of their partner, parents, and loved ones. They will feel unloved without physical contact. All of the words and gifts in the world won't change that. They need to feel closeness, not just emotionally but physically.

Our post-pandemic world has become a society where nice touches can be inappropriate. This means we must be deliberate about holding hands, tossing our children in the air, or cuddling as a family on the living room couch. Don't wait for a thunderstorm as an excuse to touch. Look for and seek out reasons to do so.

_____

_____

_____

_____

June 7
The Child Who Prayed Like Jesus

When the public schools of New Orleans were integrated under court order in 1960, four six-year-old African-American girls were chosen to attend segregated all-white schools. Three were assigned to one school. However, Ruby Bridges was sent alone to Frantz Elementary School. Federal marshals escorted her to and from school for her protection. Daily, she faced a crucible of taunts and threats, primarily from adults. White parents withdrew their children from the school until Ruby was the only child in Miss H's first-grade class. [Some accounts identify the teacher as Miss Hurley, others Miss Henry].

One morning, Miss H watched Ruby walk toward the school and stop in the middle of a screaming crowd. As she faced the mob, her lips began moving. The teacher thought Ruby was talking to them and wondered what she might be saying to people who seemed on the verge of violence. The marshals tried to move her into the building, but the six-year-old did not move until she finished what she said. Later, the teacher discussed what had happened, and Ruby explained. She said, "I wasn't talking to those people. I was praying for them." It turned out that Ruby would stop a few blocks from school each morning and pray for the people she would encounter. Her prayer went like this: "Please, God, try to forgive those people. Because even if they say those bad things, they don't know what they're doing. So you could forgive them, just like you did those folks long ago when they said terrible things about you." That morning, she had forgotten to do so until she was on the sidewalk in the middle of the angry adults.

Today may confront you with some challenging situations. You may have to deal with some mean-spirited people who are unkind or unfair. If so, perhaps we should use the Ruby and Jesus method of prayer and pray for them. It may surprise us what we can do and how their lives might change.

_____

_____

_____

_____

June 8
Does Your Investment Portfolio Include This?

Anna's story was on the front page of the denominational newspaper. The article reported the death of the ninety-eight-year-old and her generous bequest to the area organization of churches. As I read the finer details of her life, my fascination grew.

Miss Anna, who never married, was the last surviving daughter of a deceased Methodist preacher. The article quoted from her father's memoir in the 1946 Journal of The Annual Conference stated, "Brother Hensley never received more than a $1,200 salary, and most of the time far less than that; but like many other itinerants he was a miracle worker, caring for his family and educating his children."

Miss Anna was a public school teacher until retirement. Among her possessions was a photograph of one of her classes that reflected 37 smiling 5th graders. Several pictures were included in the article.

I was captivated by her story and could not help but marvel at the bequest she had made. But it is not what you are probably thinking. It wasn't the $300,000 gift but her story and the snapshots of happy children. My mind began to ponder the question: what bequest am I leaving behind?

I thought about the Preacher and his wife, who left a legacy in the lives of others and their own children. In turn, Miss Anna offered encouragement to the children she taught. Realizing many of the students in the class photos have or are approaching retirement prompted me to wonder how many others their lives have touched.

Steven B. Angus

We are already making a bequest to those around us and those who will follow. What does your investment portfolio in people reveal about your priorities?

___

June 9
High Ho! Silver!

Growing up, I wanted to be "The Lone Ranger." After watching an episode of the mysterious "Kemosabe" and his sidekick, I would tuck my pant legs into the top of my boots, put on my gun holster that held twin white-handled cap guns, tie a handkerchief around my face with slots cut out for my eyes and proceeded to run around the house shouting, "Hi ho, Silver. Away!"

Before shaking your head in disbelief, I am confident I am speaking to a former Gene Autry, Matt Dillion, Luke Skywalker, or perhaps a Catwoman or Elsa. An old saying is, "Imitation is the truest form of flattery."

Acts 4:13 states:

> *"Now when they saw the boldness of Peter and John, and perceived that they were uneducated and untrained men, they marveled. And they realized that they had been with Jesus."*

Peter and John had a hero they tried to imitate. Their desire was to become Christ-like in every aspect. In fact, the name Christian means Christ-like.

Peter had his reasons why Jesus was a hero worthy of imitation. In a small section of his sermon to the council, Peter used multiple titles to describe Jesus. Referring to Jesus as a prophet, he said, "You rejected this holy, righteous one and instead demanded the release of a murderer. You killed the author of life, but God raised him from the dead." [Acts 3:14-15, NLT]

Within his discourse, Peter called Jesus the holy, righteous One, the Christ, the author of life, God's servant, and prophet.

As Christians, we do not need to search for a hero! We already have Jesus, who is worthy of patterning our lives. When we do so, as in the case of Peter and John, others will notice a difference about us and perhaps recognize we also have been with Jesus.

How would you feel if you overheard the remark, "It is obvious [your name] has been with Jesus?"

Faith Bytes

June 10
The Thoughts of One Minister to Another

From time to time, we all need a reminder. We do not intend to forget or take something for granted, but that is our tendency. So allow me to give your memory a nudge. You do not have to punch a time card to have a calling or a ministry within the Church. A core belief among most churches is that each baptized Christian has God's call to be a minister. When I am referred to as "The Minister of the Church," I cringe. The Bible's title for the shepherd of a congregation is Pastor. This means, whether ordained or laity, compensated or volunteer, we are ministers of Jesus and His Church. John Wesley, an Anglican clergy member and the Father of Methodism, indicated the only difference among Jesus's ministers is how God has gifted us to serve.

Consider this your reminder—You are a minister! The pastors and staff of the Church you affiliate with will concur. It is not their responsibility to do the ministry for the Church but to help equip and enable you to fulfill the ministry God has called you to do in the Church.

As a pastor, let me suggest you begin with prayer by asking God for a passion for ministry. Then, look around and take note of the needs you see. When identified, ask God to show you how to minister in that circumstance. Finally, consider having a conversation with your pastor or another church leader about doing ministry instead of simply talking about it.

What are YOU waiting for? The Church needs ministers who love children to go to work immediately. For those who enjoy speaking on the phone, your ministry awaits. Those who find fulfillment in visiting hospitals and nursing homes volunteer at your Church to help it happen! Finally, for those extroverted ministers who have never met a stranger, someone is waiting for your invitation to join you in Church. Go ahead. Make that appointment today.

_____

_____

_____

_____

June 11
Change

Two caterpillars were crawling across the grass when a butterfly flew over them. As they watched the incredible feat, one nudged the other and said, "You couldn't get me up in one of those things for a million dollars."

Famous last words, right? We have said such things only to find ourselves in that very circumstance. Why is that? In a word, "change." Circumstances change. We change. Our two wormy friends had no idea they were about to have an experience that would change their entire outlook on life and transform them into a new creation.

Steven B. Angus

The Bible is one case study after another detailing change. Although change is constant, it always seems to be accompanied by surprise. When change occurs, particularly in a person or a group, others do not always welcome it. The story of Jonah is about change. With the assistance of a giant fish, God had to change Jonah's traveling plans and deposited him on the beach near the wicked city of Nineva. Forced to change his plans, Jonah half-heartedly preached the need for them to repent or else. The reluctant preacher was rooting for "else" to win out. Remarkably, an entire city chose to change their wicked ways and turn to God, much to the angst of Jonah.

Read Mark 1:14-20, and notice how Jesus' ministry centered on inviting and helping people to CHANGE. We meet such caterpillars as Peter, Andrew, James, and John, who never in a million years expected to change from being fishermen to followers of Jesus. Yet it happened, and the transformation brought meaning and direction to their lives.

In a word, Jesus is about change. The message entrusted to the Church is that things can be different and better. Jesus taught a gospel of CHANGE, and it was called Good News. What change needs to occur in your life? Who do you know who is struggling with and longing for CHANGE? Invite them to consider Jesus.

_____

_____

_____

_____

June 12
Look UP!

Where can we turn when we are in trouble and life feels like it could not get worse? Truthfully, we have all been down that unpleasant road. Psalm 121 was a song Israelite pilgrims sang while traveling to Jerusalem to worship at the Temple. The journey was exhausting and dangerous. Jesus told a story of a man traveling to the Holy City who was attacked by robbers and left for dead. If not for the kindness of a Samaritan, the man would have been another fatality.

The opening line of Psalm 121 suggests those making the journey often looked up to the hills, recognized the potential for harm, and asked, "From whence comes my help?" Regardless of our place in this world, we sometimes walk a treacherous path surrounded by dangerous mountains. Just because we are Christians with devout intentions does not guarantee a pleasant walk.

The Psalmist looked up to the hills and refused to focus on the what-ifs. Instead, he looked higher to the one who created heaven and earth. Regarding this Psalm, Eugene Peterson, the author of the Message Translation of the Bible, wrote:

> "In going to God, Christians travel the same ground that everyone else walks. . .The difference is that each step we walk, each breath we breathe, we know we are preserved by God, we know we are accompanied by God, we know

Faith Bytes

we are ruled by God; and therefore, no matter what doubts we endure or what accidents we experience, the Lord will preserve us from evil, he will keep our life." [A Long Obedience in the Same Direction, pp. 40-41.]

One congregation I served as a pastor had a unique custom when a church member died. As I led the casket from the hearse to the grave at the cemetery, someone would follow me and sing a hymn written by William Elmo Mercer. As you read some of the lyrics, imagine you are the pilgrim reflected in Psalm 121.

Each step I take, my Saviour goes before me,
And with His loving hand, He leads the way,
And with each breath, I whisper, "I adore Thee;"
Oh, what joy to walk with Him each day.

Refrain: Each step I take, I know that He will guide me;
To higher ground, He ever leads me on.
Until someday, the last step will be taken.
Each step I take just leads me closer home.

When trouble comes, where should we look? Correction, to whom do we look? Look up and beyond the hills to the one who created heaven and earth.

_____

_____

_____

_____

June 13
A Boy, Nails, and a Fence

Although Tom was just a young boy, he had already developed a terrible temper. To help his son, his father gave him a bag of nails and told him that every time he lost his temper, he must hammer a nail into the back of the wooden fence in the backyard.

At the end of the first day, Tom counted the nails and was shocked to find thirty-seven. He realized he needed to make some changes. In the weeks ahead, as Tom learned to control his anger, the number of nails hammered daily gradually dwindled. He discovered holding his temper was easier than driving those nails into the fence. Then, one evening, the boy looked at the fence and realized no nail had been placed in the wall. He told his father the good news but was surprised when his dad suggested a nail be removed when a day passed when he held his temper.

In time, Tom told his dad that all the nails were gone. The father walked with his son to the fence. He said, "You have done well, but look at the holes in the fence. The fence will never be the same. When you say things angrily, they leave a scar like this. You can put a nail in someone and draw it out. It won't matter how many times you say I'm sorry. The wound is still there."

Steven B. Angus

A verbal wound can leave a scar as harmful as a physical one.

June 14
Getting Love Right

I miss Reverend Will B. Dunn. His understanding of life and insight into the heart of God were so profound it is difficult to believe he existed in the mind of Doug Marlette and the comic strip serial KUDZU. One of my favorite episodes has a couple standing before the parson receiving the marital charge:

"Love is long-suffering and is kind. Love envieth not; love vaunteth not itself, is not puffed up. Doth not behave unseemly, seeketh not its own; is not easily provoked, thinketh no evil." By this time, the Reverend has a serious look on his face but continues. *"Rejoiceth not in iniquity, but rejoiceth in the truth. Beareth all things, believeth all things, hopeth all things, endureth all things."* Finally, with a considerable smile, the Parson delivers one of his famous Dunnisms: *"In other words, love may taketh quite a while to getteth right!"*

We sometimes think that love should come as naturally as breathing. However, we must continually work at love, and despite our noble efforts, we seldom get it right. Herein lies why love is "the greatest of these." [1 Corinthians 13:13] It doesn't give up!

Reflecting on my half-century as a pastor, I have observed a constant in all of us. It is this—We long to love and be loved. It is this pursuit that often draws us to church. There is a desire to be with the people of God because God is Love. However, I have also found that many of us believe we should get this love lifestyle correct from the start, and when we can't, then at least everyone else should. When we realize others are just like us and lack perfect love, we become dissatisfied, quit, and perhaps label the church as COLD and UNLOVING.

Yes, Reverend Will B Dunn is correct. "Love taketh quite a while to getteth right!" This means we set yesterday's mistakes aside and try to get it right today. Whether it is in our place of business or spending time with our children, let us strive to get it right. If you choose to attend a church service, do so with the mindset of love. If you have avoided church because you or someone else did not get love right, try it again. Allow yourself and the church the opportunity to get love right.

June 15
A Masterpiece!

Joseph F. Girzone wrote an excellent book titled "Joshua." Its popularity led to several other books. The series' central theme is, "What would Jesus be like if he lived in our modern world?" The names Joshua and Jesus come from the same Hebrew word, so Joshua is Jesus in this story.

In one episode, a wealthy man named Aaron watches Joshua. Amazed by his simple lifestyle, Aaron asks Joshua how he became the way he was and believes the way he did. With thoughtful kindness, Joshua explained it to Aaron. He said:

> "Each person looks at life through a different vision. Three men can look at a tree. One man will see so many board feet of valuable lumber worth so much money. The second man will see it as so much firewood to be burned to keep his family warm in the winter. The third man will see it as a masterpiece of God's creative art, given to man as an expression of God's love and enduring strength, with a value far beyond its worth in money or firewood. What we live for determines what we see in life and gives a clear focus to our inner vision."

What is the vision you have of yourself? How about your neighbor? Do we measure value based on bank accounts or what someone brings to society? When we do so, we miss the masterpieces God has created in us and around us.

A Masterpiece! This is how God sees you and, lest we forget, how God sees those we tend to deem less than lovable. No one is beyond the love of God. Consider this. Is there anything you or someone else has ever done that will prevent Jesus from entering the home of our hearts if we invite him?

_____
_____
_____
_____

June 16
Earth, Wind, or Fire?

Even those who faithfully serve God can become discouraged. Elijah, the Prophet, absolutely qualifies as an example. As a servant of God, he had put the wicked queen Jezebel in her place. Not long after the victory, Elijah questioned the wisdom of ticking off the bloodthirsty royal. Although he had every reason to feel confident, the Prophet went into hiding, seeking refuge in a mountain cave. What occurred next is found in 1 Kings 19:9-19. In the solitude of the cave, he heard God asking, "What are you doing here, Elijah?" Elijah had barely formulated his excuse when God instructed him to stand on the mountain. A series of extraordinary experiences occurred. First, there was a mighty wind that tore the mountain apart. This was followed by an earthquake, then a fire. The Bible says God was not in the wind, the earthquake, or the fire.

Demonstrating how God does not always work as we think He should, the Scripture tells us that following the fire, there was a "still small voice," or as some translations put it, "a gentle whisper."

With great insight into our human nature, Arthur DeKruyter has written, "If we had been with Elijah in the cave, waiting for God to speak, we probably would have rushed into the earthquake and tossed around a few rocks ourselves. We would have huffed and puffed along with the windstorm God sent. We would have been so busy talking about things that we probably wouldn't even have heard the still, small voice when He did speak!"

When God doesn't do things our way, we have several options. We can blame God for not paying attention to our circumstances. We can question God's love, telling ourselves that God is too impersonal to care. We always have the option to ignore the situation by convincing ourselves that it will disappear in time. Or, we can believe God loves us too much to disregard our pleas for help.

Hopefully, we will realize this option is the best. God's ways are higher than ours. God doesn't always do things the way we think God should. As difficult as it is to admit, sometimes our ideas are too narrow, our vision too limited, and our imaginations too cramped to fully comprehend the wondrous ways of God. How are you listening for God's whisper?

_____

_____

_____

_____

June 17
A Birth Felt Around the World

June 17, 1703, is a date of supreme significance for those who have roots in the World Methodist community. On this date, Susanna Wesley gave birth to her fifteenth of nineteen children in the English village of Epworth. She and her husband, Samuel, named their son John. Samuel was the pastor of the local church. An event in the church parsonage would change this child's life forever.

When John was five and a half years old, some individuals offended by his Father's bold preaching and politics set the parsonage on fire. The house, built of dry wood with a thatch roof, burned fiercely. The family rushed out of the house, but young John remained asleep in the attic. When he awoke, the staircase was engulfed in flames, so he could not escape. Showing a remarkable presence of mind, John moved a chest to the window and got the crowd's attention below. His father, believing the boy was about to die, gave his soul to God. Remarkably, John escaped through the attic window. Because of this incredible brush with death, Wesley lived the remainder of his life believing God had saved him for a specific purpose. Henceforth, he would refer to himself as a "brand plucked from the fire," as referenced in Zechariah 3:2.

John embraced the belief that God could and would use him. How about you? Have you considered the possibility that God has called you for a purpose?

Happy Birthday, John! May your brand of faith live in us.

_____

_____

_____

_____

June 18
The Mother Behind Renewal

If John Wesley is the Father of Methodism, then his Susanna is its mother. Susanna was the 25th child born to her parents. From childhood, she was exposed to many areas of learning. By the time she was a teen, she knew Greek, Latin, and French and spent many hours daily studying theology.

She was a natural teacher and taught her children at home. As soon as a child could speak, they were taught the Lord's Prayer and would say it in the morning when they got up and at night when they went to bed. On their fifth birthday, they would memorize the alphabet. Bible stories and songs were taught daily, with the oldest teaching the youngest pairing off accordingly. Susanna believed education was essential for girls and boys and treated them equally. She wrote, "The putting children to learn sewing before they can read perfectly is the very reason why so few women can read fit [idiom for well enough] to be heard."

Children were taught to ask politely for what they wanted. Lying, stealing, or playing in church should never go unpunished. In a letter to John, she stated that her principal aim was to guide children into a disciplined life where the duty to God and others was paramount.

John Wesley fathered a renewal movement built on discipline, honesty, hard work, and the constructive use of time to serve God and humanity. He discovered these qualities from his mother's instruction and example. Recognizing Susanna's leadership abilities would guide Wesley to include women in the Methodism movement.

Pause and give thanks to God for those who nurtured faith in you.

_____

_____

June 19
A Father's Legacy of Compassion

Samuel Wesley was John Wesley's father. The elder Wesley was a pastor, and although sometimes overshadowed by his wife, Susanna, he also significantly influenced his famous son. This is demonstrated in an event when Samuel was a student at Oxford.

One morning, feeling desperate, Samuel went for an early morning walk with only the equivalent of a nickel in his pocket. As he entered the park, he heard a child crying. Under a hedge, Samuel found an eight-year-old boy whose clothing had frozen to the ground. He managed to get the small boy to his feet and rubbed his hands and legs to get the circulation going again. On inquiring what had happened, the boy told Samuel that his mother had died some years previously and that his father had died three days earlier. He and his ten-year-old sister had waited in the cottage, hoping someone would come, but no one did. They had no food or money and quickly became weak. They decided that the boy's sister would go to the nearby village and beg, and he would walk into Oxford to see if he could get food. Having walked a long way with nothing to eat on a cold morning, he could go no farther and lay under the hedge. Samuel put his hand into his pocket, handed the boy his last few coins, and took him to buy bread.

The story demonstrates compassion in Samuel, which was often shown by John to the miners throughout England. How often do our children see us being generous? A compassionate heart observed can become a legacy.

_____

_____

_____

_____

June 20
A Movement is Birthed

It was never John Wesley's intention to start a new church. Ordained as a priest in the Church of England, sometimes referred to as the Anglican Church, he remained so his entire life. He was disappointed that the church he loved failed to reach out to everyone. The Methodist societies were started by Charles, John's younger brother, during his second year at Oxford. He persuaded two or three others to join him. The group initially met on Sunday evening, then two evenings a week, and eventually every evening from six until nine. Even by eighteenth-century standards, the structure of their gatherings and unconventional behavior attracted faculty and students' attention.

When John returned to Oxford as an instructor, he associated with the Society and became its leader. Their activities included the study of the Bible in the original languages, regular visits to the prison, and collecting money to help the poor and sick. They fasted on Wednesdays and Fridays. They gave considerable time to the religious instruction of children, which evolved into a Sunday School

Faith Bytes

Program. These were one-day schools for children to teach them how to read and write. The children could not attend regular schools because they worked in factories or coal mines the other six days. This Society was so different from other religious groups that they were looked upon with horror. Disparaging names were attached to the fellowship, including Bible Moths, Reformers Club, Godly Club, Enthusiasts, and the Holy Club. One day, a student referred to a group member and said, "Here comes one of those Method—ist." The name stuck. For the Wesley brothers, it was a perfect description of the work of the Society. They had a method for sharing the Gospel with the least, the last, and the lost. What will be your Method for sharing God's grace today?

_____
_____
_____
_____

June 21
Do I Know?

When John and Charles Wesley finished college, the brothers became missionaries to the young colony of Georgia in America. John accepted a chaplaincy to minister to the Indian natives and the English colonists who had settled there. They sailed with about thirty Christians known as Moravian Brethren. Unexpectedly, they encountered a severe storm. In his journal, John wrote about his fear when he thought he was about to die. He realized he was unsure about the state of his soul, but the Brethren were peacefully singing hymns with confidence. He realized they had something missing from his life: an assurance they were secure with God. They knew they were saved, while John Wesley only hoped he was.

Speaking to the Moravian Christians, they asked John: "Do you know yourself that you are a child of God? Does the Spirit of God bear witness with your spirit that you are a child of God?" This was an unfamiliar language for John. He had always done religious things and assumed he was a Christian. When John did not respond, they pressed: "Do you know Jesus Christ?" John hesitated and then answered, "I know he is the Savior of the world." A Moravian brother replied, "True, but do you know he has saved you?" Wesley could only say, "I hope he has died to save me."

No matter how long we have been walking with God or the maturity of this journey, it is always appropriate to ask ourselves—Do I know Jesus Christ? Ponder your response.

_____
_____
_____
_____

Steven B. Angus

June 22
A Fire Kindled Never to Be Extinguished.

In his journal, John Wesley was transparent about the state of his soul. He wrote, "I went to America to convert the Indians; but who shall convert me?" Returning to London, he resumed his religious duties while searching for genuine faith and the assurance of salvation. On May 24, 1738, he attended a religious society meeting on Aldersgate Street. He listened as someone read from Martin Luther's "Commentary on the Book of Romans."

At about a quarter to nine, as he listened, John Wesley later wrote that his heart was strangely warmed as he realized that he did trust Christ and was saved from the law of sin and death. Wesley said, "It pleased God to kindle a fire which I trust shall never be extinguished." With a renewed purpose, Wesley set out "to reform the nation, particularly the church, and to spread Scriptural holiness over the land." His preaching was vivid, direct, and personal.

When Wesley died, the movement he initiated included 313 preachers and 76,968 members in Great Britain and 198 preachers and 56,621 members in America. Wesley averaged preaching three times daily for over fifty years, totaling 42,400 sermons. Traveling primarily on horseback, his land journeys covered a quarter of a million miles. His writings included 400 published books, tracts, and pamphlets. Today, churches in the Methodist—Wesleyan tradition comprise more than 40.5 million in 138 countries.

Wesley's mission statement was to reform the nation, particularly the church, and to spread Scriptural holiness over the land. What fire is God kindling in you?

_____

_____

_____

_____

June 23
Need a Hug?

You may be old enough to remember when the news was delivered to your home as a newspaper. It contained details about world and state affairs and stock exchange reports. It also was the primary source of information considered necessary to be well-informed citizens. This included birth and marriage announcements, the lunch menu at the Ladies' Circle, and the boxscores of Little League Baseball and Softball games. And, of course, nestled inside the Sunday edition were the brightly colored serial comics.

One of the most popular was FOR BETTER OR WORSE. In one edition, the little girl, Elizabeth, seeing her father lying on the couch, asks, "What's the matter, Daddy?" He responds, "I don't know if I'm bored, tired, or depressed." Concerned, Elizabeth replies, "Everybody feels like that sometimes. It's nothing

Faith Bytes

to worry about." Surprised by her seriousness, Daddy asks, "What do you think you are, a doctor?" In the following scene, Elizabeth is handing him a piece of paper as she answers, "No, but I wrote you a *'perstripshun.'*" Dad reads the note, hugs his daughter, and says, "I feel better now." In the final caption, Mom enters and, seeing Dad holding a piece of paper, asks, "Is that a note from Elizabeth? What does it say?" Still smiling, he hands her the note. It read, "Take two hugs and call me in the morning."

Loving one another is best expressed by our physical presence as we offer a hug or a touch. It has been my experience that most churches do this well. As the church, we must always be looking inward and outward. Frankly, sometimes, we do a better job looking around the world and overlook those seated near us in the sanctuary or beside us in the parking lot. It takes each of us being alert to those we worship with and when they, like Daddy, seem bored, tired, or depressed and offer encouragement. What *"perstripshun"* have you delivered lately?

_____

_____

_____

_____

June 24
It Is a Blessed Miracle

A couple was preparing to celebrate their 40th anniversary. The wife was busy cleaning the kitchen while her husband sipped his coffee. He glanced up from reading the newspaper and asked, "What is the traditional gift for a 40th anniversary?" Pausing from her work, she replied, "Ruby." A few minutes passed, and he asked. "What about the 25th anniversary?" She said, "Silver." Moments later, he asked, "Then what is the 30th?" With a sigh, she answered, "Pearl. And before you ask, 35 is jade, and 45 is sapphire." Just as she returned to her task, he asked, "Then what will our 50th anniversary be?" With great exasperation, she declared, "It will be A BLESSED MIRACLE!"

We have known those who express their marriages this way. Usually, they consider all the ups and downs, the joys and heartaches, the accomplishments and failures, the faithfulness and unfaithfulness, and say, "It is a miracle we have made it this long." The truth regarding this litany of experiences is they are intimately connected to the last two: faithfulness and unfaithfulness. The ups and downs, joys and heartaches, etc., are the harvest of the sown seeds of faithfulness or unfaithfulness.

Whether we call it loyalty, fidelity, trustworthiness, or faithfulness, our world needs it and is desperately longing to witness it. Specific attributes should be visible in the life of a Christian, and one is faithfulness.

"It is a blessed miracle." Can you think of a better term to describe the love relationship between God and His people? God's love always keeps its promises. On the other hand, we realize the same cannot be said of us. What motivates us is learning how often we have been the beneficiaries of God's

Steven B. Angus

blessed miracle. Amazed by miraculous love, we attempt to be faithful promise-keepers.

How does God's blessed miracle of love encourage you to be faithful?

___

June 25
A Bee's Life

My grandfather had many interests. Among them was maintaining colonies of bees. As a boy, I gave little attention to the tiny creatures other than keeping my distance lest I encounter an angry bee. As an adult, I wish I had spent time learning the fascinating world of beekeeping from my grandfather.

When it comes to the Bible, there are more than sixty references to bees and the fruit of their labor, honey. Bees are referenced in the Book of Judges in the story of Deborah. She was a prophetess and the only female judge of the Israelites. Her name comes from a Hebrew word that means "bee." She demonstrated the wisdom, resourcefulness, teamwork, and hard work that characterize bees. God used Deborah to free the Israelites from a cruel king.

Perhaps God has included the bee in Scripture to encourage us when we wonder if the little we do in a world needing so much makes a difference. Consider this. An average beehive produces one hundred to two hundred pounds of honey annually. That sounds substantial, especially when we add hot biscuits and butter. What is most astonishing is a single bee in that hive will produce about one-twelfth of a teaspoon of honey during its lifetime! It takes somewhere between 80,000 and 90,000 bees to accomplish this impressive feat.

The bee's life is another example of how little is much in God's hands. The acts of kindness, the comforting words, a smile—in isolation may seem insignificant. But combined with similar actions from other Christians, it becomes something sweet and nourishing as honey. A little is much in God's hands. In a world needing so much, what are you offering today to bring something sweet to those who have forgotten what it is like?

June 26
Jesus's Greatest Desire

"I am the good shepherd; I know my sheep, and my sheep know me." [John 10:14]

In John 10:11-18, Jesus speaks about his relationship with his followers. He describes himself as the Good Shepherd and his disciples as his sheep. In doing so, the Lord discloses a truly extravagant love. He goes on record so that all generations of his followers can rest assured of his care. His declaration teaches us at least three things about himself. First, he is willing to give his life for his sheep. Second, he knows each of us intimately. And third, there are other sheep whom he also loves. His words demonstrate a heart longing for a relationship between shepherd and sheep.

I have known very few shepherds, which is probably true for you. In some ways, this metaphor of shepherd and sheep is not easy for us to appreciate. Then, I thought about my daughter Amanda's relationship with our cat, Purrs. The two were inseparable. I remember what occurred because it began a few days before Easter. For reasons known only to Purrs, he decided to go AWOL. This was not the first time he had done so; thus, we were not overly concerned. However, Amanda greatly missed her sleeping companion and confidant. As the days mounted, the tears began to flow. Amanda and her siblings organized a search and produced a circular to go into the community. The neighborhood children were all quizzed about Purrs. Whenever I spoke to Amanda, the first thing out of her mouth was, "Did Purrs come home?" And speak of prayer! Purrs must have been the most prayed-for cat in history. However, after two weeks, with no sign of Purrs, we had all just about given up hope of his return. Then, one Sunday morning, I heard something while lying in bed. I rushed to the door, and when I opened it, Purrs sashayed in as if a king. I would have considered killing that darn feline if he wasn't cherished by five ecstatic children.

We may not understand sheep, but we can appreciate the bond of a pet. If something happens or they go missing, we worry about them. Granted, this pales in comparison to Jesus' concern for us, but maybe it is a start. Jesus is the Good Shepherd. My! What a relationship he desires with us. How does it make you feel when you say, "The Lord is my Shepherd?"

Steven B. Angus

June 27
What's Your Meaning?

I appreciate it when someone shares an article or story with me. I came across one such clipping that had turned brown with age. It was titled "Medical Dictionary of the South." I found it hilarious, and since I am a native Tennessean, it is okay for you to laugh with me. Here are some of the medical terms and southern definitions.

ARTERY...The study of paintings. BACTERIA...The backdoor of a cafeteria. BARIUM...What doctors do when patients die. CESAREAN SECTION...A neighborhood in Rome. ENEMA...Not a friend. HANGNAIL... A coat hook. NODE...was aware of. PELVIS...A cousin of Elvis. RECOVERY ROOM...a place to do upholstery. VARICOSE...nearby. And my personal favorite: DILATE...to live long.

Lists such as this serve as a reminder of how vital and fragile communication can be. We do not consistently communicate what we assume we are. The lack of communication or miscommunication has destroyed many relationships. Merely using words is not always enough. Our actions must demonstrate what our language suggests. Communication problems can occur in the church and between the church and society. We use words like *love, welcome, concern, sorry,* and others, but the accompanying actions do not match.

Today, consider the words you speak. What do those phrases actually mean? Are your actions modeling what you say?

_____
_____
_____
_____

June 28
Lord, Teach Me to Play

When we think of vacations, days off, or leisure, we seldom consider it something high on God's checklist. In fact, we tend to boast about how little of it we have due to our constant work. We act as if leisure is opposed to the CHRISTIAN WORK ETHIC.

Perhaps we need to reconsider our PLAY ETHIC. Is it possible our subsequent request of Jesus should be, "Lord, teach me to play?" We need to remind ourselves that God is not opposed to our leisurely enjoying life. Even Jesus took the time to consider the lilies and to attend dinner parties. We each have some free time, so how should we use it?

Dr. Leland Ryken, the author of "Work and Leisure in Christian Perspective," has suggested four steps in achieving "excellence in leisure." The first step is to consciously choose how to spend our leisure time. If we do not, we will allow our free time to drift into mediocrity. Second, our leisure will be better if we deliberately pursue goals for our relaxation. For example, if family unity is a goal, we must assemble the family. Third, we must realize that we derive our identity from our leisure just as much as from our work. We need to choose leisure pursuits that enhance our individuality and talents. If your abilities are connected to sports, then try softball. And finally, our leisure will be its best if we pay attention to what activities bring us the most satisfaction. This does not mean every leisure moment needs to be completely satisfying, as some moments must be for recovering from the wear and tear of daily living. Our goal should be that some of our leisure rises above recuperation.

Spend some leisurely time pondering these questions. What is the status of leisure in my own life? Do I have enough of it? If not, what are the things that prevent it? Am I satisfied with the quality of my leisure? How can I make work and leisure enrich each other? How does my faith affect how I use my leisure and vice versa?

_____

_____

_____

_____

June 29
If It Represents You

The pastor addressed the congregation and made a financial appeal for a worthy cause. Following the service, a woman handed her a check for $50, asking if her gift was satisfactory. The pastor immediately replied, "If it represents you."

After a moment of soul-searching, she asked for the check to be returned. A few days later, she returned, handing the pastor a check for $5,000. Again, she asked, "Is my gift satisfactory?" The pastor responded as before, "If it represents you." After a few moments of hesitation, she retrieved the check and left.

Later in the week, she came again with a check. This time, it was for $50,000. As she placed it in the pastor's hand, she said, "After earnest, prayerful thought, I have concluded that this gift does represent me, and I am happy to give it."

In his Sermon on the Mount, Jesus addressed the daily needs of life with the invitation, "Consider the lilies of the field." It was a call to give "earnest and prayerful thought" to our giving, asking God what we should do. Giving is a spiritual matter. It is something between each of us individually and God. It is not about accepting a piece of the financial pie. When we approach our giving through prayer and in a spirit of trust, we can say with the woman above: I have concluded that this gift represents me, and I am happy to give it. When you give, how do you decide what it will be? What lilies do you consider?

_____

_____

Steven B. Angus

June 30
The Kitchen Table Prayer

In her book, "The Silent Cry: Mysticism And Resistance," Dorothy Soelle recounts an event in Montgomery, Alabama, when Martin Luther King, Jr. was 27 years old. Having received death threats, he was trying to think of a face-saving way to leave his pastorate there. The young preacher considered calling his father, also a minister, for advice. However, something inside him said, "You can't call Daddy now. He's up in Atlanta, a hundred and seventy-five miles away. You have to call on that something, that being that your Daddy told you about, this power that finds a way where there is none." King realized he had to get to know God for himself. Sitting at the kitchen table, he began to pray aloud: "O Lord, I'm down here trying to do what is right... The people are looking to me for leadership, and if I stand before them without strength or courage, they, too, will falter. I am at the end of my powers. I have nothing left. I can't face it alone."

Reflecting on what occurred at the kitchen table, Dr. King said an inner voice offered quiet assurance:

> *"Martin Luther, stand up for righteousness. Stand up for justice. Stand up for truth. And lo, I will be with you even unto the end of the world."*

He believed it was the voice of Jesus telling him to keep up the struggle. Then King began to sing: "He promised never to leave me, never to leave me alone." He often said he felt God's presence like never before. His fears and uncertainty vanished. He was ready to face anything and did not resign from his church or mission.

We can gain much from Dr. King's prayer. We also have those occasions when we feel we have nothing left. We may be dealing with health issues or finding that our way of life is changing drastically from what it has been. Whatever our circumstances, we need to hear the message Dr. King heard, "He promised never to leave me, never to leave me alone."

When have you heard God say something similar to "I promise never to leave you alone?" What might you attempt if you embraced such a promise?

Steven B. Angus

JULY

July 1
Who Is In the Kitchen?

When reading about the Church in the New Testament book of Acts, many things create a sense of excitement for the reader. One significant trait often overlooked is its diversity. The church, born in Jerusalem, was comprised of people with varying backgrounds. When we hear a worship leader read the events of Acts 2, we immediately thank God that we are not the ones charged with the task. Acts 2:9-11 reads like a roll call in the United Nations. Those in attendance included—"Parthians, Medes, and Elamites; residents of Mesopotamia, Judea and Cappadocia, Pontus and Asia, Phrygia and Pamphylia, Egypt and the parts of Libya near Cyrene; visitors from Rome; Cretans and Arabs."

In summary, they differed in almost everything, from food to clothes. The languages they spoke and the color of their skin reflected a multiplicity of cultures. These early Christians had differing occupations and financial resources. They probably disagreed on many things about life and maybe even how the church should be structured or worship services conducted. Yet, this diversity is intended to accentuate another trait at the forefront of their new faith: they became one! They became the church! They were a church comprising all nations whose mission was to go to all nations!

How did this occur? They loved Jesus. They knew he looked not at the external makeup of a person but at the heart. Because they loved him, they allowed the Holy Spirit to take their diversity and make it something beautiful. We could say the Holy Spirit became the master chef. He took a dash of this and a pinch of that, stirred it all up, made it into a delicious entrée, and served it to the world. And consider this—The cook is still in the kitchen!

How might the Master Chef use you to reach a spiritually hungry culture?

_____

_____

Steven B. Angus

July 2
Conversion: I will become a.......

Acts 9 is the story of a man on a mission. He was an expert in religious law, possessing a warrant to arrest anyone in Damascus who identified as a Christian. His original purpose is diverted by a major pothole in the road. Standing in his path is the resurrected Jesus, startling his horse, leaving the fellow on the ground and blind. It was a spectacular transformation for Saul, who became known as Paul. The experience gave rise to the phrase "A Damascus Road experience" to describe a dramatic conversion to the faith.

On this date in 1505, a young law student returned to the university on horseback after a trip home. During a thunderstorm, a lightning bolt struck near the young man. Later, he told his father he was terrified of death and divine judgment and cried out, "Help! Saint Anna, I will become a monk!" He came to view his cry for help as a vow he could never break. He left the university, sold his books, and fifteen days later, he entered St. Augustine's Monastery. The young man was Martin Luther. Like the Apostle Paul, he continues to profoundly impact the Christian faith.

Take some time to remember your coming to faith in Jesus. No matter how it occurred, it was a dramatic event. Give thanks to God, the Father, Son, and Holy Spirit for his love, grace, and fellowship.

_____

_____

_____

_____

July 3
Our Four-Stanza Anthem

It is impossible to know the number of times we have heard and sung the National Anthem. We are all familiar with the words Francis Scott Key penned in 1812. It became our National Anthem on March 3, 1931. The familiar lyrics include: "O say, can you see, by the dawn's early light...O'er the land of the free and the home of the brave."

Francis Scott Key was an attorney and a devoted Christian. In a letter to a cousin, he wrote: "Nothing but Christianity will give you victory...Until a man believes in his heart that Jesus is His Lord and Master and joins in the earnest and eloquent application of the convert's prayer, 'Lord, what will you have me to do?' his course through life will neither be safe nor pleasant."

Perhaps you know that our National Anthem has four stanzas. I cannot recall an occasion when I have heard them sung. Realizing the importance of Key's faith to him amplifies the plea of the fourth stanza. He wrote:

"O THUS BE IT EVER, WHEN FREE MEN SHALL STAND
BETWEEN THEIR LOVED HOMES AND WAR'S DESOLATION!

Faith Bytes

BLEST WITH VICTORY AND PEACE, MAY THE HEAV'N-RESCUED LAND
PRAISE THE POW'R THAT HATH MADE AND PRESERVED US A NATION!
THEN CONQUER WE MUST, WHEN OUR CAUSE IT IS JUST;
AND THIS BE OUR MOTTO: "IN GOD IS OUR TRUST!"
AND THE STAR-SPANGLED BANNER IN TRIUMPH SHALL WAVE
O'ER THE LAND OF THE FREE AND THE HOME OF THE BRAVE!"

May we "Praise the Power that has made and preserved us a nation!" And let us pray to God we will be "Blest with peace."

Are there phrases in this stanza that resonate with your soul?

_____

_____

_____

_____

July 4
Made in the Shade

Charles Allen was a pastor who grew up in a minister's home. He often heard his father preach a sermon titled "The Second Mile." Later in adulthood, Allen said the only thing he could remember about the sermon was an illustration, which he frequently used in his sermons.

It is a story about a man renting a house with no trees. His wife suggested they plant some. It would have been easy to walk down to the woods, dig up a few small trees, and set them out in the yard. But he refused, stating it was his duty to pay the rent and nothing else. The years passed, and the fellow never set out any trees. Every month for twenty-five years, he paid the rent. Then, one day, he bought the house, and it belonged to him. His only complaint? There were no trees in the yard.

Allen said that if the man had gone just a little beyond his duty, shown some generosity and kindness, and went the second mile, he would have ended up with nice trees to give him cooling shade. But he didn't. (Charles L. Allen, "Prayer Changes Things," p. 117)

As we celebrate the blessings and freedom we enjoy as citizens of this great nation, I wonder if Allen's parable might speak to us. When it comes to our government, do we think only of ourselves? Are we short-sighted when it comes to many issues? We would be wise to go the second mile as citizens. Indeed, we may not be the ones to enjoy the shade, but our children and grandchildren could be blessed or suffer from our actions or lack of it.

What tree will you plant? Can you visualize your children climbing it and someday resting in its shade?

_____

_____

Steven B. Angus

July 5
Do You Believe? Then Get In.

If you have visited Niagara Falls, you have likely heard stories and seen photographs of individuals who crossed the gorge on a tightrope. The last person to do so was Nik Wallenda. He walked the half-kilometer, five-centimeter-width cable on June 15, 2012, becoming the twelfth person to cross the Niagara River on a suspended cable. The Niagara Parks Commission only considers applications for stunts once per generation.

The most famous of Niagara's daredevils was Jean Francois Gravelot, a Frenchman better known as "The Great Blondin." In 1859 and 1860, he made many crossings while performing various stunts, including carrying his manager across on his shoulders. Great crowds watched and applauded as he performed one incredible feat after the other. One of his most famous performances was to push a wheelbarrow across the suspended wire. One day, he observed a boy whose amazement was clearly shown on his face. The man asked, "My boy, do you believe I could put you in this wheelbarrow and push you over the falls?" "Oh, yes," said the boy. Gravelot said, "Then get in." Instantly, the boy ran away. It would seem the lad was also wise beyond his years!

How many of us are like this boy regarding our faith in God. We say we believe, but our actions come up short. Hebrews 11 contains the names of men and women the author felt were role models of faith. Among the examples were Abraham and Isaac. Nineteen times in this chapter, these heroes do what they did "by faith." These people did not just believe in God; they lived based on this belief. Within their own experiences, they had learned to recognize the voice and the love of God.

What, then, is Christian faith? Faith is active. It says, "I believe this and will live my entire life based upon this belief." Faith is trust!

What are ways your faith is active? Are there wheelbarrows you are running from?

_____

_____

_____

_____

July 6
The Genesis 15 in Each of Us

It was a sultry day when sitting around and doing as little as possible was best. This is precisely why Abraham had put his tent in the shade of some trees. As he sat at the entrance, possibly sipping on a skin of Old Testament Gatorade, the Lord, accompanied by two others, stopped to pay Abraham a visit. Of course, Abraham did not realize who his guests were. However, attempting to be a hospitable host, he invited them to join him as Sarah, his wife, brought some refreshments. As they ate, the guests asked Abraham where Sarah was. Abraham told them that she was in the tent. Then, the Lord told Abraham that he would return the following year, and Sarah would have given birth to a son. It just so happened that Sarah was eavesdropping. She laughed as she thought, "I am an old woman, and Abraham is older than me. It just can't happen." Hearing her, the Lord asked Abraham why Sarah was laughing. He then asked the question whose answer is what truly mattered: "Is anything too hard for the Lord?"

Are we really surprised that Sarah laughed? It was comical at her age until we realized who was saying what would occur. The story of Abraham and Sarah is a reminder that the answer to the Lord's question is—there really isn't anything too hard for God! And yet, we often stifle a chuckle of doubt over things far less unfathomable circumstances than gerontological pregnancy.

When confronted with seemingly impossible circumstances, we typically ignore them, hoping they work themselves out or go away. If forced to deal with them, we usually decide based on our resources and experiences. When we pray about it, we often ask for power to do what we think is best.

As you think about your life, what would you attempt if you were sure that the Lord would intervene to help? Have you avoided something by saying, "Oh, that's impossible?" Is it?

_____

_____

_____

_____

July 7
The God Who Keeps Promises

Genesis 22:1-14 is the most revered and read story in Jewish tradition. Every morning, devout Jews read this passage. In addition to occurring once in the regular reading cycle, it is also part of the reading on the Jewish New Year, Rosh Hashanah. This means the story of Isaac being placed on the altar is read 367 times annually. In Hebrew, this story is known as the "Akedah," or "the binding of Isaac." In the Jewish tradition, the emphasis is not on testing Abraham but as a reason for hope in the face of the constant threat they have endured. The knife is poised to strike, but God suddenly stops it.

Christians also believe Genesis 22 is an important story referred to twice in the New Testament: James 2:21-24 and Hebrews 11:17-19. In the Church of the Holy Sepulcher in Jerusalem, the traditional site of the crucifixion, near the altar that marks the place where the cross is thought to have stood, on the ceiling to the right of the altar, is a painting of the binding of Isaac next to the mosaic of Christ on the cross.

The story begins when God says to Abraham, "Take your son, your only son—yes, Isaac, whom you love so much—and go to the land of Moriah. Go and sacrifice him as a burnt offering on one of the mountains, which I will show you."

Steven B. Angus

We hear the words "burnt offering" and realize it means death, but understanding what was being asked of Abraham requires reading Leviticus 1 and thinking—my child. This offering wasn't as simple as dropping a few dollars into a collection plate.

This story is significant to Jews and Christians because it demonstrates Abraham's faith that God would keep God's word. God had promised Isaac to Abraham and Sarah. Furthermore, God said that through Isaac, he would bless the world. Abraham truly believed that God was trustworthy and would see to it. This complex story requires us to ask: Do we believe God will keep his promises to his people? It has been stated that there are over 800 promises to Christians in the New Testament. If God had not kept his promise to Abraham, we would have reason to doubt God's faithfulness to keep any of them. Why don't you research God's promises and identify those most significant to you?

_____

_____

_____

July 8
All On the Altar

When Abraham placed Isaac on the altar, it was the ultimate act of faith. His actions proved he believed God was who God said he was and was a promise keeper. Does this mean God will ask us to do the same thing with our children? No! This story is not to be literally applied to our world. In fact, one of the teachings of Judaism is how this event occurred partly to demonstrate God's disgust with Judea's heathen neighbors who regularly committed such atrocities. God was saying—No!

However, the story of the binding of Isaac turns the question back on us. God has demonstrated his trustworthiness, but what about us? Do we take God at his word? Do we trust God? Are we willing to do what God says? Does anything mean so much to us that we cannot relinquish it?

Imagine standing before the altar of God. What do you need to place upon it? Possibly, it is our problems, which may include illness or the lousy report received from the Doctor. Can we lay it down? What is it that you most fear? Losing a spouse either by death or divorce? Abraham believed and named the place Moriah, which means "The Lord would provide" and "the Lord will see to it."

Hopefully, we have noticed that Abraham was presenting his best to God. Isaac was not sick. There isn't any indication that Isaac was an unruly child. Abraham was offering the best he had. Isaac was what he cherished most. This is the ultimate act of faith - do we trust God enough to give God those things we love the most? God does ask us to offer him the best of who we are. Where is the best of you located? Is it on the altar of God?

Faith Bytes

July 9
The Jonah Factor

Ask a child about their favorite Bible story, and we will hear David and the giant, Zacchaeus sitting in a tree, and Jonah and the big fish. Almost every child under ten has seen that skinny stalk of asparagus in the lead role of the Veggie Tales movie "Jonah." However, it isn't just the young who are fond of him. Even when he behaves as if he is the best thing to come along since Jack Sparrow, we adults tend to cut him slack. He reminds us of that grumpy family member who complains about everything. Maybe, just maybe, Jonah reminds us of ourselves.

From the opening line, we find that God had a plan for Nineveh, which included Jonah. God instructed the preacher to go to the city of Nineveh and tell them that God had seen the bad things they had done and must repent. God provided a purpose for Jonah's life. This may be a revelation for some of us, but God also has a purpose for our lives. We often contemplate, "Why am I here?" We lament, "If only I had a reason for living." God intends us to hear Jonah's story and realize if God had a purpose for ole grumbling Jonah, then God surely has a purpose for us.

Jesus is clear about the ultimate purpose of our life when he says:

> "A new commandment I give to you, that you love one another; as I have loved you, that you also love one another. By this all will know that you are My disciples, if you have love for one another." [John 13:34-35]

You and I were created to love God and our neighbor as ourselves. This is both our purpose and identity as Christians. Jesus clarified our mission when he commissioned us to "Go therefore and make disciples of all the nations, baptizing them in the name of the Father and of the Son and of the Holy Spirit, teaching them to observe all things that I have commanded you." [Matthew 28:19-20].

Jonah demonstrates what can happen when we lose sight of our purpose. Jonah disapproved of the Ninevites' lifestyle and believed they were unworthy of God's kindness—or his. When we, like Jonah, replace God's agenda with ours, we move away from God.

God has established your purpose. Does Jonah's actions seem familiar?

Steven B. Angus

July 10
Jonah and the. . . Second Chance?

As you read the Book of Jonah, did you find it ironic how God spoke to a fish, a bush, a worm, the wind, and a heathen? God gives instructions one time, and they immediately obey. On the other hand, God speaks to the man of God, and he tries to run away. The human, who happens to be a prophet, cannot seem to grasp that when God speaks, God means business. Just as we feel the urge to shake our heads in disbelief, we suddenly realize that although the book bears this human's name, the main character is God. Located almost at the story's center, we learn something significant about God. Jonah 3:1 states matter of factly, "The word of the Lord came to Jonah a second time."

When Jonah finally arrived at Nineveh, he entered a city of 200,000 people, so large it usually required three days to walk across. Jonah doesn't bother going to the center of town. Instead, he traveled one day and preached an eloquent sermon, which required a lot of preparation. He said, "Forty days more, and Nineveh shall be overthrown!" [3:4]. Eight words. We cannot but wonder if his voice sounded urgent or delighted.

The point of the story isn't Jonah's childishness. It is God's nature, which is to never give up on people. God is all about giving second chances, even the Ninevites. Jonah delivered the message half-heartedly, and the people repented.

Did Jonah deserve a second chance? Did Nineveh? What about us? No. We do not deserve a second chance or even a first chance. These opportunities are called "grace." Although undeserved, God will give us a second, third, fourth, and so on chance. Jonah said,

---

"I know that You are a gracious and merciful God, slow to anger and abundant in lovingkindness, One who relents from doing harm." [4:2].

When has God given you a second chance? When have you extended a second chance?

_____

_____

_____

_____

Faith Bytes

July 11
The Lord's Prayer—One Size Doesn't Fit All

Regardless of what the ad would have us believe, one size does not fit everyone! The item, whether a vehicle, a house, or clothing, may come close to meeting our needs but inevitably is too long, short, tight, or ugly! And yet, we are often forced to make do. Regarding prayer, we can feel like the frustrated airline passenger who attempts to squeeze a six-foot, three-inch body into a standard seat as we tell ourselves if we want to reach our destination, our only option is to suck it up [or in] and endure it.

However, prayer was never intended to be a one-size-fits-all template. It isn't a spiritual sugar cookie created by someone armed with a celestial cookie cutter. Our prayers were never meant to be pre-fabricated petitions rolling off the press of some otherworldly machine shop. As distinctive as the human race, so it is with our conversations with God.

If you haven't formerly met, I would like to help you become reacquainted with a dear friend. This ally has walked beside followers of Jesus for two thousand years. We know it as The Lord's Prayer.

I hope we can resist the temptation to transform the Lord's Prayer into a legalistic set of dos and don'ts and find it to be that rare friend who is as familiar as a snuggly blanket we wrap around ourselves until the chill passes. When we are distressed to the point of despair and surrender, may the words be so embedded within our spiritual DNA that they flow soothingly upon our spirit as if they were a soaking spring rain bringing refreshment to a freshly plowed and hungry field.

Go ahead! Take the Lord's Prayer out for a test drive.

> *Our Father, who art in heaven, hallowed be thy Name, thy kingdom come, thy will be done, on earth as it is in heaven. Give us this day our daily bread. And forgive us our trespasses, as we forgive those who trespass against us. And lead us not into temptation, but deliver us from evil. For thine is the kingdom, and the power, and the glory, forever and ever. Amen.*

How does it handle?

_____

_____

_____

_____

July 12
The Lord's Prayer—The Thirty-Second Faith Lift

How was your test drive with the Lord's Prayer? Did you try it on the open road when the weather is pleasant and the highway is straight? How did it handle the potholes and hairpin turns of life? Did you notice its durability when you had to downshift as you approached that mountain on the horizon? Undoubtedly, you felt its strength when you slammed on the brakes as a broken relationship or a shattered heart fell across the way. Frankly, the Lord's Prayer is the finest all-terrain vehicle available.

The Lord's Prayer consists of sixty-eight words. How long did it take to speak the words? I am guessing about—half a minute? Its brevity is one of its strengths. Think of the Lord's Prayer as a thirty-second faith lift. If you find yourself in the heat of life and cannot pause to read the 176 verses of Psalm 119, then wrap yourself for thirty seconds in the Lord's Prayer. As you focus on the prayer, thirty seconds here and thirty seconds there, you will soon find your faith lifted and your spirit replenished.

How did you feel as you prayed the Lord's Prayer? Which part spoke to you most significantly?

_____

_____

_____

_____

July 13
The Lord's Prayer—A Gift For the Rest of Us

Discussing prayer can make me nervous. Perhaps nervous isn't the best word. It is like the uneasiness you feel when you sit down to take a test. The anxiety isn't because I do not know the subject matter. Instead, in that moment, I am keenly aware of my deficiencies. Regarding prayer, I lack the boldness of the Apostle Paul and would never say as he did—be an imitator of me.

Do not misunderstand. I pray and have seen the difference it has made in my life and the lives of those for whom I have prayed. My uneasiness stems from what I have learned about myself because of prayer. It is hard for me to be still, and because I have ADHD, my thoughts are in constant motion. When I pray, my mind, well—let me give you an analogy. Imagine I'm holding a Jack Russell, and you have a Chihuahua. In a moment of lunacy, we put them in the same pet crate. Please don't try that at home!

Sometimes, when I pray, I struggle to find the right words, to the point that my prayer becomes the work of constructing a carefully researched monologue. Prayer—as language becomes tiring and can leave me exhausted. I am guessing I am not the only person who struggles with—not the significance of prayer but with doing it with joy and enthusiasm. I envy those who seem to pray in such a way that their conversation with the Almighty simply rolls off their tongues with eloquence.

Does any of this resonate with your experience of prayer? If so, the Lord's Prayer is a gift Jesus made available to help us. However, it is not intended to be a legalistic formula for approaching God. When sincerely offered by a group of believers, it can breathe life into a church. Yet, it can move mountains when prayed in the solitude of a closet or in the mind of one surrounded by the noise

Faith Bytes

and chaos of an ER. The Lord's Prayer is always alive—always breathing renewed life into the one who, through its words, is leaning into God.

Try praying the Lord's Prayer throughout the day. If you are alone, say the words aloud. If you are working on the computer at the office, standing in the check-out lane at the grocery store, or sitting in a doctor's waiting room in the privacy of your mind, take thirty seconds and give your faith a lift. What was your experience?

_____

_____

_____

_____

July 14
The Lord's Prayer—When Praying Feels Awkward

If you want to learn about prayer, then the writings of Reverend E.M. Bounds are required reading. His experiences as a Methodist preacher and chaplain during the Civil War are remarkable. However, it was in retirement that he made a lasting gift to Christians. During those seventeen years, he wrote eight books in a series on prayer, only two of which were published during his lifetime. He states that the Lord's Prayer is the perfect prayer. Jesus, he said, gave "us a form and an outline that can be followed, and yet one that can be filled in and enlarged with our needs and convictions as we may decide as we pray." What he means is the Lord's Prayer can breathe life for each of us. [The Complete Works of E. M. Bounds, Kindle Locations 11849-1185]

Even before unpacking the words of the Lord's Prayer, its appearance is a source of encouragement. The prayer is recorded in two places in the Bible. We find it in the Gospel of Matthew 6 as part of a larger body of teachings Jesus gave his disciples known as "the Sermon on the Mount." The other occasion is found in Luke 11:1-13. Jesus is responding to a request by one of his disciples, who was acting as a spokesperson for all of Jesus' followers, including those in the future. Having observed Jesus's unique prayer life characterized by an intimate, almost casual relationship with God, asked him, "Lord, teach us to pray."

The disciples' request can offer us hope, particularly for those who find prayer—awkward. We can learn to pray. Interestingly, the disciple who wished to learn how to pray does what he requests—he asks. Learning to pray is learning to ask. Do not be afraid to ask Jesus. What are you asking God?

_____

_____

_____

_____

Steven B. Angus

July 15
The Lord's Prayer—Mindfulness

The Lord's Prayer is recorded in Matthew 6 and Luke 11. The context of the two passages is unique, but one thing they have in common is Jesus' introduction to the prayer. In each account, Jesus said to his disciples, "When you pray." "When" is a reference to time. More specifically, "time that is made" or "making time." The implications of "when" are enormous. When we make time, it suggests mindfulness. When we make time for our family or place the kickoff time of a football game on the calendar, it indicates our being mindful to prioritize it.

At the very least, The Lord's Prayer teaches us—we must be mindful of God. When we pray together or as individuals, it is an acknowledgment of our mindfulness that God is in the room. In his book, "A Plain Account of Christian Perfection," John Wesley wrote: "Whether we think of God or speak to God, whether we act or suffer for him, all is prayer, when we have no other object than his love, and the desire of pleasing him. . .All that a Christian does, even in eating and sleeping, is prayer, when it is done in simplicity. . . In souls filled with love, the desire to please God is a continual prayer."

Prayer does not require us to close our eyes, launch into a formalized petition, or quote a Psalm. Prayer is our mindfulness that God is present—that God is God. In his book, "The Practice of the Presence of God," Brother Lawrence wrote:

> "[God] does not ask much of us, merely a thought of Him from time to time, a little act of adoration, sometimes to ask for His grace, sometimes to offer Him your sufferings, at other times to thank Him for the graces, past and present, He has bestowed on you, in the midst of your troubles to take solace in Him as often as you can. Lift up your heart to Him during your meals and when you are in company; the least little remembrance will always be the most pleasing to Him. One need not cry out very loudly; He is nearer to us than we think."

The Lord's Prayer teaches us that prayer is our mindfulness of God. How will you make being mindful of God a priority today?

_____
_____
_____
_____

July 16
The Lord's Prayer—The Power in Our

The average first-century Jew understood God as distant. Jesus was pursued by so many people because he presented God as warm and inviting. When the Disciples observed Jesus' interaction with God, they encountered a welcoming God. As expectantly as a thirsty traveler nearing a cool mountain stream, they asked Jesus for a drink—"Lord, teach us to pray."

Faith Bytes

The Disciples were familiar with the teachings of other rabbis, even referring to John the Baptist instructing his followers. They had been taught to pray at mealtimes and at the traditional hours of prayer at nine, twelve, and three. Although spoken sincerely, the language of these prayers was often read or spoken in (high church) high temple Hebrew. It differed from the Aramaic spoken in the villages outside the Temple in Jerusalem.

Responding to their request to be taught how to pray, Jesus said, "When you pray, say, 'Father in heaven.'" These words had the same cosmos-changing effect as Copernicus's presentation of a solar system replacing the earth as the center with the sun. With his words, "Our Father, who art in heaven," Jesus rewrote the book on prayer. He replaced the formal Hebrew language associated with religion and brought prayer into the center of daily life.

The words "Father in heaven" reveal a God who speaks our language and hears us in our voice. Are you wanting to talk to God but worry you do not know how to express yourself or fear you may say something incorrectly? How do you speak to your best friend? What do you say to your spouse or children before going to sleep? That's how you begin. Give it a try.

_____

_____

_____

_____

July 17
The Lord's Prayer—Our Father

You probably noticed that The Lord's Prayer found in Matthew 7 and Luke 11 are not identical. They also differ from those we say in church worship, a composite of these two texts. Luke's prayer does not begin with the traditional "Our Father." It just starts. "Father." Recognizing that Jesus spoke Aramaic is helpful. The word he used for Father is "Abba." In English, the terms father and mother are formal words more in keeping with a title. When we address our parents, we typically use the more affectionate momma or daddy. "Abba" is speaking to God as "daddy." This information can help us to be more effective pray-ers. Jesus' use of Abba wasn't a whim. Nor was it an isolated occurrence. 169 of the 170 times in the Gospels when Jesus addressed God as Father, he said Abba. [The one exception was Jesus' prayer from the cross.]

Notice the wording of the first line of the prayer in Luke 11:2. Jesus said, "Father, hallowed be your name." Jesus' intention is our prayers should demonstrate honor and respect towards God. We do this by treating God's name as holy. But which name? Is it Jehovah? Yahweh? Perhaps Elohim? In this context, it seems logical that Jesus refers to the name he just invited his disciples to use. When cascading off the lips of a loving child, the endearing Father, Abba, or Daddy renders the name of the Almighty—"Holy."

Instantly, Jesus transformed prayer into a relationship. How would addressing God as "Our Abba" or "Dad" affect how you relate to and with God? Consider writing a prayer address to God this way.

_____

_____

_____

_____

July 18
The Lord's Prayer--Our Father Isn't That Father

When we hear the opening words of The Lord's Prayer, some of us must contend with feelings of shame, guilt, and anger. In truth, many of these deep-seated emotions cannot be adequately labeled. When the words "Our Father" are voiced in corporate worship, instead of solidarity with our sisters and brothers, it is experienced as isolation. Often in silence, some ask, "How could God be Father if the only father I knew was cruel and abusive?" Some of us have suffered severely at the hands of men who were father figures. The pain is genuine, the unseen scars can run deep, and I am not communicating in the third person.

When speaking with someone who has difficulty using the word Father to address God in the Lord's Prayer, I usually encourage them, as hard as it may be, to focus on the word that precedes Father. It says, "Our Father," and isn't speaking about your father. Immediately following the Lord's Prayer in Luke 11, Jesus said:

> "You fathers—if your children ask for a fish, do you give them a snake instead? Or if they ask for an egg, do you give them a scorpion? Of course not! So if you sinful people know how to give good gifts to your children, how much more will your heavenly Father give the Holy Spirit to those who ask him."[Luke 11:11-13, NLT]

Jesus indicates that using any human idea to compare God will always be incomplete. Even the best of humanity cannot stack up to God. I believe the following advice from another pastor has merit. "Our Father is not the father who violated you. It's our Father in heaven, our Father who has no abuse in Him, who will never violate anyone. We all need to learn to use this phrase and transfer to God the positive attributes that we so earnestly desire and so seriously miss in our earthly fathers."[R.C. Sproul. The Prayer of the Lord].

When we say "Our Father," we are reminded that we are not alone. Although there are occasions when addressing God as "My Father" is appropriate, why do you think Jesus said, "Our Father?"

_____

_____

_____

_____

Faith Bytes

July 19
The Lord's Prayer—Our Abba

"Our Father in Heaven." What would these words suggest if we were unfamiliar with Jesus' teaching concerning prayer? We would likely think quite literally of God in heaven. We might point upward and say, God is there, and we are here. Or something like—God is above us, withdrawn from us. God is virtually unapproachable, and for all practical purposes, God is distant.

However, the perspective changes when God is "Our Abba" in heaven. In heaven now, our Father has a better vantage point to watch over us. Our Father God would never allow us to wander far from his watchful eye.

When I was a young pastor, I had a church member who was of Dutch descent. Even now, I can almost hear his wonderful accent as he would try to encourage me with his favorite statement—"Pastor, remember, our Father owns the cattle of a thousand hills."

Perhaps our confusion and uncertainty as Christians is due to an identity crisis. To be politically correct, we have forced ourselves to avoid speaking of God in a paternal sense. An unexpected consequence is we have inadvertently cast ourselves as orphans. If we have mother or father issues—and we all do to some extent—how does divorcing ourselves from an Abba-God do anything but cause an even more profound sense of not belonging.

How does saying "Our Father in Heaven" influence your understanding of God?

_____

_____

_____

_____

July 20
The Lord's Prayer—Hallowed Be Thy Name

In the Lord's Prayer, Jesus mentions six petitions that should be included in our conversation with God. The first is "Our Father who art in heaven, hallowed be thy name."

Hallowed is a word seldom used today. It is an old English word that means "to honor as holy." It is not a prayer asking God to "be holy" because God is already holy. This first petition is that God will be honored and glorified as the Holy One. It is not a phrase included to make the prayer sound religious. It is a request that the awesome holiness of God would be recognized and acknowledged by everyone.

When you consider the occasions when you felt the most profound and significant harm, what was the source? If my experience is the barometer, it is when we feel disrespected by those who love us most dearly. Perhaps we should be reminded to whom Jesus was speaking. It was his disciples, which included us. John Calvin said that because Jesus felt the need to have this petition in the Lord's Prayer demonstrates our great disgrace. More to the point, you and I fail to treat God with respect and honor.

This is a reminder. God is our "Abba." However, our closeness to God may lead us to disrespect God if we are not careful. Although the Lord's Prayer reflects our intimacy with God, it isn't an invitation to slap God on the back as if he were one of the boys.

As we pray that God's name be honored as holy, how can we make it so in our lives and how we pray? Here are a few possibilities. We can avoid being rude and acknowledge God's presence. We can be intentional about learning who God is. We can honor the holiness of God by trying to become like him. We can honor our "Abba" by putting away childish things and growing up.

How will you apply these suggestions to honor God as holy?

_____
_____
_____
_____

July 21
The Lord's Prayer—Thy Kingdom Come

Although the Lord's Prayer is brief, it contains six specific petitions. The first three appeals to God for "thy" glory to be brought to bear in the world. We pray "hallowed be thy name," "thy kingdom come," and "thy will be done." When these petitions are realized within and around us, our world will be radically different.

What does the request "Thy kingdom come" mean? The word "kingdom" is used approximately 154 times in the New Testament. Jesus says it 56 times in Matthew alone. When we pray, "Thy kingdom come," we do so as if it is one of several items on a prayer list. However, each part of the prayer addresses some facet of God's kingdom. If all the requests occurred, then God's kingdom would be achieved.

When we say or hear Thy kingdom come, we often interpret it as our placing an order for a kingdom to be constructed and, when it is completed, to deliver it. When asked when the kingdom would come, Jesus answered, "The kingdom of God does not come with observation; nor will they say, 'See here!' or 'See there!' For indeed, the kingdom of God is within you." [Luke 17:20-21, NKJV]

The petition implies a Kingdom already exists, and we request God incorporate us into it. When our prayer is Thy kingdom come, it is not only a request. It is an invitation for it to come in and around us.

The "Thy" of the petition makes the request very specific. The parameters of "Thy Kingdom" have already been defined. This domain already has a king. "Thy kingdom" is not a democracy; there shall never be another monarch. When we make this appeal, it is an acknowledgment that God has a plan and an agenda for His world, and we want to help bring it about.

As you pray, reflect on the petition, "Thy Kingdom come," and consider how to apply it to your circumstances. For example, we could pray, "Your kingdom come—as I have a difficult conversation with my friend or parent." "Your kingdom come today in my relationships at the office or with my civic organization." "Your kingdom come especially for _____, who is having such a hard time right now." "Your kingdom come. . ."

_____

_____

_____

_____

July 22
The Lord's Prayer—Thy Will Be Done

"Thy will be done." Four words—a mere thirteen letters in the King James Bible, fourteen in modern English, "Your will be done." In isolation, each word is ordinary. Three of the four words appear on lists of the one hundred most-used English words. Seldom is a sentence spoken or written that does not include one or a combination of these words, but rarely do all four appear in this sequence unless addressed to God. In other words, "Your will be done" is chiefly a prayer.

This grouping of the words is unique; therefore, it cannot be a coincidence whenever they appear together. We would be committing a grave error by not seeing a relationship between the prayer Jesus taught his disciples in Matthew 6 and the one he prayed during his agonizing night spent in the Garden of Gethsemane.

The events in the garden occurred soon after Jesus and his disciples shared the Last Supper in the Upper Room. It was a grove of olive trees, and as they entered, Jesus instructed his disciples to remain where they were and to pray. He then invited Peter, James, and John to go farther into the garden and keep watch with him. When Jesus stepped aside to pray, had they remained awake, they would have seen Jesus at his most vulnerable moment. He prayed, "My Father! If this cup cannot be taken away unless I drink it, your will be done." In total, he would plead his case before his Father three times. Taken in isolation, "Thy will be done" would appear to be a foolhardy statement of submission that ultimately gave way to profound disappointment, a possibility only surpassed by pain.

However, we return to the Lord's Prayer when the petition is prefaced by—"Our Father." Jesus is not inviting us to pray "thy will be done" to Caesar but to our Abba. In the Garden of Gethsemane, it was to Abba that Jesus submitted. Jesus often invited those who would follow him to become like children. He was speaking about a child's ability to trust. Praying "Our Father, thy will be done" is such trust!

Steven B. Angus

Why is trust significant to prayer?

July 23
The Lord's Prayer—Trust

If we believe God's will is best, why are we reluctant to say it to God? As I considered this question, I thought of a movie credited with making James "Jimmy" Stewart a star. No, it wasn't "It's a Wonderful Life." Instead, it was "Mr. Smith Goes to Washington," which garnered eleven Academy Award nominations. Stewart portrays a naive Jefferson Smith, who is sent to Washington to serve the remaining term of a senator who has died. Initially, Smith is considered a hopeless country bumpkin and an embarrassment. However, visiting the Lincoln Memorial reminds him of what he hopes to accomplish: a national camp for boys. Smith eventually has a showdown with corrupt Senator Paine, who had presented himself as a mentor to Mr. Smith. Outraged, Paine sets out to destroy the young idealist. Smith's secretary encourages him to filibuster while his friends attempt to advertise the real story. While Smith holds the floor, his Boy Rangers print up and try to distribute their own newspaper, but Senator Paine's henchmen stop them. Smith holds the Senate floor and speaks for twenty-three hours as the older Senator attempts to persuade him to yield the floor. Nevertheless, the young Senator had been burnt in the past by trickery and refused because he had learned that some people cannot be trusted.

We must yield our will to God to pray Thy will be done. Like Mr. Smith, we have been burnt as people who do not know us have tried to use us for their gain. Sometimes, family and those we thought were our friends have ambushed us. Fear and hurt have made us reluctant to trust anyone, including God. We have withdrawn into ourselves as if we are protected in some Kevlar bulletproof vest for the soul. "Thy will be done" is moment by moment, choice by choice. Every day, we are confronted with "our will?" or "God's will?" As we grow in our trust in God, we find that God's will has become "our will."

Are there areas of your life where your will and God's will are in opposition? Why is trust important?

Faith Bytes

July 24
The Lord's Prayer—Give Us This Day

Jesus speaks to the full spectrum of our lives with the least words possible. The Lord's Prayer consists of six petitions which address our every need. The first three have as their subject the honor and holiness of God. Although these requests have as their subject what God deserves, they are addressing a need within us and not something lacking in God. In other words, God does not need to be holy because God is holy. It is us, God's children, and society who possess a need to honor God as such. God does not require a Kingdom, as He is already King. However, humanity has needs that only God's kingdom can fulfill. As for God's will, it shall come to pass. Our need is to trust that God's will for us is best. These three requests acknowledge our need for God's holiness, reign, and will.

We now move into the second part of the prayer. Jesus is still concerned about our needs. Let us not forget that Jesus introduced the prayer by saying, "Therefore do not be like them. For your Father knows the things you have need of before you ask Him." [Matthew 6:8]. This knowledge is evident in the subsequent petition as Jesus teaches us to pray, "Give us this day our daily bread."

Before rushing forward, consider the words—"Give us this day." Jesus is the ultimate wordsmith; therefore, each word is like a weight-bearing wall in a building. We speak the prayer so quickly we tend to hear these clarifiers as if they only relate to bread. I suggest we apply them to each of the following requests. In other words, Jesus instructs us to ask, "Give us this day—'forgiveness of our trespasses as we forgive others today." It means, "Give us this day"—the willpower to combat temptation, that is, "victory over evil and the spiritual forces of this world." Each petition represents our need for today.

"Give us this day" is our prayer of faith. We are not eyeing the future solely but look to God daily for our provision. "Give us this day," is saying to God, "I trust you with the only thing I have with any certainty, which is this moment."

_____

_____

_____

_____

July 25
The Lord's Prayer—Our Daily Bread

Are you surprised by the inclusion of something so simple as bread? Just a few breaths ago, this prayer had us ascending through the highest heavens while reflecting on kings and kingdoms. Now, we are discussing first-century Palestinian bread made from a handful of flour from whatever grains were in season, a pinch of yeast, and a splash of water. It was baked by placing the dough on preheated stones or a platter resting on an open flame. A loaf? Visualize a patty about the size of a pancake on a short stack at IHOP. The bread was the primary staple at the two daily meals of a first-century Middle Eastern home. The amount of adequate food daily was three loaves for a man and his family. Fruits, dates, and fish would supplement. For snacks, children and those working outdoors could eat all the grasshoppers and crickets they could catch! The bread was essential to life.

For fun, count the number of words in the first section of the prayer. "Our Father, who art in heaven, hallowed be your Name; your kingdom come; your will be done; on earth as it is in heaven."

How many did you count? Now, do the same with the second section. "And forgive us our trespasses, as we forgive those who trespass against us. And lead us not into temptation, but deliver us from evil." How many words? Nestled between these two sections is the petition: "Give us this day our daily bread." What we may consider small and take for granted is the center of the perfect prayer.

An essential lesson about prayer is this—nothing is too small or insignificant to bring to God. Jesus realized that the stuff of day-to-day living is exactly where our most extreme pain and our deepest fears reside.

Have you thought, "God is too busy to be bothered with my trivial issue?" When something wounds our heart, the need for a morsel of bread, anxiety about the unpaid light bill, fear about an exam at school, the apprehension about our spouse's upcoming medical tests—whatever it is, Jesus picked it up and placed it directly at the center of the prayer of all prayers. We are invited to make these and countless others a part of our prayer.

July 26
The Lord's Prayer—What is Daily Bread?

If you wonder if I have overstepped the intent of Jesus' use of daily bread, know that we are not the first to ponder the question, "What does daily bread mean?" In his "Small Catechism," Martin Luther arrived at the following conclusion.

Luther stated that Daily Bread is—"Everything that nourishes our body and meets its needs, such as: Food, drink, clothing, shoes, house, yard, fields, cattle, money, possessions, a devout spouse, devout children, devout employees, devout and faithful rulers, good government, good weather, peace, health, discipline, honor, good friends, faithful neighbors and other things like these."

Aren't you glad Jesus did not forbid us to ask for the small things? Richard Foster said that if God had declared we could only talk to Him about the weighty matter and profound issues, not the trivialities of everyday life, "We would be orphaned in the cosmos, cold, and terribly alone. But the opposite is true: he welcomes us with our 1,001 trifles, for they are each important to him." [Prayer, p. 186].

Faith Bytes

The Lord's Prayer teaches us to depend on God in everything. Remember, "give" is a God word best defined as grace! "Give us" is the essence of prayer offered in faith.

_____

_____

_____

_____

July 27
The Lord's Prayer—The Forgiveness Clause

Scott Calvin was the character portrayed by Tim Allen in the movie "The Santa Clause." Scott was a divorcee who was spending Christmas Eve with Charlie, his son. After reading "The Night Before Christmas," he tucked him into bed. That night, Santa lands his sleigh on their roof. Scott assumes it is an intruder and rushes outside, startling Santa, who loses his balance and falls off the roof. You get the picture. Scott finds a card in the pocket of Santa's suit that states, "If something should happen to me, put on my suit, the Reindeer will know what to do." Scott does so and has a beautiful night delivering gifts. What he didn't realize until later, printed in tiny letters on the card, is "The Santa Clause," making him the new Santa. Scott is unhappy about the clause, believing he was tricked. Scott's life changes drastically, but he eventually discovers "the clause" was the best thing to have occurred.

Sometimes, we feel this way about the Lord's Prayer and forgiveness. Although we may agree to forgive is probably good for us, it carries with it some things we had not anticipated. We may plead we had not understood the fine print of the "Forgiveness Clause." Yes, we love the part about God forgiving our sins. Still, forgiving others causes us to heartily agree with C.S. Lewis when he said: "Everyone thinks forgiveness is a lovely idea until he has something to forgive."

However, unlike Scott, we cannot plead ignorance or appeal to the notion that Jesus hid the problematic details in small print. It is right there and as bright as day. In fact, in an effort for full disclosure, Jesus circles back to the subject after he has completed the prayer and stated for the record:

> "For if you forgive men their trespasses, your heavenly Father will also forgive you. But if you do not forgive men their trespasses, neither will your Father forgive your trespasses." [Matthew 6:14-15].

Evidently, forgiveness is a big deal for Jesus. Is there someone you need to forgive?

_____

_____

_____

_____

Steven B. Angus

July 28
The Lord's Prayer—Quid pro quo?

The Lord's Prayer is a gift to the Church that is a means of grace to everyone. A person doesn't have to be a Christian to pray it. However, it means something different for a Christian and someone who isn't. It is a means of grace that can lead someone to faith in Jesus. It demonstrates a need for Christ and is an invitation to confess one's sin and become a Christian. The Lord's Prayer is a gift to the world. Still, Jesus primarily intended it for those who, by faith, address God as Father. Jesus is teaching Christian disciples how to pray. This is important because asking for forgiveness by someone becoming a Christian is not the same as a Christian asking for forgiveness. Although we tend to mix sins altogether, there is a difference in Sin with a capital S and sins. We take all the sin stuff, mix it, and formulate a list of sinful actions. Once compiled, we proceed to rank them under particular classifications such as "sins," "big sins," and "you can smell the flames of hell sins." The Bible makes a distinction between acts of sin and our sinful nature.

For the individual coming to faith, "forgive us our trespasses" is seeking forgiveness for the big S Sin. This acknowledges, "Not only do I miss the mark—I am a sinner." Although specific acts of sin may come to mind, we realize our soul needs forgiveness. We need to be born again. A Christian has been forgiven of Sin with the capital S and changed allegiances. When a Christian asks for forgiveness, it is like a child sitting down with a parent and coming clean about specific ways we have fallen short of God's best for us.

Does this part of the Lord's Prayer qualify as quid pro quo? Jesus' petition is not suggesting, "I forgive so and so, now you forgive me." It is not a principle of cause and effect; instead, it is a statement about what we are doing. Even as God forgives us, we forgive others. We forgive like God forgives us. We will have issues if this is not our life's natural routine. Why? Because unforgiveness is a sin. Sin gets in the way of God's best for us. If we choose not to forgive, our actions contradict entirely what we profess to believe.

Perhaps the intent of this petition can be understood as God has covered our debt. Now, God gives us the privilege of becoming like our heavenly Father as God allows us the honor of extending forgiveness to others.

_____
_____
_____
_____

July 29
The Lord's Prayer—Keep me safe from me

My uncle loved to tell the story of a young boy who accompanied him while working on his farm. As my uncle worked, he noticed the boy getting close to an electric fence. So he called to the chap, "Now don't touch that fence, or it will bite you." My uncle watched out of the corner of his eye because he knew what would happen next. Sure enough, the boy eased closer to the fence, looking over his shoulder to see if my uncle was watching. The boy gingerly extended his hand and, finally, grabbed the wire. When he did, he yelled and ran to my uncle in tears. Until the day my uncle died, he enjoyed telling this story about me. This event introduced me to the enticing world of temptation. Temptation is a course in which humans appear to excel.

When we pray the Lord's Prayer, we are accustomed to saying, "And lead us not into temptation but deliver us from evil" and not "Deliver us from the evil one." While studying the Bible, I typically consult numerous translations and original language material. The three translations I use in worship are the New Living, New Revised Standard, and English Standard. Two of these use the phrase "evil one" and the other "evil." Each includes a footnote stating another possibility is the opposite of how that particular translation rendered it.

The point is that although the two parts of the petition "lead us not into temptation but deliver us from the evil one" are related, they are also distinct. Eugene Petersen's rendering in "The Message" is quite helpful. He translated the petition as "Keep us safe from ourselves and the Devil."

Temptation and Sin are often of our own creation. Our coworker has a beautiful new F-350 pickup truck, and we want it and have nasty thoughts about how we deserve ownership, not them. That is on us, and we cannot, honestly, lay the responsibility at someone else's doorstep. Asking God to keep us safe from ourselves is in order. It is incredible how many electric fences we choose to touch daily. Our saying, "God, keep me safe from me," is an honest appeal for guidance.

_____
_____
_____
_____

July 30
The Lord's Prayer—The Adversary

We now come to the second part of this petition:" Deliver us from evil "or "Deliver us from the evil one." Eugene Petersen's "The Message" translates the request as "Yes, I believe in the existence of the Evil One, but I have no intention of giving him any credit for his wicked ways."

Is there someone in scripture who can help us understand the Evil One? The individual I think of was present when Jesus taught the Lord's Prayer. Jesus once told him: ""Simon, Simon! Indeed, Satan has asked for you, that he may sift *you* as wheat. But I have prayed for you, that your faith should not fail; and when you have returned to *Me,* strengthen your brethren." [Luke 22:31-32]. If anyone understood the danger of temptation and the Evil One, it was Peter. He put his expertise to work in the Epistle of First Peter 5, using his most ardent words to warn Christians of the Devil's sinister methods. Without mincing words, Peter warns:

> *"Like a roaring lion your adversary the devil prowls around, looking for someone to devour." [5:8]*

Peter calls the Devil an adversary. The Greek word he used suggests physical and mental intensity brought to bear by an adversary in a lawsuit. If we are in a court of law, we want an attorney who is tenacious and uses every maneuver at his disposal to win. When words fail, what becomes the best course of action? To prolong the proceedings and keep the judgment in limbo. The goal is to wear an opponent down until the other side is willing to settle. Peter intentionally applies this image to describe the Evil One. What is at stake is salvation, a person, or the witness of a Christian. The Devil is cut-throat and will use every ploy necessary to make life miserable. His strategy is to keep applying pressure; perhaps our resistance will weaken over time, and we sin.

Ellsworth Kallis stated: "The most descriptive name [for Satan] is the basic biblical term—the adversary. [He] is the ultimate perpetrator, the one who really has it in for us and wants most to discomfort, disrupt, disassemble, and destroy us. The adversary."

Peter relates this adversary to a lion on the prowl whose sole purpose is to devour. This brings us back to our petition and Jesus' prayer instruction: "Lead us not into temptation but deliver us from the Evil One." We would be wise to take the sage advice of Reverend Dr. Ellsworth Kalas to heart and remember: "This adversary is helpless without our cooperation."

July 31
The Lord's Prayer—Who Has the Last Word?

If you are a Protestant and have attended a Roman Catholic service, you probably were surprised, perhaps embarrassed, when you joined the congregation in praying the Lord's Prayer. They stopped at "evil," and you did not. Maybe you have noticed that almost every translation of the Bible has a footnote at the end of Matthew 6:13, which states that some manuscripts include "For thine is the kingdom, and the power and the glory forever. Amen." This means that the oldest texts we have of the New Testament do not include this statement. The earliest manuscript of the Gospel of Matthew to include the extended ending of the Our Father is a late fourth or early fifth-century parchment called Codex Washingtonensis. The first usage of the extended ending of the Lord's Prayer is found in a document written around 95 AD called "The Didache."

Faith Bytes

Frankly, I am pleased these early second-century Christians included this closing to the Lord's Prayer. It is theologically correct and demonstrates how the Holy Spirit continues teaching Jesus's disciples. Evil nor the Evil One should have the last word. So, could you identify the key phrases included in the closing of the Lord's Prayer? We hear "Father, Son, and Holy Spirit" in Trinitarian fashion and cadence. The adversary may be like a roaring lion on the prowl to destroy. Still, he has more in common with a toothless kitten than Abba, Jesus, and the Holy Spirit. When we pray this prayer, we declare this is God's kingdom. We know who has the power. We affirm the glory of God, which is forever. When we state, "Yours is the kingdom! The Power! The glory forever!" we declare who God is!

We have come full circle. We began the Lord's prayer with a declaration of who God is. We transitioned to a time of praise and worship as we declared, "Hallowed be thy name." We have returned to worship as we proclaim, "For thine is the kingdom, the power, and the glory, forever and ever." This precious prayer, given to us by a loving savior, is strategically positioned between the bookends of praise and worship.

_____
_____
_____
_____

Steven B. Angus

AUGUST

August 1
Back to School Wisdom

In 1872, at 16, a former slave, Booker T. Washington, decided he wanted to go to school. He walked 500 miles to Hampton Institute in Virginia and presented himself to the head teacher. Washington later recalled, "Having been so long without proper food, a bath, and change of clothing, I did not make a very favorable impression upon her, and I could see at once that there were doubts in her mind about me." She sent him with a broom to a classroom needing cleaning. The menial work would have insulted some, but Washington recognized it as his big chance. He swept that room three times, dusted it four times, and even cleaned the walls and closets. When he reported to the head teacher, she examined the room like a drill sergeant, including taking a handkerchief test. When she could not find a single dirt particle, she said, "I guess you will do to enter this institution." As a 16-year-old, Washington realized he could not do many things but could clean a room.

Booker T. Washington became one of the foremost leaders in our nation's history. As an educator, he founded what is now known as Tuskegee University. He became an advisor to Presidents Theodore Roosevelt and William Howard Taft.

As some of you will return to the classroom in preparation for students' arrival, perhaps these quotes by Dr. Washington will find a place on your bulletin board.

"I have learned that success is to be measured not so much by the position that one has reached in life as by the obstacles which he has had to overcome while trying to succeed."

"I will permit no man to narrow and degrade my soul by making me hate him."

"Those who are happiest are those who do the most for others."

Faith Bytes

August 2
Thank a Woman

I have encountered those who say that women should not be the pastor of a congregation or have leadership over men inside or outside of the church. Those same individuals are often surprised that the Christian Church and Methodists have a rich history of women leading in the church. John Wesley appointed women lay preachers and class leaders from the movement's earliest days. His mother, Suzanne, was known to preach for her husband and was considered a much better speaker.

August 2020 marked the 100th anniversary of ratifying the Nineteenth Amendment, which guaranteed the right of a woman to vote. It was the fulfillment of a journey seventy years in the making. In 1848, the first organized women's suffrage convention was held at Wesleyan Methodist Chapel in Seneca Falls, New York. The advocates for women's rights and the abolition of slavery worked closely together. Sojourner Truth, a former slave who began her ministry as an itinerant Methodist preacher, was an activist for both causes.

Under the leadership of Frances Willard, the Women's Christian Temperance Union did more than encourage abstention from alcohol. They helped improve factory working conditions, institute an eight-hour workday, raise the age of consent for girls, and secure women's right to vote. They saw the vote as a necessary tool to address these needs. [Hann, Heather. Methodists crucial in the fight for women's vote. Aug. 18, 2020, | NASHVILLE, Tenn. (UM News)]

Pause and join me in giving thanks to God for those women who have made our churches and our country a better place.

_____

_____

_____

_____

August 3
The Rule that Governs

On August 3, 1846, in Wales, a boy was born into a family influenced by the Wales Calvinistic Methodist Church. The denomination claimed the Reverends George Whitfield and John Calvin in its family tree. At the age of three, his family immigrated to the United States. The boy received only a few years of education from his mother, primarily from scripture and Methodism.

It is doubtful Mrs. Jones would have believed her boy, Samuel Milton, would someday be known to millions as "Golden Rule" Jones. At the age of ten, he went to work doing odd jobs in sawmills and steamboats and eventually in the Pennsylvania Oil Fields. Having saved a small nest egg, Jones moved to Ohio and purchased oil fields. He eventually opened a factory that manufactured oil

Steven B. Angus

equipment, making him a millionaire. When he opened his factory, the workmen were greeted with a sign over the door. It read,

> *"The Rule that Governs This Factory: Therefore Whatsoever Ye Would That Men Should Do Unto You, Do Ye Even So Unto Them."*

Although he opened during a depression, he paid his workers a living wage. He instituted an 8-hour day, a 48-hour week, a week's vacation with pay, health insurance, and a 5 percent bonus at Christmas. Lunches were provided at cost in The Golden Rule Dining Room. Paychecks were accompanied by printed sermons on applied Christianity written by Jones. Eventually, "Golden Rule" Jones was elected mayor of Toledo, Ohio, and tried to lead the city by the Golden Rule. He established an 8-hour day for city workers. He opened playgrounds, golf links, and kindergartens and offered free concerts at the "Golden Rule Music Hall." He worked for fair treatment of the poor and social outcasts. Oddly, he faced opposition to his reform from pastors and business leaders. After being re-elected three times, Jones died in office on July 12, 1904. It was reported that 50,000 people filed by his open casket to pay tribute, including pickpockets, prostitutes, factory workers, businessmen, and politicians.

Sort of makes someone wonder if there may be something to this "Golden Rule" thing.

___

August 4
The Gold[en] Standard

Because Jesus was called teacher, we visualize him saying to his disciples [students], "Okay, take out your papyrus and quill and write this down. Luke 6:31, this is what I refer to as the Golden Rule." We know better but are still surprised to learn that the earliest known usage of the phrase "Golden Rule" for Jesus' words was by two Anglican priests, Charles Gibbon and Thomas Jackson, in 1604. Four hundred years is a long time, but it is less than 20% of the time since Jesus spoke the words.

The term, Golden Rule, was born when gold was the currency standard. Just as gold directed and allowed for economic relationships, this statement was the standard for how people could live justly and peaceably with one another.

John Wesley stated, "[the Golden Rule] commends itself, as soon as [it is] heard, to every [person's] conscience and understanding; no one can knowingly offend against it without carrying [its] condemnation in his own breast." Wesley meant that when we apply Jesus' "Golden Standard," we realize some things are wrong. Therefore, John Newton, a former Slave trader and author of the hymn "Amazing Grace," began his book titled "Thoughts Upon the African Slave Trade" with the words of the Golden Rule.

If possible, Father Wesley would have shouted "Glory" if he could have heard these words of Frederick Douglass, a former slave:

> *"I love the religion of our blessed Savior...which makes its followers do unto others as they themselves would be done by. If you demand liberty for yourself, it says, grant it to your neighbors. If you claim a right to think for yourself, allow your neighbors the same right. It is because I love this religion that I hate the slave-holding, the woman-whipping, the mind-darkening, the soul-destroying religion that exists in the southern states of America."*

Sort of makes someone wonder if there may be something to this "Golden Rule" thing.

August 5
Cheap or Costly Grace?

Since we have unofficially declared this the week of the "Golden Rule," do you remember what it is?

"Remember the Golden Rule" is the title of a collection of "The Wizard of Id" newspaper cartoons by Brant Parker and Johnny Hart. In one sketch, a king declares, "Remember the Golden Rule!" A peasant asks: "What the heck is the Golden Rule?" A musician replies: "Whoever has the gold makes the rules." We often confuse the musician of Id's Golden Rule with the one Jesus taught. Jesus put it this way: "Do to others as you want them to do to you."

How can we state Jesus's Golden Rule to help us in this anxiety-ridden season? The legendary New York Yankee catcher Yogi Berra, known for his pithy Yogi-isms, paraphrased the rule: "Don't do nothin' you wouldn't want done to ya." Eugene Petersen, the author of "The Message," a paraphrase of the Bible, translated Jesus' words: "Here is a simple rule of thumb for behavior: Ask yourself what you want people to do for you; then grab the initiative and do it for them!" Not bad, not bad at all.

A small book, "The Cost of Discipleship," was published in 1937. The author attempted to explain Jesus's Sermon on the Mount and the Golden Rule by referring to cheap and costly grace. He stated we can only understand Jesus' teachings and the Golden Rule when we define them this way: "When Christ calls a man [sic], he bids him come and die." On April 9, 1945, only days before the American liberation of his POW camp, the author of these words, 39-year-old

Steven B. Angus

Lutheran pastor Dietrich Bonhoeffer was hanged for treason by preaching against Nazism. His last words were: "This is the end—for me, the beginning of life."

His actions cause me to believe there just may be something to this "Golden Rule" thing. I pray for the costly grace to live by it.

August 6
Golden Isn't Simple

Have you actively pursued ways to apply the Golden Rule? Like the proverbial warning on the side of the package, "some assembly required," being Golden doesn't equate to simple.

John Wesley refused to accept Jesus's instruction, "Do to others as you want them to do to you," as some catchy Christian slogan. He did not believe the Golden Rule could be understood apart from Jesus' statement: "If you love those who love you, what credit is that to you? For even sinners love those who love them."

In his "Explanatory Notes on the Bible [Luke 6:32]," Wesley stated: "Our Lord has so little regard for one of the highest instances of natural virtue, namely, the returning love for love, that he does not account for it doesn't even deserve thanks...Even those who do not regard God or taken one step in Christianity may do this."

Father Wesley was correct. We don't need to be instructed to love our friends. It comes easier. When it comes to an enemy, our natural instinct is to hate.

How does someone become our enemy? Typically, it concerns how we feel about an actual or perceived offense against us. It may also have to do with our feeling guilty of having caused injury to them. We respond to these uncomfortable emotions with a more satisfactory reaction—hatred. What is least satisfying is reacting to offenses with forgiveness. The hatred of an enemy is easier. Yet, hatred breeds more hatred.

Perhaps now is the time to return to today's initial question: Have you actively pursued ways to apply the Golden Rule?

Faith Bytes

August 7
What is Your Mettle?

Wow! This Golden Rule stuff must be priceless because it isn't for the faint of heart. The following statement in a commentary on the Old Testament story of Naaman the Syrian seems to apply. "Then she shows the metal she is made of. To try the spirit of men, of what mettle they are made of."

When Daniel Rogers wrote these words in 1642, the two spellings, "mettle" and "'metal,'" were virtually interchangeable. By the turn of the century, the two spellings had begun to separate. 'Mettle' was usually reserved for 'character,' in other words, "the stuff a person is made of."

What is the material that a Jesus follower is made of? In a sermon by Theophilus Brown Larimore, published in 1903, titled "The Iron Rule, the Silver Rule, and the Golden Rule," he describes each and asks, "What is your mettle?" The Iron Rule is about power. Its motto is: "Might makes right." The Silver Rule may sound familiar as it holds the idea if you do not wish something done to you, do not do it to others. The silver rule declares, "It's not my problem, and I will mind my own business if you do the same." In practice, it is basically Golden Rule Light. To the casual listener, this may sound like the teaching of Jesus. However, what makes the golden rule golden is its emphasis on action, not passivity. Jesus said, "Do unto others."

As an illustration, Larimore uses Jesus's Parable of the Good Samaritan. The robbers represent the Iron Man, the religious leaders the Silver Man, but the Samaritan is Golden. Jesus's instruction at the end of his parable is to go and be the Golden man.

Gold has value because it is pliable. Pure gold is liquid. It will only hold form when something is added. Thus, the number of carats is determined by the amount of additives. As a follower of Jesus, we must avoid being rigid while maintaining form. What is it that gives us form without becoming hard? It is the Father, the Son, and the Holy Spirit at work in us.

What is your mettle? Will those you spend time with today see something golden?

_____
_____
_____
_____

August 8, 2020
Making Buddies Out of Bullies

Israel "Izzy" Kalman, a School Psychologist and author of "Bullies to Buddies - How to Turn Your Enemies into Friends!" mentions a letter sent home by a school principal informing parents and students that the school would operate by the Golden Rule. The note concluded: "So you have to live by the GR in school, and if you don't, we will have no choice but to punish you." Kalman concluded that some intelligent, educated people believe the Golden Rule means we must do to others exactly what we want for ourselves. In truth, the Golden Rule does not mean we must give someone everything they want. We can hurt people by doing so, enabling them to become bad people. The Golden Rule requires us to say "no" sometimes, but nicely and without anger. It really means that we should be nice to people even when they are mean to us. We often teach our children that anti-bully means we don't act like a bully, but the Golden Rule also means not to act like a victim!

Kalman concludes that the Golden Rule is the ultimate act of empowerment. We must act independently of the bully's actions, treating them like friends even when they treat us like enemies. Loving our enemies is the real purpose of the Golden Rule.

Kalman flips the discussion, asking how we would feel if our enemies loved us. Before long, they wouldn't be our enemies. So, just as we would like our enemies to love us, we need to love our enemies. If we were to replace our zero-tolerance-for-bullying policies with this expression of the Golden Rule: "Love your enemy (bully); be nice to people even when they are mean to you," bullying would disappear.

The Golden Rule is another example of why we call Jesus our teacher.

_____
_____
_____
_____

August 9
Finding Hope in the Dust

Is today one of those days when you question your ability to take even one additional step? We each have those days. Where can we find the strength, spiritually speaking, to stand and place one foot in front of the other? When this occurs, the experiences of others can inspire us.

Alexander Solzhenitsyn, a brilliant teacher of mathematics who possessed a photographic memory, was incarcerated in one of the Gulag camps in Siberia for expressing a dim opinion of Stalin. Of his eight years of imprisonment, he said the thought of suicide entered his mind once. After several years of hard labor, Alexander set his shovel aside, moved sluggishly to a crude workbench, and sat down. After a few moments sitting with head bowed, he lifted his eyes and saw a skinny, old prisoner squat beside him. The man did not speak but, with a stick, traced a cross in the dirt at Solzhenitsyn's feet. The man stood and returned to his work. Solzhenitsyn sat, staring at the cross. Solzhenitsyn said, "At that moment, I realized that Jesus shed His blood for me on that cross. It reminded me that God loved me. This knowledge gave me the courage to live through my imprisonment. I found the strength to stand, pick up his shovel, and return to work. The purpose of my existence dawned upon me."

Faith Bytes

Nothing around him changed, but inside, he received hope. He experienced what many discouraged Christians have found to be true:

> *"For the message about the cross is foolishness to those who are perishing, but to us who are being saved, it is the power of God." [1 Corinthians 1:18, NRSV]*

How does this message help prepare you for the day?

_____
_____
_____
_____

August 10
You Must Preach to Us!

Barbara heard John Wesley preach numerous times in her native Ireland. She combined a zeal for Jesus and a fiery Irish temperament with every situation. Barbara Heck and her family immigrated to the colonies a year after her cousin, Philip Embury. He was a Methodist preacher in England and arrived in America on August 10th or 11th, 1760. Rev. Embury felt he was too busy trying to make a living in New York to take up church work. However, the no-nonsense Barbara believed it was a sin to trifle away time.

One day, returning to the home she shared with her cousin, she was appalled to find a card game in progress. She gave them a piece of her mind, threw the cards into the fireplace, and went to her knees in prayer. Appealing to her cousin, she said, "Philip, you must preach to us, or we shall all go to Hell together, and God will require our blood at your hands!" He responded that he could not do so because he did not have a church building or a congregation. Unphased, Barbara said, "Preach in your own house first and to our own company."

Philip relented and preached what is believed to be the first Methodist sermon given in America. The congregation consisted of five people in his own rented house. Services were held every Thursday evening and twice on Sunday. In response to their success, John Wesley sent missionaries to America.

Christians are compelled to share the Gospel. Whether in a break room, a home, or under a carport, we must not forget the urgency of Barbara Heck's appeal: "You must preach to us!" How are you sharing the Good News?

_____
_____

Steven B. Angus

August 11
Depression is Real

No one saw it coming. Well, none of us watching from a distance. Always full of joy, his energy caused us to visualize a bounding jackrabbit or a curious Jack Russell terrier. When he was to appear as a guest on late night television shows hosted by Johnny Carson or David Letterman, I made the effort to stay up. My children identified him as Peter Pan and Mrs. Doubtfire. My generation remembered him as Mork from Ork. When it was reported on August 11, 2014, that Robin Williams had died, many of us grieved.

We wonder if anyone could see beyond the slapstick humor and the mischievous grin and recognize the pain on the other side of those inquisitive blue eyes. Depression is real. It can be produced by a chemical imbalance or situationally triggered by anxiety associated with stress. I am personally acquainted with each of these forms of depression. Although some days are challenging, I carry on because of understanding family and friends, the counsel of medical and mental health professionals, and leaning into God's means of grace, such as prayer.

The serenity prayer written by Reinhold Niebuhr has been vital to many. A portion of the prayer petitions God:

> *"God, grant me the serenity*
> *To accept the things I cannot change;*
> *Courage to change the things I can;*
> *And the wisdom to know the difference.*
>
> *Living one day at a time;*
> *Enjoying one moment at a time,*
> *Accepting hardship as the pathway to peace;*
> *Taking, as He did, this sinful world As it is, not as I would have it;*
> *Trusting that He will make all things right*
> *If I surrender to His Will;*
> *So that I may be reasonably happy in this life*
> *And supremely happy with Him*
> *Forever and ever in the next. Amen."*

_____

_____

_____

August 12
Day of Invention

I checked my email and was greeted by the caption: "August 12: Day of Invention." Soon, I was zipping across the internet universe, hoping to discover why it merited the distinction. It didn't take long to see the merit of the statement.

Faith Bytes

Astrologists suggest that on this date over two thousand years ago, the planets of Venus-Jupiter came so close together in the night sky visible over Bethlehem that Magi identified it as a new star to be followed.

On August 12, 1851, Isaac Singer patented his sewing machine; in 1877, Thomas Edison completed the first model of the phonograph; in 1908, Henry Ford's company manufactured the first Model T car. In 1930, a fellow named Birdseye received a patent for a method for packaging frozen foods. Remember this tonight when you take out the frozen pizza for dinner. In 1977, the Space Shuttle Enterprise made its first free flight, launching the technology era. IBM introduced its first Personal Computer with DOS version 1.0 four years later.

On this date in 1959, a tiny baby weighing 10 pounds, 15 ½ ounces, was born. Rumor has it his birth was the inspiration for the number one song on that date by Elvis Presley with The Jordanaires titled "A Big Hunk O' Love." It was the day I looked up from my hospital nursery crib and requested of the nurse, "Seconds, please."

On this day of inventions, I hope you will pause and remember that you are a unique creation of God. The Psalmist said:

> "You made all the delicate, inner parts of my body
> and knit me together in my mother's womb.
> Thank you for making me so wonderfully complex!
> Your workmanship is marvelous—how well I know it."
> [139:13-14 NLT]

August 13
Do You Feel It?

You may recognize Sally Field as the surfer girl named "Gidget" or as the nun whose superpower was a habit that rendered flight. Despite a stellar career in show business, she will always be remembered for her acceptance speech for her second Academy Award in 1984. Millions observed her contagious exuberance as she said, "You like me, you really like me."

Most of us prefer history as we remember it, not for what occurred. What the actor actually said was about her not "feeling" her first Oscar, but "This time," she said, "I feel it. And I can't deny the fact that you like me. Right now, you like me!"

Steven B. Angus

As I read Jesus' prayer in John 17, particularly verse 23, I thought about the misquote attributed to Sally. When I discovered her actual words, I found them to be more in the spirit of what Jesus expressed. Jesus prayed, "May they experience such perfect unity that the world will know that you sent me and that you love them as much as you love me." [NLT].

Did you hear Jesus' message? God loves you. God actually likes you. And here's the kicker—God loves you as much as he loved Jesus. I know. We hear this message all the time. But do we feel it? Repeat the words, "God loves me as much as God loves Jesus." Perhaps as it was with Ms. Field, the first time may not have registered. Say the words aloud: "God loves me as much as God loves Jesus."

Do you feel it? Someone advised John Wesley, "Preach faith until you have it, and because you have faith, preach it."

Right now, do you feel it?

_____

_____

_____

_____

August 14
The, I'll never walk away from you, love.

"Even if the mountains walk away and the hills fall to pieces, My love won't walk away from you."[Isaiah 54:10, The Message].

This has to be one of God's all-time great "Be My Valentine" messages! Let God's promise take root in your Spirit: "My love won't walk away from you." Virtually everything can change except for God's love for us.

Robert Munsch's children's book is probably a favorite of every mom. It begins with a mother holding her newborn and slowly rocking him back and forth as she sings to him:

"I'll love you forever
I'll like you for always,
As long as I'm living
My baby, you'll be."

The baby grew until he was two years old, causing havoc around the house, pulling books off shelves and food out of the refrigerator. Sometimes, his mother would say, "This kid is driving me crazy!" However, when the two-year-old was

Faith Bytes

asleep, she opened the bedroom door, crawled across the floor, and looked into the bed. If he was sleeping, she picked him up. Then, while she rocked him, she sang:

> *"I'll love you forever*
> *I'll like you for always,*
> *As long as I'm living*
> *My baby, you'll be."*

The story continues through each stage of her son's life, but the message never wavers: "I'll love you forever." This is what God means when God whispers in our ear: "Even if the mountains walk away, my love is an I'll never walk away from you, love."

August 15
Apples of Gold

For many readers, "Apples of Gold" is the title of a book by Jo Petty, published in 1962. It contains gems of inspiration sorted into nine categories based on the biblical fruit of the Spirit. Almost every mom or grandmother has received a copy of the gold-covered hardback as a Mother's Day gift. Therefore, it is a staple at any respectable neighborhood garage sale. However, few realize its long history.

On February 23, 1862, Charles Spurgeon preached "A Sermon for Spring." He said, "The things which are seen are types of the things which are not seen. The works of creation are pictures to the children of God of the secret mysteries of grace." And this is the sentence I really appreciate. "God's truths are the apples of gold, and the visible creatures are the baskets of silver." [www.spurgeon.org] Spurgeon's dual description is weighty in its simplicity. Yes, God's truths are Apples of Gold. Still, you and I are also valuable as we are compared to a superbly crafted receptacle of fine silver.

However, this grand portrait predates Petty and Spurgeon. It reaches back to a time long before Jesus walked the earth. They appear in the Biblical book of Proverbs 25. It says:

> *"A word fitly spoken is like apples of gold in a setting of silver. Like a gold ring or an ornament of gold is a wise rebuke to a listening ear."* [Proverbs 25:11-12, NRSVUA].

Steven B. Angus

I wonder, do students still give apples to teachers? As school begins, I want you to be the teacher as I present you with an Apple of Gold harvested from the book of wisdom titled "Proverbs." Its wealth of knowledge has inspired such persons of faith as the late Billy Graham to read one of its chapters each day corresponding to the month's date. I invite you to open your hand and allow Proverbs to drop into it a serving of God's grace. Go ahead and turn the book's pages, pausing to taste the sweetness of its wisdom.

August 16
The Beginning of Wisdom

Are you ready to receive today's Apple of Gold? The book of Proverbs begins with an invitation to be taught wisdom. Just how earnest is our instructor's desire to teach us? Based on his choice of words, very. He used the words "wise" and "wisdom" 133 times [NLT]. A tweet on his Twitter [X] account would be wisdom in all capitals. He is not timid to tackle what seems impossible. He believes The Apples of Gold can help us live a successful life by doing what is right, just, and fair. This wisdom can guide the simple and offer discernment to the young. The wise can grow in understanding.

A math teacher said the difficulty in math is not that some get it and others don't. Math is relentlessly sequential. New skills are built on previously learned concepts. You may get by for a while, but eventually, you will hit a wall, and the frustration begins.

Is there a starting place for wisdom? Proverbs 1:7 states: "The fear of the Lord is the beginning of knowledge, but fools despise wisdom and instruction." This is where the infant, whose name is Wisdom, is birthed. The beginning of wisdom is the belief in God. Some say this is the thesis statement of Proverbs. Yes, "the fear of the Lord is the beginning of knowledge," but here is today's Gold Apple. Verse 7 finds completeness in Verse 23. The teacher invited us to "Come and listen to my counsel. I'll share my heart with you and make you wise." [NLT]

Biblical wisdom already knows there is a God who wants to have a relationship with us. This wisdom isn't related to intelligence or education. A wise person hears and accepts God's invitation to come and listen as God shares His heart. That is? That's Golden!

Faith Bytes

August 17
Half-hearted Trust?

In October 1850, Reverend Mark R. Watkinson began his ministry as Pastor of the First Particular Baptist Church of Ridley, Pennsylvania. Later, he would pastor a congregation near Richmond, Virginia. When the Civil War began, Watkinson returned to Ridley and soon became the supply pastor of his home church, receiving a salary of $5 a week. During this time, he wrote a letter dated November 13, 1861, to the Secretary of the Treasury: "One fact touching our currency has hitherto been seriously overlooked. I mean the recognition of the Almighty God in some form on our coin." Because of his efforts, the slogan IN GOD, WE TRUST, first appeared on the 1864 two-cent coin. Almost one hundred years later, in 1956, a law was passed declaring this statement the motto of the United States. The phrase first appeared on paper currency in 1957.

The writer of Proverbs stated:

"Trust in the Lord with all your heart,
And lean not on your own understanding;
In all your ways acknowledge Him,
And He shall direct your paths." [Proverbs 3:5-6]

Trust. What is it? Based on this passage, it is leaning on God and not oneself. It acknowledges that God's understanding is better, and ultimately, His direction is superior to ours. If the author wanted to save his expensive papyrus paper, he could have simply stated, "Trust in the Lord." However, he didn't and appealed that we "Trust in the Lord with all our heart." Which begs the question: What is the difference between wholehearted and halfhearted trust?

Halfhearted trust is a belief or action based on our perception of circumstances. Wholehearted trust is the ability to wait or to act, believing God will direct us rightly.

Here is today's Golden Apple: Half-hearted trust is like wholehearted doubt. In other words, there really isn't such a designation. We either trust God or we don't. Which is it for you?

Steven B. Angus

August 18
Friendship Isn't a Game

The book of Proverbs has so many Golden Apples we could spend a lifetime strolling underneath the branches of a single tree in its grand orchard. It would be easy to overlook many of them. For example, this Golden Delicious variety is found in Proverbs 18:24. "Some friends play at friendship, but a true friend sticks closer than one's nearest kin." [NRSV]. This is one of seventeen references to friendship in the book.

In a Harvard Business Review article, Vivek Murthy Waltz, former Surgeon General, stated that loneliness is a public health concern, with over 40% of American adults reporting feeling lonely. The actual number may well be higher, particularly among men. As a male and as an introvert, I understand how hard it is to make a friend. Of the many words Jesus could have used to describe his relationship with us, he chose to express it this way.

"I do not call you servants any longer...but I have called you friends." [John 15:15, NRSV]

Consider this today—How does it make you feel to hear Jesus call you friend?

August 19
Friends Who Enfold You Like a Blanket

What are the attributes of friendship? Before she passed away, a friend gifted me some of her unpublished poetry. Faye Kautz wrote this poem about friendship. It reflects the sentiment of Proverbs 18:24: "Some friends play at friendship, but a true friend sticks closer than one's nearest kin." [NRSV]. Faye wrote:

Friends are those who help to calm
The storms within one's soul
That's like a raging sea at night
And has somehow lost control

They lift you up with loving hands
And carry you to shore
And hold you safe within their arms
While you let the teardrops flow.

Faith Bytes

They stay with you and let you lean
While floodgates open wide;
Until the raging storm is calmed
And then stand by your side.

We do not know the purpose
Of many things that happen in our lives;
But we do know we're not alone
With our sadness and our strife.

So I thank God for angel friends
That He's sent to help me cope
And know that in my darkest hours
They'll be there to bring me hope.   Faye Kautz [January 9, 2001]

Today, give thanks for God's friendship and the Angel Friends in your life.

_____

_____

_____

August 20
Apples of Gold in Settings of Silver

John Wesley and one of his preachers were eating lunch in the home of a wealthy family who had just heard him preach. The daughter of the house, a beautiful girl, was much impressed with Mr. Wesley's preaching. As Wesley spoke, his companion noticed she was wearing several rings. Knowing Wesley's reputation for not approving Methodists wearing jewelry, the fellow took her hand, held it up for Wesley to see, and asked, "What do you think of this, sir, for a Methodist's hand?" The girl was embarrassed. However, Wesley smiled and said, "You have such beautiful hands." It was enough. She never wore jewelry again. His gentle and kind words captured her for Christ. [The Tyndale Series of Great Biographies: The Journal of John Wesley]

I wonder if Wesley thought of these words from Proverbs as he spoke. It says: "A word fitly spoken is like apples of gold in a setting of silver. Like a gold ring or an ornament of gold is a wise rebuke to a listening ear." [25:11-12, NRSV]

"The NIV Women's Devotional Bible" tells the story of Mary, who was teased for her poor speech caused by a cleft palate. All the children in Mary's class liked their schoolteacher, but she grew to love Mrs. Leonard. In those days, teachers administered a hearing test to their students. Unfortunately, Mary was partially deaf in one ear. Not wanting to be teased, she had a plan to pass the "whisper test." She covered her bad ear and turned her good one toward her teacher. As she listened, a smile appeared as she heard seven words that changed her life. She heard Mrs. Leonard's whispered words: "I wish you were my little girl."

Steven B. Angus

Solomon called such words "apples of gold in settings of silver." They are filled with love and acceptance that can erase years of pain and sorrow. They are priceless to those who hear them. What Apples of Gold will you speak today?

_____
_____
_____
_____

August 21
The Power to Bring Death or Life

The one-line zinger moves the laughter gauge on the sitcom. Political debates and elections have been decided by them. Even if they aren't true, we arm our children with them as a defense against the bully. Does the saying, "Sticks and stones may break my bones, but words will never hurt me," sound familiar?

The Proverbs would lose all credibility if they did not address the most potent instrument in society—words. They have launched wars, devastated marriages, ended friendships, destroyed business relationships, guided the stock market, split churches, and set the course of a child's life. This is power.

Emphasizing the proper use of words dominates the Proverbs. Over 150 times, it uses terms such as tongue, lips, and speech. Substantial. Here is a sampling—

> "You have been trapped by what you said, ensnared by the words of your mouth." [6:2, NIV]
> "Too much talk leads to sin." [10:19, NLT]
> "Fools' words get them into constant quarrels." [18:6, NLT]

Such statements leave the smell and taste of fermenting, rotting apples. In their place, Proverbs offer these Apples of Gold for the wise person who draws near to God to taste.

> "Anxiety weighs down the heart, but a kind word cheers it up." [12:25, NIV]
> "Gentle words are a tree of life; a deceitful tongue crushes the spirit." [15:4, NLT]
> "Pleasant words are like a honeycomb, sweet to the soul and health to the body." [16:24, KJV]

The wise person recognizes their words can "bring death or life." [18:21, NLT] Therefore, the wise person will choose carefully.

_____
_____
_____
_____

Faith Bytes

August 22
Invitation to a Celebration!

According to legend, the citizens of an ancient village in Spain learned that the King was coming for a visit! The villagers were excited because a monarch had never graced their hamlet. Everyone was in agreement that this called for a grand celebration. However, it was a poor village, and there weren't many resources. Finally, someone put forth a suggestion. Since many of the residents made their own wines, why not bring a large cup of their choice wine to the town square, pour it into a large vat, and offer it to the King? The consensus was that it would be the best he had ever tasted.

The day before the King's arrival, hundreds of people lined up to make their offering to the honored guest. They climbed a small stairway and poured their gift through a small opening at the top. Finally, the vat was full! The King arrived, was escorted to the square, given a silver cup, and told to draw some wine, representing the best the villagers had. He placed the cup under the spigot, turned the handle, and drank the wine. But instead of wine, it was nothing more than water. Every villager seemed to reason, "I'll withhold my best wine and substitute water, what with so many cups of wine in the vat, the king will never know the difference!" The problem was that everyone thought the same thing, and the King was greatly dishonored.

This parable hits home more than we care to admit. It describes our inclination to offer less than the best, especially when we think we can. Like these villagers, we have reason to celebrate. Part of that celebration is expressed in our times of worship. It should be said that every Sunday's worship service, at some level, is a time of celebration. After all, we worship on Sundays because we continuously celebrate the resurrection of Jesus. Everything we bring to or do during that worship should never be less than our best. The taste of the festival depends on whether we present the best we have to offer to (King) Jesus. Here's to celebrating!

_____
_____
_____
_____

August 23
Who Has Your Ear?

It was a hot August morning on this day in 1920. However, it appeared every citizen of Tennessee had gained entrance into the state capitol. The question on everyone's mind: How would Tennessee legislators vote on women's right to vote? Ratification of the 19th Amendment to the U.S. Constitution required the approval of 36 of the 48 states. Thirty-five states had already done so. However, most of the state's neighbors had rejected the measure, and the Tennessee legislators felt pressured to do the same. Four states had yet to vote, but three

Steven B. Angus

refused to call a special session of their legislature, but Tennessee agreed to do so. For all practical purposes, the amendment's fate rested on this vote.

Those gathered in the gallery who dared to hope for ratification knew the numbers. Only 47 of the 96 legislators in attendance were committed to their cause. They had little hope that eastern Tennessee Rep. Harry T. Burn, the state's youngest legislator at age 24, would join their ranks. In his lapel was a red rose, the symbol of opposition to the amendment. Mr. Burns had initially intended to vote for the amendment. Party leaders and constituents from his district overwhelmingly opposed women's suffrage, so he began to side with the Anti-Suffragists. These facts were well-known to observers.

What they could not see was the letter concealed in his pocket. It contained advice from his Methodist mother: "Dear Son: Hurrah, and vote for suffrage! Don't keep them in doubt." Burn's sudden "aye" tied the vote and encouraged a fellow legislator to give the decisive 49th assent. Thus, Tennessee secured women citizens a voice in their nation's democracy, including that year's presidential election.

Senator Burn entered the House Journal, explaining his decision to cast his vote as he did, stating, "I knew that a mother's advice is always safest for a boy to follow, and my mother wanted me to vote for ratification." [wikipedia.org/Harry_T._Burn]

Today, many voices are eager to tell us what we should or should not do. Whose will you listen to?

_____

_____

_____

_____

August 24
A President, A Monk, and A Prayer

February 2, 1984, President Ronald Reagan spoke at the Annual National Prayer Breakfast at the Washington Hilton Hotel. He began his remarks by saying: "We all in this room, I know, and we know many millions more everywhere, turn to God in prayer, believe in the power and the spirit of prayer. . . I wonder if we have ever thought about the greatest tool that we have, that power of prayer and God's help." [reaganlibrary.gov]

The President then told the story of a fourth-century monk to illustrate the power of prayer. The Asian monk Telemachus lived in a remote village, spending most of his time praying or tending the garden from which he obtained sustenance. One day, believing he heard the voice of God telling him to go to Rome, he set out. Weeks later, he arrived, having traveled most of the way on foot.

A festival celebrating the Roman triumph over the Goths was occurring. Telemachus followed a crowd into the Colosseum. In this great gathering, he saw the gladiators stand before the Emperor and say, "We who are about to die salute you." The small monk realized they would fight to the death for the entertainment of the crowds. And he cried out, "In the name of Christ, stop!" But his voice was lost in the tumult there in the great Colosseum.

As the games began, he descended through the crowd, climbed over the wall, and dropped to the arena floor. The crowd saw this scrawny little figure reaching the gladiators, repeatedly saying, "In the name of Christ, stop." They thought it was part of the entertainment. When they realized it wasn't, they grew belligerent and angry. And as he pleaded with the gladiators, one of them plunged his sword into his body. As he fell in death, his last words were, "In the name of Christ, stop."

Suddenly, a strange thing happened. The gladiators stood looking at this tiny form lying in the sand as silence fell over the Colosseum. And then, someplace up in the upper tiers, an individual made his way to an exit and left. In the dead silence, everyone left the Colosseum. That was the last battle to the death between gladiators in the Roman Colosseum. One tiny voice that could hardly be heard above the tumult. "In the name of Christ, stop." We could be saying this to each other throughout the world today.

_____

_____

_____

_____

August 25
The King Who Had It All..... Almost

To be referred to as the king of anything seems to invite disaster. The title typically leads to the construction of a glass house, and when the king stumbles, the resulting crash is devastating. We can quickly formulate a list of kings who started well but finished tragically—Michael Jackson, the king of Pop. OJ Simpson, the king of the gridiron. Bill Cosby, the king of comedy. And Elvis, the King of Rock and Roll.

The Bible speaks of a king who seemed to have it all when suddenly his life imploded. His name was Solomon. When he became king, he was young but realized his father, David, had left some big shoes to fill. Solomon asked God for wisdom to govern justly when given the opportunity. God was pleased with Solomon's humility and promised to bless him in many other ways. Not only did he demonstrate wisdom, but he also had incredible talent as a writer. The Bible credits him with writing 3000 poems, 1005 songs [1 Kings 4:32], Proverbs, the Song of Solomon, and Ecclesiastes. His grasp of mathematics and engineering enabled him to oversee the Temple's construction, incorporating the finest lumber, gold, and precious gems. He appeared to have the Midas touch, but it turned to dust. The warning signs were there when he began forming alliances with countries with different values, usually sealing the deal by marrying into the family. These treaties led to compromising his beliefs and ignoring God's instructions. He began to swindle partners who had trusted him. It wasn't long

Steven B. Angus

until he developed an obsession and addiction to pleasure, having 700 wives and 300 concubines. These foreign wives persuaded him to worship other gods. Having left God entirely, we witness the birth of a cynic whose life lacks purpose.

How did things get so bad? Solomon forgot his relationship with God! Ultimately, the wise king said: "Let us hear the conclusion of the whole matter: Fear God and keep His commandments, For this is man's all. For God will bring every work into judgment, Including every secret thing, Whether good or evil." [Ecclesiastes 12:13-14]

How is your relationship with God? Are you compromising your principles and trusting something above God?

_____

_____

_____

_____

August 26
Maud and Agnes

To my knowledge, Maud and Agnes never met. Each had a deep love for Jesus, and although they lived on opposite sides of the globe, they would have a profound impact on their part and, consequently, the entire world. August 26 was significant to each. On this date in 1910, Agnes was born. In 1948, Maud died at the age of 83.

Maud began helping those in need as a young girl, assisting her pastor father and mother in a London slum. She married Ballington Booth, whose father was William Booth, founder of the Salvation Army. Taking her husband's first and last name, they came to the United States to work with the Salvation Army. However, following a disagreement concerning some of the methods of the Army, they formed the rival Volunteers of America. Believing Jesus was the answer to personal and societal problems, Maud created the Parent-Teacher Association and was instrumental in significant prison reform, which led to the establishment of a parole system.

Agnes, unlike Maud, was reared primarily by her mother, who instilled in her a concern for the poor. She counseled Agnes, "My child, never eat a single mouthful unless you are sharing it with others." At age eighteen, Agnes set off for Ireland to join the Sisters of Loreto in Dublin. She took the name Sister Mary Teresa.

Summing up her life in a characteristically self-effacing fashion, Mother Teresa said, "By blood, I am Albanian. By citizenship, an Indian. By faith, I am a Catholic nun. As to my calling, I belong to the world. As to my heart, I belong entirely to the Heart of Jesus."

Maud Booth and Mother Teresa were profoundly different. Yet, as sisters in Christ, they continue to bear testimony to the ministry of all believers whose hearts belong entirely to Jesus. How will you share the heart of Jesus today?

Faith Bytes

August 27
Monica and Her Son

Monica was a Christian. Although her husband wasn't, this did not prevent her from praying for him and her children. She worried about her son, whose lifestyle was anything but Godly. Turning to a pastor, she tearfully asked him to speak to her son. Finally, he told her, "Go your way; live as you are living. It cannot be that the son of these tears should perish." She accepted his answer as being from heaven. Eight days before Monica's death, her son came to faith. She died a happy woman as her husband and son became Christians. When her son remembered his life, he credited it to his mother's prayers.

The church celebrates the Feast Day of St. Monica on August 27 and her son, St. Augustine, on August 28. No one has shaped the church's teaching outside the Bible more than St. Augustine. For example, these are a few of his statements explaining love.

> "What does love look like? It has the hands to help others [and] feet to hasten to the poor and needy. It has eyes to see misery and want [and] ears to hear the sighs and sorrows of men. That is what love looks like."

> "Love is not breathlessness, it is not excitement, it is not the promulgation of promises of eternal passion. That is just being in love, which any of us can convince ourselves we are. Love itself is what is left over when being in love has burned away."

> "If you are silent, be silent out of love. If you speak, speak out of love."

St. Augustine described a Christian as "a mind through which Christ thinks, a heart through which Christ loves, a voice through which Christ speaks, and a hand through which Christ helps."

In gratitude for Monica and Augustine, ask God to help you be such a Christian as Augustine described.

Steven B. Angus

August 28
Shelia. Sheila Caldwell. What is Your Dream?

Sheila. Sheila Caldwell. At least, I believe that was her name. Reaching back over fifty years to when I entered first grade leaves room for doubt.

Today, I would be tagged as socially disadvantaged. I spent my first five years living on tenant farms and had little interaction with children my age. I have some good memories of first grade—particularly recess and being able to climb the monkey bars. However, I never understood why the teacher would strike my left hand whenever I attempted to use it to write.

I am pretty sure the little dark-skinned girl was named Sheila. Sheila Caldwell. I was often confused during "coloring" time. The teacher said, "Draw a picture of yourself," only to be spanked as she told me, "You are not a stick person." Years later, I understood her intent, but definitely not her methods. Did I mention I was socially and culturally backward? Sheila was one of my first friends. We shared the same table. I was curious because she was the first black person I ever met. Looking back, I am sure we liked each other because we both felt awkward, but for different reasons. We ate cake together on Columbus Day. For Christmas, I gave her a coloring book, and she gave me a book of Life Saver candies. I never understood why the teacher moved me to a different seat when we came back after the holidays.

It would be years before I learned who Dr. Martin Luther King, Jr. was. Nor did I realize that on this date in 1963, he delivered his "I Have a Dream" speech to an audience of 200,000 in Washington, D.C. In large part because of his sermon, my first-grade class was the first integrated class in my county, and I met Sheila. I told her, "Someday, I am going to be a preacher." What is your dream?

_____

_____

_____

_____

August 29
When God is the Last Resort

Everything seemed good for Judah and its King, Hezekiah, until the King of Assyria and his army appeared on the horizon, threatening to destroy them. God had promised to help and protect Judah, but Hezekiah turned to Egypt as an ally instead of trusting God. At the last moment, Egypt reneged, and Judah was left alone. Meanwhile, the Assyrians kept coming, gobbling up real estate. As the army drew nearer, the Assyrian king demanded a bribe to not ransack Jerusalem. Hezekiah realized the deck was stacked against him, but instead of turning to God, Hezekiah panicked and decided to pay. Desperate, he withdrew all the gold and silver from his banks and looted the Temple of its gold and silver, including stripping the plated metal off the doors of the Temple. How humiliating it must have been to watch as chests filled with "God's treasure" exited the holy

Faith Bytes

city. Like the playground bully who demands our lunch money, it is never enough. Smelling the aroma of fear and eyeing a potential golden goose, the Assyrian King advanced his army surrounding Jerusalem. Hezekiah had been double-crossed. He requests a pow-wow to discuss terms for peace. But the King of Assyria has no interest whatsoever in withdrawing. His chief of staff sends this message to Hezekiah: This is what the great king of Assyria says: "What are you trusting in that makes you so confident?" [2 Kings 18:19, NLT].

Perhaps this taunting of a pagan warlord is why God recorded it in three different books of the Bible—2 Kings, 2 Chronicles, and Isaiah. Could there be a more poignant question for Hezekiah or us than this? Words intended as trash talk form the question we must answer daily— "What am I trusting in that makes me so confident?"

Initially, Hezekiah trusted God and led his people back to Him. Hezekiah lost focus and began to trust his ability to handle Assyria's king. It was not until he had nowhere else to turn that he looked to God.

The Scottish author and clergyman George McDonald wrote: "How often we look upon our God as our last and feeblest resource. We go to Him because we have nowhere else to go, and then we learn that the storms of life have driven us not upon the rocks but into the desired haven."

_____
_____
_____
_____

August 30
Hurry Up and Wait!

It was a Sunday afternoon. We made a trip into the city and completed our task early. It was a beautiful fall afternoon, and the children quietly chatted in the back seat. We occasionally checked the score of the Tennessee Titans game on the radio. All was calm as we discussed a rare night without a church meeting and the possibility of watching something on Netflix as a family. Suddenly, as we approached our exit, the traffic came to a grinding halt. After several hours, we realized that our evening was shot. There were moments when we felt we would never reach our destination.

As we sat in that stagnant ocean of chrome and fumes, I recalled the ancient fable about the tortoise and the hare and how the tortoise faithfully kept up his pace and eventually reached his destination. I also thought of David the Shepherd, who was the source of many of the Psalms. As a youth, he was anointed by the Prophet Samuel to be the King of Israel. Yet it was years accompanied by countless heartaches before he assumed the throne. I reflected on how some aspects of my life seemed to move slower than I had hoped or expected.

Steven B. Angus

However, the proverbial tortoise did cross the finish line. David did become King, and my Clan arrived home safely Sunday night. Perhaps none of these things occurred as quickly as the traveler involved would have liked, yet it happened.

Most of us are not where we want to be spiritually, in our relationships, or in many other areas of our life. However, we must keep moving even if it appears at a snail's pace. More often than not, we encounter God in the slow moments. The advice of the Apostle Paul, another person who understood what it meant to hurry up and wait, is helpful. He wrote: "Not that I have already obtained all this, or have already arrived at my goal, but I press on to take hold of that for which Christ Jesus took hold of me." [Philippians 3:12 NIV]

___

August 31
"As I walk'd through the wilderness of this world."

When hearing the titles of such literary masterpieces as "Don Quixote," "The Gift of the Magi," "Crime and Punishment," or the names of Chaucer, Wilde, or Bonhoeffer, we unlikely associate them with—Incarceration. Aren't you relieved that a jail sentence isn't a prerequisite to being a Christian? Yet some of God's most reliable servants had a prison record.

The first person mentioned in the Bible who spent time behind bars was Joseph, and the last was Paul. Nestled between them were such convicts as John the Baptist, Jeremiah, Silas, and [lest we forget] Jesus.

One of the most significant pieces of Christian fiction, "Pilgrim's Progress," was written by John Bunyan while in prison. Within 20 years of its publication in 1678, over 100,000 copies were in circulation. Some report it is presently second only to the Bible in copies sold.

Prison may have contributed to the book's opening sentence, which begins, "As I walk'd through the wilderness of this world." It is the story of Christian, who flees the City of Destruction and journeys to the Celestial City. On his expedition, he encounters characters such as Worldly Wiseman, Ignorance, the Giant Despair, and others whose names identify their personality traits. He travels the Slough of Despond, the city of Vanity, and the Valley of the Shadow of Death, finally crossing the River of Death and entering heaven. Not everyone he meets wants to harm him but offers encouragement so he does not abandon his journey.

John Bunyan's faith would land him in and out of prison. Like his character, Christian, Bunyan never gave up on his quest for heaven or his work as a pastor. On this day in 1688, he died from a cold he caught while riding through the rain to reconcile a father and son. His faithfulness encourages us that although the journey may be difficult, God provides what we need.

Faith Bytes

SEPTEMBER

September 1
His voice caused women to weep and men to tremble

Today is the birthday of a man who helped to bring Jesus to the American frontier. If we could construct our spiritual pedigree, his name would likely appear. In 1785, Peter Cartwright was born. As a boy, his family moved to Logan County, Kentucky, known to harbor the roughest of society. Soon, Cartwright became a leader. At sixteen, he attended a camp meeting and pleaded with God for hours seeking forgiveness. Within two years, he was a licensed Methodist preacher.

Cartwright's toughness would serve him well. An example occurred when he warned General Andrew Jackson that he would go to Hell as quickly as any other man if he did not repent. When someone apologized to the General for Cartwright's bluntness, the future president responded that Christ's ministers ought to love everybody and fear no mortal man, adding he wished he had a few thousand officers like Peter Cartwright.

While traveling throughout Kentucky, Tennessee, and Illinois, crowds flocked to hear his three-hour sermons. His booming voice caused women to weep and strong men to tremble as tens of thousands came to Christ.

The life of a circuit rider was tough, with a life expectancy of 29. Few married; however, Cartwright did. Concerned his daughters might grow up to marry a Slaveowner, he asked the Bishop to move him to Illinois. With only his horse for a companion, his circuit consisted of three-quarters of the state. Eventually, Cartwright ran for the Illinois legislature. He defeated a fellow named Abraham Lincoln. The two-faced each other again in an election for Congress. The outcome was different, with a win-win for all Americans. A nation received a great president. The church gained a tremendous voice for Jesus. God has a way of raising up those most needed.

Steven B. Angus

September 2
Now what?

So, you are a Christian. Now what? Perhaps you became a follower of Jesus years ago and are still pondering this question. If so, meet Thomas. Thomas attended Oxford, studied theology, and earned his doctorate in Civil Law. Soon after his ordination in the Church of England, he was expelled from his parish because of his "Methodistical" leanings. His parishioners celebrated by ringing the church bells and opening a keg of cider. Soon after, Thomas met John Wesley and became one of his most trusted assistants. When Wesley recognized the urgency for Methodist pastors in the United States, he asked the Anglican Bishop of London to ordain priests who could serve as pastors in the newly formed country. The Bishop refused. Wesley, now eighty, realized he could not make a trans-Atlantic trip. Recognizing the need, he felt his only option was to personally ordain two preachers, appoint Thomas as the American Methodists' superintendent, and deploy them to their mission field on the other side of the Atlantic.

Artist Kenneth Wyatt has painted a marvelous rendering of the September 2, 1784 event. The painting portrays the two newly appointed pastors and general superintendent on a ship about to sail for the recently formed United States. John Wesley stands on the pier, speaking to Thomas, who is onboard. The five-foot-six-inch Wesley must have loomed a giant to the five-foot-one-inch Thomas. The print captures the moment Thomas asks Wesley, "What do I tell them?" It was his "what now" question. Wesley responded, "Offer them Christ, Thomas." The man Wesley nicknamed "the flea" because he always seemed to be hopping around on his missions did just that. Thomas Coke and Francis Asbury would become the first Bishops of the American Methodist. If you wonder what to do next, consider these three words, "Offer them Christ."

_____

_____

_____

_____

September 3
What Day Is It?

As a child, I thought daylight savings occurred by magic. When I discovered my dad changed the clock, it lost its glamor.

The time change can offer intrigue to Sunday worship. I recall a lovely older couple entering the Sunday morning service as we were singing the closing hymn. As they slowly walked the middle aisle towards their typical second pew seat, we all heard him say, as they both were hard of hearing, "They are singing the opening hymn. I told you we are not late." As they squeezed by the couple standing in the pew, he asked, "What page are we singing." "Just give me a minute," she said as the congregation recognized her confusion. When the

Faith Bytes

benediction was pronounced, and they realized what had occurred, he said, "I told you we were going to be late."

If one hour causes a disruption in our lives, imagine the reaction of the citizens of Great Britain and her American colonies having gone to bed on September 2, 1752, to awake and learn that instead of September 3, it was September 14. Folklore reported streets flooded by angry subjects demanding the king return the ten days of their lives he had stolen.

Two hundred years earlier, most nations had switched to the Gregorian Calendar. However, England refused, not wanting to acknowledge the Catholic Church. A world with two calendars did result in some unique situations. For example, William Shakespeare and Miguel de Cervantes died on the same date, April 23, 1616. However, the Spanish writer actually died ten days before the English one. Confusing, I know.

What isn't confusing is today is September 3. It is the day that the Lord has made. Let us rejoice and be glad in it.

_____

_____

_____

_____

September 4
Trailblazers of Faith

Perhaps you have noticed my passion for history. The Letter to the Hebrews states that we are surrounded by a Great Cloud of witnesses. We can think of these as spiritual Daniel Boones, who have blazed a trail that can lead us to God's best on earth as it is in heaven.

On this day in 1633, a ship sailed into Boston Harbor with three stowaways aboard. This was not uncommon. However, this trio was not your typical fare. It wasn't a daily occurrence that prominent Puritan ministers found their way to the American frontier, even those facing arrest for refusing to accept the authority of the Church of England. The three were John Cotton, Thomas Hooker, and Samuel Stone. Bostonians were hopeful they could help forge a New England on the American continent, boasting [if Puritans could do such a thing] that they now had "Cotton for their clothing, Hooker for their fishing, and Stone for their building."

Thomas Hooker became the most influential, typically referred to as "the Father of Connecticut." He became the pastor of the First Parish Church of what today is Cambridge. His parish became known as "Mr. Hooker's Company." Considered an accomplished pulpiteer, he had been expelled from the pulpit in England for refusing to perform many of the Liturgical forms associated with the Church of England, such as kneeling to the bread and wine of Holy Communion. Despite his nonconformity, forty-seven Church of England priests signed a petition asking he be allowed to continue preaching. The authorities ignored their request.

Steven B. Angus

Thomas Hooker died from an "epidemical sickness" in 1647 at age 61. As he approached death, someone remarked to him, "Sir, you are going to receive the reward of all your labors," to which Hooker retorted, "Brother, I am going to receive mercy!" The wisdom of this trailblazer of faith for us can be found in his words:

"Prayer is my chief work, and it is by means of it that I carry on the rest."

_____

_____

_____

_____

September 5
I'm Tired!

It looks like I will be working on Labor Day weekend. It happens every year. Suppose you happen to find yourself in the same dilemma. In that case, you will appreciate the wisdom of the fellow who stated: I never understood why it is called Labor Day when so many people have the day off except for me. Lately, it seems everyone is interested in how I'm doing. When they ask, I smile and say, "Fine." Truth is—I'm tired. There, I said it. Yes, I'm tired. For years, I've been blaming it on my age, an iron deficiency, lack of vitamins, air and water pollution, saccharin, obesity, dieting, underarm odor, and a dozen other maladies that make you wonder if life is worth living.

But now, I find out it isn't that. I'm tired because I'm overworked. The population of this country is over 200 million. Eighty-four million are retired, leaving 116 million to do the work. There are 75 million in school, which means 41 million to do the work. Of this total, 22 million are employed by the [federal] government. That leaves 19 million to do the job. Four million are in the armed forces, which leaves 15 million to do the work. Take from that total the 14,800,000 people working for the state and city governments, which means 200,000 remain to do the tasks. Considering there are 188,000 in hospitals, there are 12,000 to do the work. Now, don't forget there are 11,998 people in prisons. That leaves just you and me to do the work. And you're sitting there reading this. No wonder I'm tired!

It's a good thing you and I trust in the Lord. We can lean into his promise in Isaiah 40:31:

"Those who wait on the Lord shall renew their strength; they shall mount up with wings like eagles; they shall run and not be weary; they shall walk and not faint."

Faith Bytes

September 6
It's Football Time!

All across the United States, College football fans are wearing their school's sports apparel and daring to dream that this will be the year they will win it all! I am excited because I just learned that my wife, Cheri, has purchased tickets for Saturday's game involving my Alma Mater, the Vanderbilt University Commodores!

Even if you are a casual football fan, you recognize the name Tom Landry. It is a name that is synonymous with professional football. He coached the Dallas Cowboys for years, leading them to countless victories. He was asked what he attributed to his success as a coach. Responding to a crowd of more than two thousand students at Baylor University, he stated, "In 1958, I did something everyone successful must do. I determined the priorities for my life—God, family, and then football."

The Coach's advice is worthy of our consideration as it pertains to sports and anything we are "fan" atical about. Does this mean we must observe an athletic fast and stop checking the box scores of our favorite team or player? No, but it is a call to monitor our priorities. As we get pepped up for the big game, it may be an opportunity to call a time out and review what matters in our lives. What does the box score of your priorities reveal?

_____

_____

_____

_____

September 7
Welcome To the Garden

On this day in 1911, my Grandmother Rennie McGee Angus was born. About this time of year, the unmistakable feel of fall was in the early morning air. The last garden vegetables had been "put up" in recycled mason jars and stored in the root cellar to be enjoyed during winter's cold and barren days. In addition to raising eleven children, no one had a thumb greener than my grandmother.

My first memories of visiting my grandparents included traveling down a dusty driveway at the top of Apple Hill in north Giles County, Tennessee. At the end of the road, we would be greeted by Granny's flower garden just before arriving at their home. As a child, I wasn't sure how big an acre was, but her colorful floral paradise must have numbered in the hundreds. Of course, it was far more modest. I thought it was a magical garden because of the thousands of butterflies it attracted. The only occasion I remember my Grandmother raising her voice at me was forbidding me from capturing her butterflies in one of those recycled Mason jars. I later understood the secret to her many blooms was the butterflies and my Grandfather's honeybees.

Steven B. Angus

I have long since associated my Grandmother's flowers with Galatians 5:22-23. This passage describes an equally magnificent garden with nine identifiable fruits. They are love, joy, peace, patience, kindness, generosity, faithfulness, gentleness, and self-control. Indeed, you agree, this garden must be grand. The only place such a garden can exist is in the life of a person who loves Jesus. This is you and me.

Now that fall is in the air, join me as we sample this luscious fruit.

_____

_____

_____

_____

September 8
Recognizing the Fruit

How do others see you as a Christian? John Wesley, ever methodical, believed that Christians should hold each other accountable, and he offered three questions to guide the process. They were: "Have they faith? Have they gifts? Have they fruit?" The intent was for these questions to be personal. Perhaps you would like to reflect upon them. Do I have faith? Do I have gifts? Do I have fruit?

Perhaps you recognized the natural progression. First, there must be faith in Jesus. Where there is such faith, God bestows gifts. Although an oversimplification, one could venture the formula, faith + gifts = fruit. This trinity of faith, gifts, and fruit comes from God. In the days ahead, let us explore the question: Do I have fruit?

Jesus said, "Therefore by their fruits you will know them." [Matthew 7:20] He also said,

> "For a good tree does not bear bad fruit, nor does a bad tree bear good fruit. For every tree is known by its own fruit. For men do not gather figs from thorns, nor do they gather grapes from a bramble bush. A good man out of the good treasure of his heart brings forth good; and an evil man out of the evil treasure of his heart brings forth evil. For out of the abundance of the heart his mouth speaks." [Luke 6:43-45]

As an industrial society, we may incorrectly assume that what our work produces is another way of understanding fruit. A technician operating a machine manufactures a product. This illustration doesn't work because what the device assembles isn't fruit. Although intense labor is expended for a tree to have the best environment to yield fruit, what occurs is natural. The fruit Jesus describes grows out of the natural process of following Him. Perhaps the Genesis creation story can help.

> God said, "Let the earth bring forth grass, the herb that yields seed, and the fruit tree that yields fruit according to its kind, whose seed is in itself, on the earth; and it was so." [Genesis 1:11]

Faith Bytes

Only a Christ follower can produce Christ-like fruit. What fruit are you bearing in your life?

_____
_____
_____

September 9
Who Wants to Be a Banana?

In those alone moments when you are driving to and from work, walking or running through the neighborhood, or perhaps during your quiet time with Jesus, I hope you have asked yourself, "Am I bearing fruit?" Not the fruit manufactured by our effort, such as writing a card or visiting someone. These actions are often expressions of the fruit in your life, but they aren't the fruit itself. This begs the question, are there specific fruit we must look for in our lives?

In Galatians 5 is a list of the fruit that becomes evident as we draw closer to Jesus. This fruit is love, joy, peace, patience, kindness, generosity, faithfulness, gentleness, and self-control. You counted correctly. There are nine.

Perhaps this may help us remember them. Grapes and bananas grow in clusters. We can think of the fruit of the Spirit as growing in three groups of three.

The first cluster of three is primarily inward aspects of a life devoted to Jesus. During the next 24 hours, I want you to look inside yourself. Is what you find characterized by love, joy, and peace? Hmmm... Do I sense some extra Jesus time in your future?

Let me leave you with the lyrics of a song I hope you will sing throughout the day.

The Fruit of the Spirit's not a banana
The Fruit of the Spirit's not a banana

You want to be a banana
You might as well hear it:
You can't be a fruit of the Spirit
Cause the fruit is

Love, joy, peace, patience,
Kindness, goodness, faithfulness
Gentleness and self-control

Love, joy, peace, patience,
Kindness, goodness, faithfulness
Gentleness and self-control

_____
_____

Steven B. Angus

September 10
The Greatest of These is Love

"The Fruit of the Spirit's not a banana...." I hope this Bible School song has helped to etch the Fruit of the Spirit in your memory more permanently than the masterpiece your toddler scribbled on the dining room wall with the Sharpie you thought out of reach.

The first cluster of fruit is love, joy, and peace. This grouping is similar because they are not dependent on external forces. Life may bear the opposite of love, joy, and peace upon our bodies, minds, and emotions, but this holy cluster is unaffected. They flow out of us from a source of living water.

Pollsters consistently report when asked, "What are you looking for most in life?" the results, while including materialistic goals, find the top three things people want in life are love, joy, and peace, which happens to be the first three fruits of the Spirit! God knows what we truly need.

You are unlikely surprised that love is at the top of the list. The Apostle Paul, who identified the fruit of the Spirit in Galatians 5, also wrote: "And now abide faith, hope, love, these three; but the greatest of these *is* love." [1 Corinthians 13:13] God is love. God's love is unconditional. God loves everyone, even those who do not return His love. When Jesus said, "Love your enemies," [Matthew 5:44] he used the Greek word, Agape, which encompasses this God-like love.

Although the list of fruits is not a ranking of importance, we cannot ignore the fact that love is mentioned first. Some have suggested that there is only one fruit of the Spirit: love. If so, the eight words that follow it are ways love manifests in our attitudes and actions. Although the text does not suggest this, it requires our consideration today. In other words:

> JOY IS LOVE'S STRENGTH.
> PEACE IS LOVE'S SECURITY.
> PATIENCE IS LOVE'S ENDURANCE.
> KINDNESS IS LOVE'S CONDUCT.
> GOODNESS IS LOVE'S CHARACTER.
> FAITHFULNESS IS LOVE'S CONFIDENCE.
> GENTLENESS IS LOVE'S HUMILITY.
> SELF-CONTROL IS LOVE'S VICTORY.

How will the fruit of love be observed in your life today?

_____

_____

_____

_____

Faith Bytes

September 11
Where?

If you recognize the lyrics, feel free to sing along. "I've got the joy, joy, joy, joy. (Where?)" Along with love and peace, joy forms the first cluster of the fruit of the Spirit. These three flow from within a Christian and out into the world. They are not dependent on external circumstances.

What would you include if you wrote a list of adjectives to describe joy? Is there someone you visualize as definitely having joy? When we see a life that is indeed joyful, it abides in our memory.

After spending a few minutes with Billie, you would have forgotten the initial spasm you felt in your stomach when you saw her gnarled body cradled in her bed. Although her osteoarthritis was painful, the more significant concern was the realization that any sudden movement could snap another unrepairable bone.

I loved Billie. We discussed faith but also such things as her passion for parakeets and cockatiels. In fact, she eventually gifted her cockatiel to me. She introduced me to Bob Ross and convinced me to start painting. Occasionally, she would surprise me by sharing a canvas she had painted after convincing someone to force a brush between her thumb and curled index finger. However, these circumstances could not conceal the joy that gushed out of her. Her joyful smile was like a candle calling out to a moth, yet knowing you were safe in its warmth.

The Bible distinguishes between joy and happiness, mentioning happiness 67 times but joy over 450 times. Billie taught me the difference. Circumstances must be near perfect, and we may be able to grasp the golden ring society calls happiness. But joy comes from that place inside an individual who believes God is in control, working all things "together for the good of those who love him."

"I've got the joy, joy, joy, joy, (Where?)"

_____

_____

_____

_____

September 12
There is a Place of Quiet Rest

Galatians 5:22-23 identifies nine fruits of the Spirit. We can think of them as three clusters of three. The first cluster, love, joy, and peace, flow from within a Christian and isn't dependent on external circumstances.

Jesus said, "Peace I leave with you, My peace I give to you; not as the world gives do I give to you. Let not your heart be troubled, neither let it be afraid." [John 14:27] Jesus quickly clarifies that his peace differs from what is commonly associated with it, such as the absence of war or discomfort.

Steven B. Angus

A Rabbi told a story of a fellow who, when he got up in the morning, found it so difficult to find his clothes that he hesitated going to bed at night for fear of the trouble he would have on waking. One evening, as he undressed, he made a note to remind himself where he had placed everything. The following day, all went well as he took the slip of paper and read: "cap" -- there it was, and he set it on his head. "Pants," and so it went until he was fully dressed. Then, puzzled, he asked, "Where in the world am I?" He looked and looked but could not find himself. "And that," said the rabbi, "is how it is with us."

The peace Jesus offers flows from within a person and can be thought of as knowing we are never lost or misplaced. If today, you feel restless, even fearful, perhaps these lyrics of a familiar hymn can soothe your soul.

> "There is a place of quiet rest, Near to the heart of God
> O Jesus, blest Redeemer, Sent from the heart of God
> Hold us who wait before thee, Near to The Heart Of God."

Peace is the fruit associated with knowing where we are.

September 13
"Billy, Just Calm Down!"

The second cluster among the fruit of the Spirit is patience, kindness, and goodness. Together, they describe how the Holy Spirit can influence our relationships with others. We often associate patience with the ability to wait for something in the future. This is only partially true. In this context, woven into the fabric of patience is another word: tolerance. The King James Bible uses the term "longsuffering." Realizing God has been patient with us, we, therefore, are willing to suffer long with the shortcomings of others.

A fellow stopped by the market and noticed a father trying to shop with an uncooperative three-year-old in the cart. The first time they passed, the child repeatedly asked for a candy bar. The dad said, "Now, Billy, this won't take long." Passing in the next aisle, the child's plea had increased several octaves, but the father quietly said, "Billy, just calm down. We will be done in a minute." As they passed the dairy case, the kid was screaming uncontrollably. Dad remained unruffled, and in a soothing voice, he said, "Billy, settle down. We are almost out of here." When they reached the checkout counter, the boy had pulled out all the stops, screaming and kicking. The stalwart dad still gave no evidence of losing control as he calmly repeated, "Billy, we will be in the car in just a minute, and then everything will be OK." The bystander was impressed, and as they exited, he said to the long-suffering dad, "Sir, I couldn't help but watch how you handled little Billy. You were amazing." The dad replied, "You don't understand. I'm Billy!"

Faith Bytes

Indeed, we have tested God's tolerance. Now, we must be patient with one another. Today, may the fruit of patience be evident in you.

September 14
The Light Everyone Can See

"If you see your brother standing by the road
With a heavy load from the seeds he's sowed
And if you see your sister falling by the way
Just stop and stay you're going the wrong way

You got to try a little kindness
Yes show a little kindness
Just shine your light for everyone to see
And if you try a little kindness
Then you'll overlook the blindness
Of narrow-minded people on the narrow-minded streets."

The song is only two minutes and thirty-three seconds, but in 1969, propelled by the voice of Glen Campbell, it was a hit on three music charts. Its simple message resonated with those tired of meanness. Wouldn't it be wonderful if someone could offer a lyrical message today that would inspire our world to be nice to each other? Kindness is one of the fruits of the spirit that can influence our relationships with others.

I have been told sixty percent of the adult human body is water. I wonder if coffee counts. This reminds me of the morning as I was seated in my car waiting to receive the cup of coffee I hoped would give me the boost to tackle the day. As I waited for the slow line to move, I realized I was growing anxious to get on with my day. Finally, when it was my turn, the server handed me my order as I extended my two dollars. Instead of taking my money, she smiled and said, "The driver in front of you paid for your coffee and said to pass it forward." This simple act of kindness had an enormous impact on me. Author Charles Swindoll wrote, "Kindness is a language that deaf people can hear, and that blind people can see." I would add it is also how we can demonstrate to others the nature of our God. "Yes, show a little kindness. Just shine your light for everyone to see."

Steven B. Angus

September 15
More Precious

Goodness. Simply stated, a person whose life is controlled by the Spirit will be a good person. No higher compliment can be said of a Christian than, "She is a good person." Yes, goodness. However, it is more than doing the right thing. The person is actually good.

In one of his sermons, Peter summarized the life of Jesus, stating: "Jesus went about doing good." [Acts 10:38] Like the fruit on a vine, goodness doesn't occur because one continually thinks, "I must be righteous in this situation." Typically, our disposition aligns with the goodness modeled by Jesus. Goodness is love in action, so consistently, it defines the person.

It has been said that a righteous person could follow the standard and evict a widow for failure to pay her rent, but goodness would pay the bill for her. In the Epistle of Third John, we are compelled to avoid evil and actively "Model the good. (Why?) The person who does good does God's work." [The Message].

When Hurricane Katrina devastated the Gulf Coast, my community began collecting supplies. Schoolchildren were encouraged to collect and bring items to school that people needed. One young boy was delighted to bring in a tube of toothpaste. There was one slight glitch. It was a half-used tube. The administration was hesitant to accept it but quickly realized that, for this child, it was probably his only tube of toothpaste. The boy wanted to do something good, and his teachers, in turn, did so as well.

Writer and philosopher Will Durant stated, "A good [person] who is not great is a hundred times more precious than a great [one] who is not good."

_____
_____
_____
_____

September 16
"Good Morning, Beautiful People."

Patience, kindness, and goodness are fruits of the spirit demonstrated toward others. They are attitudes others see in us that hopefully will cause them to want to have a relationship with Jesus.

Alice Gray tells how a beauty product company invited people to send pictures and brief letters about the woman they considered the most beautiful. Within a few weeks, thousands of letters were submitted. One letter stood out and was passed on to the company president. It was written by a young boy from a broken home in a run-down neighborhood. With spelling corrections, an excerpt from his letter read: "A beautiful woman lives down the street from me. I visit her every day. She makes me feel like the most important kid in the world. We play checkers, and she listens to my problems. She understands me, and when I leave, she yells out the door that she's proud of me." He ended his letter by saying, "This picture shows you that she is the most beautiful woman. I hope I have a wife as pretty as her."

Intrigued, the president asked to see this woman's photograph. Looking back at him was a smiling, toothless woman, well-advanced in years, sitting in a wheelchair. Sparse gray hair was pulled back in a bun, and wrinkles formed deep furrows on her face, which were somehow diminished by the twinkle in her eyes. "We can't use this woman," he explained, smiling. "She would show the world that our products aren't necessary to be beautiful." [More Stories to Warm Your Heart (Sisters, OR: Multnomah Publishers, 1997)]

The true beauty of a Christian life is found in a heart overflowing with the Holy Spirit. This heart can only be cultivated by spending time with Jesus.

Years ago, I had a colleague who never failed to greet an audience with a smile as he said, "Good morning, beautiful people." May you be such a person today.

___

September 17
Number One on That List is . . .?

The Bible mentions nine fruits of the Spirit, which can be thought of as three clusters of three. Have you noticed the priority system embraced by the three clusters? The first cluster is love, joy, and peace. These flow from within a person because of their relationship with God. The second cluster consists of patience, kindness, and goodness. These fruits are evident in our connection with others. The third bunch emphasizes self-discipline reflected in the fruits of faithfulness, gentleness, and self-control.

The path of a Christian has long taught the JOY principle. Jesus is first. Others are second. And finally, ourselves [You] are third. God expects to be first in our lives. Contentment occurs when we maintain these priorities.

Author Bruce Larson tells of Clay Shiver's experience when he played center for the Florida State Seminoles football team. Standing 6-foot-2-inches and weighing 280 pounds, Clay was acknowledged as one of the nation's best. One magazine wanted to name him to their preseason All-American football team. This presented a problem for the future NFL standout. The magazine was Playboy, and Clay is a Christian. Shiver knew this would promote his career. Such publicity never hurts an athlete who aspires to go to the next level. However, when he was informed that Playboy had made their selection, Clay Shiver declined. He stated he did not want to embarrass his mother and grandmother by appearing in the magazine or giving old high school friends an excuse to buy that issue. He added, "I don't want to let anyone down. Number one on that list is God."

Are we bearing fruit in our lives? If the fruit seems to be suffering from drought, perhaps our priorities are out of sync.

September 18
A Lifetime, One Day at a Time

Included in the list of fruits of the Spirit is faithfulness. Other words that express its appearance in a person are trustworthy or loyalty. The Greek word is *"Pistis"* [pronounced peace-tis] and often refers to fidelity in marriage. As Christians, when we bear the fruit of faithfulness, we are trustworthy in our relationship with Jesus and reliable in our commitment and lifestyle with those around us. At the end of the day, there is no doubt about our fidelity.

The late Fred Craddock was a renowned professor of preaching. Speaking about the practical implications of consistent faithfulness, he said, "To give my life for Christ appears glorious. To pour myself out for others. . . to pay the ultimate price of martyrdom -- I'll do it. I'm ready, Lord, to go out in a blaze of glory."

Craddock stated many Christians understand that giving their life to the Lord is similar to placing a $1000 bill before God and saying, "I'm giving it all. Instead, Jesus sends us to the bank to exchange it for $l,000 in quarters. We go through life putting out twenty-five cents here and fifty cents there. Listen to the neighbor kid's troubles instead of saying, 'Get lost.' Go to a committee meeting. Give a cup of water to a shaky old man in a nursing home. Usually, giving our life to Christ isn't glorious. It's done in all those little acts of love, twenty-five cents at a time. It would be easy to go out in a flash of glory; it's harder to live the Christian life little by little over the long haul."

This is faithfulness. It is fidelity. Living the Christian life encompasses a lifetime of one day at a time, starting today.

Faith Bytes

September 19
Gentled for God's Purposes

The first years of my life were spent on a Walking Horse ranch. My parents have photos of me sitting on several World Champions. It goes without saying I have a fondness for horses. One of my favorite movies is "The Man from Snowy River." Central to the plot is a beautiful free-roaming stallion. When galloping down the rocky terrain of a mountain, his powerful muscles bulge. Rearing up and standing on his back hooves is to observe grace in motion. However, despite his natural abilities, the creature is out of control, a menace, leaving destruction in its path and leading other horses astray. It isn't until the hero captures the stallion and tames his power that the creature achieves its potential. The strength was always present but needed to be guided by an understanding and firm hand.

The Greek adjective translated as gentleness or meek among the fruit of the spirit is *"PRAUS"* [pronounced, prowl oos]. It was an equestrian term to describe an animal that has been tamed.

Christians often encounter those who believe we must be passivist in all matters. For them, meek is just another word for weak. This is a belief most of us need to reject. The strength of the Lord is upon us, but it has been gentled for God's purposes.

The Scottish theologian William Barclay said that the beatitude rendered "Blessed are the meek, for they shall inherit the earth" should be reworded. He suggests a more precise statement:

"Blessed is the one who is always angry at the right time and never angry at the wrong time."

Perhaps as we consider the fruit of gentleness in our lives, we must ask, "What makes me angry?" Is it the perceived mistreatment of ourselves or the violation of the dignity of others? Anger is a useless emotion unless it leads to a positive response.

_____
_____
_____
_____

September 20
Our Personal Trainer

Standing almost 6 feet 4 inches, President Lyndon Johnson was known as the big man from Texas. Incredibly proud of his body, he tried to maintain a body weight of 183 pounds and often used it to intimidate his opposition. During his term as President, he put on some extra weight. One day, his wife, nicknamed Lady Bird, challenged him with this blunt assertion: "You can't run the country if you can't run yourself." Respecting her wise observation, the President lost 23 pounds.

In his book, "Momentum for Life, "Michael Slaughter wrote: "If you can't lead yourself, you won't be effective in leading others. Self-leadership precedes strategic leadership." When Suzanna Wesley's son John was a student at Oxford, she sent him a letter stating: "Anything which increases the authority of the body over the mind is an evil thing." Sounds like the mom of a college freshman, doesn't it?

This is at the heart of the fruit of the spirit of self-control. If we cannot lead ourselves, we cannot effectively lead others. Just as the word implies, when it comes to our body, mind, and spirit, there may be external motivators, but only we can control ourselves.

The term self-control seems to suggest we have a choice in the matter. Doesn't the author, the Apostle Paul, understand that our lives are dictated by someone else? Actually, he does. Perhaps he mentioned this fruit last because those that proceed it build to a crescendo, where self-control is the natural response to allowing Jesus to live in us through the Holy Spirit. The Holy Spirit transforms us in such a way that we have the mind of Christ. We aren't even conscious of it as we grow in Christ and exhibit self-control. We are merely living as Jesus would. Do you recall how fruit occurs naturally?

Most good athletes work hard to discipline their bodies. However, the great ones typically have fantastic personal trainers. Ours is the Holy Spirit. What do you need your personal trainer to help you with today?

_____

_____

_____

_____

September 21
Is It Corn or Johnson Grass?

By now, you can identify the nine fruits of the Spirit. I hope you have recognized them in your life. I want you to know that as a follower of Jesus, to desire them is a good thing. However, the fruits mentioned in Galatians 5:22-23 are not displayed in a basket at a farmer's roadside market, allowing us to squeeze them like a Mellon, choose the ones we want and place them in a paper bag and take them home where we enjoy them at our leisure. Instead, they must grow in us.

Is it possible for our heart to be a greenhouse that encourages this fruit to grow? Jesus addresses this very topic in John 15:1-11. If we wish to grow, bloom, and bear fruit, this is where we must begin. Jesus' opening statement is the gardening tool necessary to break ground. Unless the soil contains the nutrients required for the yield we seek, we will be disappointed. The fruit of the Spirit begins with Jesus' declaration, "I am the true vine, and my Father is the vinegrower." [15:1] This fruit can only come from Jesus, who identifies himself as the true vine. If he is the genuine vine, this means some vines are not.

I worked as a field hand in high school at a University Agricultural Experiment Farm. As the title suggests, we did experiments to determine which practices provided the highest yield. One day, I was working with a horticulturist on a plot of corn. I was operating an expensive piece of farming machinery called a hoe. I was unmercifully whacking away at the weeds when my supervisor said, "Hey, Little Bull." This was my nickname by way of my last name, Angus. Pointing at what I had just decapitated with my hoe, he asked, "What is that?" I identified it as a stalk of corn. He said, "Little Bull if you are going to work with me, you must learn the difference between Johnson Grass [a weed] and corn." In fairness, they look alike, but the yield is different.

Are you hoping to experience joy by harvesting Johnson Grass? Jesus said, "I am the true vine." He is the source of lasting and fulfilling fruit of the Spirit.

_____
_____
_____
_____

September 22
Stay Connected

The fruit of the Spirit is love, joy, peace, patience, kindness, goodness, faithfulness, humility, and self-control. In John 15:1-11, Jesus teaches us how to be a greenhouse that encourages this fruit to grow.

I doubt there is ever a need in your home or workplace for someone to repeat themselves. However, if your supervisor repeated a phrase, say ten times in seven sentences, would you assume it was important? This is precisely what Jesus does in John 15:4-10. He used the Greek word *"mino"* [pronounced me-nose]. It means to stay in a given place or in proximity to someone. Have you ever told your kindergartener, "Stay here beside me and don't move?" That is the idea Jesus is conveying. Most Bible translations rendered *"mino"* as "abide" or "remain." Jesus is instructing us to stay beside him and not move. He elevated it to the urgency of a category five emergency by repeating it ten times. It is suddenly tittering on the edge of life or death. Why did Jesus consider remaining in the relationship so vital? Listen to what he said.

- *Remain with me "because (by doing so), you will bear much fruit." [v.5]*
- *Abide with me "because apart from me, you can do nothing!" [v. 5]*
- *Furthermore, "If you remain with me,...ask for whatever you wish, and it will be done for you." [v.7]*

Remaining with Jesus isn't merely something to be considered. It is essential. If Jesus were addressing us today, he possibly would borrow an image from the world of technology. He would call us by name, "Steven. Stay connected to me. You are the electronic device. I am the network. Do not go offline."

Are you bearing fruit? Can you hear Him now? If not, then check your connection.

September 23
Bloom and Grow

When I moved into my new home, I was thrilled it came with several rose bushes. When I gave them a closer look, I recognized the neglect. Realizing I couldn't do more harm, I happily retrieved my pruner. Identifying a dead branch—*clip*. Seeing the withered residue of a bloom—*snip*. Like a barber high on coffee, I trimmed away. Someone with an untrained eye would have thought I had scalped the bushes. Satisfied, I collected the trimmings and discarded them into the burn pile.

A few weeks later, I noticed the green of new growth. Prominent on the tip of several branches were the unmistakable burgundy of a rose bulb preparing to greet the world. Then, I noticed colorful petals protruding from a tightly wound bud. Breaking it off, I peeled away the sepals. Then, I offered it as a gift to a friend. In a matter of days, the bushes were ablaze with red flowers. I soon removed fading blooms and nonessential growth that would divert nutrients from the next flower.

In John 15, Jesus refers to this necessary process as pruning. Suppose we long for the fruit of the Spirit to bloom in our lives. In that case, we must allow the vinegrower, God, to prune us by clipping the old growth, trimming the branches, and cutting off the unnecessary "suckers." We need this pruning even if we are bearing fruit. Jesus said, "Every branch that bears fruit he prunes to make it bear more fruit." [15:2] The good news is we do not prune ourselves. Jesus says this is the task of the vinegrower, who is God.

Go ahead. Be bold. Trust the vinegrower. Ask God to prune you so the fruit of the Spirit can grow and bloom in you.

Faith Bytes

September 24
Encouragement From Prison

If you were confined to a prison cell, how would you use your time? If we depended on Hollywood to tell us what most inmates do, every parolee would re-enter society with the physique of Dwayne *The Rock* Johnson from spending every waking moment pumping weights. This isn't a topic most of us would want to consider. Time in prison is the last thing we want to imagine. However, the Apostle Paul spent many nights in jail. Refusing to focus on his difficulties, he used those hours of isolation to write many of his letters to various congregations and colleagues in ministry. One of those letters was addressed to a group of Christians facing persecution. They were a minority group living in a culture that did not like anything they stood for. The Church was located in a region called Galatia, and the document is identified as the Epistle to the Galatians.

Try to imagine Paul sitting in a cold, dingy dungeon. All things being equal, we would assume he was the one who needed reassurance. With a pastor's heart, Paul wants to say something to sustain their faith for the long haul. Setting his pen aside, he gazes at his bleak surroundings as he ponders how to express to these young believers his own love and loyalty to Jesus. Then it hits him! It had been staring him in the face all along. It was on the walls and the table and chair. It was even embroidered on the guards' uniforms. Each had something in common. They bore the mark of Caesar. No one could question or deny ownership of these items.

As we journey through the Letter to the Galatians to discover the Marks of a Christian, ask yourself: Can others recognize who you belong to? What are the things about your life that others see that identify you as loving and belonging to Jesus?

_____
_____
_____
_____

September 25
Branded For Jesus

As Paul looked around his prison cell, almost everything he saw had the mark of the Roman Empire. Seeing these things, he realized he was also a marked man. Just as the insignias signified to the world that these things belonged to Caesar, there were marks on his body indicating Paul belonged to Jesus. Paul wanted the Galatians to know he understood the hardship they endured as recent converts to Christianity. He wrote, "From now on let no one trouble me, for I bear

Steven B. Angus

in my body the marks of the Lord Jesus." [Galatians 6:17] Various Bible translations render the word "marks" as "scars" branded upon his body.

Paul's meaning is clear. The bruises, cuts, and scabs proved he belonged to Jesus. Many of these marks were literally branded onto his body. Each scar told a story that confirmed his loyalty. He did not want anyone to doubt his love for the one who transformed his life. However, his marks went beyond what the eye could see. He bore spiritual scars that were just as vivid.

One of John Wesley's published sermons was titled "The Character of a Methodist." In the sermon, he declared that there are "distinguishing marks" of a Christian. He asserted the world decides whether we are Christians, not only by what we say we believe but by the spiritual marks guiding how we live daily. What would you include if you were to compile a list of these traits?

_____

_____

_____

_____

September 26
Conversion

I have a friend who is a Hospice Care volunteer. As I asked her questions about her work, she stated that during her training, it was emphasized that a volunteer should never impose their personal religious ideas. My friend recalled her visit with her first client. She stated that shortly after their meeting began, the patient asked, "Are you a Christian?" In light of her training, I inquired how she responded. Thoughtfully, she said, "I said, 'Yes.'" Then added, "I have found that when someone approaches death, they have a way of getting to the point. They focus on the things important to them, and usually, it concerns faith."

Is there a character, a mark that is above all other marks? There is. When we are baptized, we demonstrate the mark of conversion. Some call it "being born again," while others call it "being saved." John Wesley called it "Justifying grace." It means that we have been made right with God. Some define justified as "just as if I'd never sinned."

What these terms describe is a personal encounter with Jesus. Conversion means we have moved beyond knowing about Jesus to knowing him. We can understand the facts about Jesus and not be a Christian. Conversion comes when we know Jesus can be trusted as our Lord and Savior. The first mark of a Christian is Conversion.

_____

_____

Faith Bytes

September 27
The Mark of Loyalty

Theodore Roosevelt said, "It is better to be faithful than famous." When asked what is most important in a friendship, J K Rowling of Harry Potter fame responded, "Tolerance and loyalty." In the traditional Christian marriage ceremony, each spouse is asked: "Will you love him (or her), comfort him, honor and keep him in sickness and health, and forsake all others, be faithful to him as long as you both shall live?"

It seems we place a high priority on loyalty. We live life hoping to experience it. But what exactly does it mean to be loyal and faithful? According to "Webster's New World Dictionary," loyalty includes "allegiance, fidelity, trustworthiness, integrity, honesty, reliability, and truthfulness." If this is what it means to be loyal, it should be a mark associated with a Christian's character.

The Bible is filled with examples of men and women who exemplify the characteristics of loyalty. Among these is the Apostle Paul. He was a loyal servant from the day he met Jesus on the Damascus Road until he was beheaded in Rome. He could have avoided the suffering he encountered. The stripes that marked his body that he referred to in Galatians 6 could have been avoided. All he had to do was renounce his faith in Jesus. Instead of the humiliation and shame of prison, he could have been lauded as a great Jewish Rabbi, except for one thing. Jesus meant more to him than anything this world had to offer. Paul could honestly say, "You can do to me what you will, but I will remain true to Jesus."

The mark of a Christian is loyalty. Considering the characteristics of loyalty mentioned above, which best describes Christian loyalty? Is there a distinction?

_____

_____

_____

_____

September 28
The Mark of Humility

Humble. Before Jesus came into the world, you would call them humble if you wanted to insult someone. It was a term reserved for a slave. Jesus changed all of that. Because of the life Jesus lived, one of the highest compliments a Christian can receive is to be called humble.

What does it mean to be humble? Consider the word humility. The root word is "*humus*," from which we also get the word human. "*Humus*" literally means "of the earth." We could think of humility this way. Visualize a level plain on the

Steven B. Angus

Earth. Humility is that plain. Humility is neither above it nor below it. Humility is "of the earth;" therefore, someone with it is grounded. Humility is not putting oneself down, nor is it thinking too highly. We are neither puffed up nor grovel in the dirt. It is having a modest estimation of ourselves.

A little boy came running to his father excited. "Daddy! Guess what? I am 8 feet 4 inches tall!" The dad said, "Are you sure? I know you have had a growing spree, but I don't think you are 8 feet tall yet." The boy said, "You can measure for yourself," and handed his father a six-inch ruler.

This is often what we do. We measure ourselves with the wrong measuring stick. I once heard humility described as "Standing as tall as you can against something bigger than you are." Our standard is Jesus. We should never degrade ourselves but stand as tall as we can beside him.

In Colossians 3:12-13 Paul says Christians have a wardrobe we should try to wear daily. He names some of the garments. He says: "clothe yourselves with tenderhearted mercy, kindness, humility, gentleness, and patience."[NLT] There is the word humility. And then he says: "Make allowance for each other's faults and forgive anyone who offends you."

This is what the mark of humility in a Christian does. It makes allowances for imperfection. It is tolerant and forgiving. It's not about us. It's all about Jesus.

_____
_____
_____
_____

September 29
Courage –A Matter of the Heart

There are many synonyms we use to identify courage. We speak of bravery, valor, or simply "guts." I have always appreciated Ernest Hemingway's definition of courage. He described it as being "grace under pressure." When we try to live Christ-like lives, we will be different, requiring genuine grace under pressure. We must never take for granted those Christians worldwide who bravely live for Jesus, realizing it could cost them their lives. This is courage.

A young soldier was home on furlough before being sent to the front lines. He visited his grandfather, who suffered from a painful disease. Both were Christians, so they had a good time discussing spiritual matters. As he prepared to leave, the boy said to his grandfather, "Grandpa, pray for me that, if necessary, I'll have the courage to die." The old man looked up from his bed through eyes that revealed his pain and said, "I will, and please pray for me that I'll have the courage to live."

Faith Bytes

It takes courage to die! Sometimes, it requires more courage to live. You may understand what this means. When a Christian dies, we go to be with Christ. This can bring us great peace and hope. But to live day after day, year after year, with pain or difficult circumstances is another matter. To give thanks to God in a land of plenty when there is apathy takes courage. The authentic Christian heroes are those who are sick, their bodies wrecked with pain, yet continue to trust the Lord. That is courage for living. The true hero is the spouse who cares for that sick loved one. Days, even weeks, pass, and they never see that spark of recognition in the eye of their life partner. This is courageous living. Those believers who have prayed about something for years and have never seen their prayer answered as they had hoped, yet they keep trusting God's love. That is courage for living.

The word courage comes from the Latin word "*cor*," which means "heart." In other words, courage is a matter of the heart. We cannot have hope for lasting courage if our heart is not right with God. Courage is possible when Jesus is in charge of your heart.

_____

_____

_____

_____

September 30
Grace to Suffer Long

How much patience do you have? Most of us live in a "Hurry up; I want it yesterday world." During the Middle Ages, the Church included "Patience" as one of the great virtues. If patience is indeed a virtue, most of us would have to say we are not very virtuous.

What is patience? Instead of "patience," the translators of the King James Version of the Bible used the word "long-suffering." The Greek word literally meant "willing to suffer long." It also suggests "self-control," which is the "ability to keep one's feelings and emotions in check." Patience helps us avoid rushing into something.

The Bible introduces us to various people who demonstrated this kind of patience. One such person who bore the mark of patience was the Apostle Paul. Paul revealed a very intimate detail about himself in a letter to the Church at Corinth. He told them he suffered from what he called "a thorn in the flesh" that hindered his work for Jesus. Although he did not reveal the infirmity, some have suggested it may have been a bad temper, poor eyesight, or a speech impediment. All we know is the Apostle was frustrated by it, believing it hindered

Steven B. Angus

his ministry. He was so discouraged that he asked God to remove it on at least three occasions.

According to Paul, God responded, "No, I will not remove the thorn, but I will give you the grace you need to live with it." [2 Corinthians 7:7-10] During this struggle, Paul learned to say, "I would rather have the thorn with God's grace than not have the thorn with less grace." This is an example of patience at work in the life of a Christian. With God's grace, Paul was able to suffer long. He learned to trust that God knew what was best for him.

Do you feel you have a thorn? The reality of the situation may remain, but God can offer something most precious: His grace to endure. Sometimes, God will take our wounds and transform us into compassionate servants that someone who does not understand could not be.

_____
_____
_____
_____

Faith Bytes

OCTOBER

October 1
Gratitude—Oh, what a relief it is!

The most attractive mark in a Christian's life is gratitude. When we are around someone genuinely thankful, we notice a glow in them. If we want to learn gratitude, then we should observe a grateful person. Someone in the Bible who exemplified exuberant thankfulness was the Apostle Paul. Thankfulness is a dominant theme in his writings, with at least 43 references. Almost all include a combination of three words: "I thank God."

Paul expressed gratitude to God because he remembered life before meeting Jesus. God's love radically changed him, and he could not help but express his gratitude to God. Do you remember what life was like before you became a Christian? Do you recall a time when you were out of God's will? I can, and I was washed over with guilt. I felt out of alignment with God. But when I asked Jesus to forgive me, things changed. It had a Holy Spirit Alka Seltzer effect. It was as if my spirit could sing, "Oh, what a relief it is!" Gratitude is the only word to describe it.

This must have been what Paul had in mind. God literally reached down, dusted him off, and set him free. The response: gratitude. Paul was so thankful he could say: "Rejoice always, pray without ceasing, give thanks in all circumstances." [1 Thessalonians 5:16-18, NRSVUE] To give thanks in all circumstances is radical Christianity!

Perhaps some clarity is in order regarding the Apostles' statement. Paul did not say, "Give thanks for all circumstances." Using "in" makes a huge difference. Paul endured some harsh experiences in life. He was imprisoned, ship wretched, beaten to within inches of his life, and saw friends die for their faith. If Paul applied the hindsight is 20/20 rule, we might understand how Paul could thank God for the good that eventually came from those circumstances. However, Paul was in trouble when he wrote those words. Remembering life before God's grace led him to Jesus and how God provided grace in the thorns of life; he, therefore, could be grateful during anything this world hurled at him. What Paul was thankful for was God's love and presence. When we are truly grateful to God for rescuing us from our sinful selves, the stuff of life takes on a new perspective.

Steven B. Angus

October 2
Generosity—Beyond the Expected

One day, Jesus and his disciples entered the Temple in Jerusalem, sat near the offering box, and watched people drop in their money. Some of the gifts were quite large. However, a particular woman, a poor widow, caught his eye. Approaching the offering box, she reached into her purse and removed what represented everything materially she owned. Without a hint of hesitation, she dropped it in the box. Her gift was two coins valued at less than a penny. Moved by her actions, Jesus said to his disciples, "Assuredly, I say to you that this poor widow has put in more than all those who have given to the treasury; for they all put in out of their abundance, but she out of her poverty put in all that she had her whole livelihood." [Mark 12:43-44] The woman demonstrated the true meaning of generosity by doing more than expected of her.

In the Sermon on the Mount, Jesus indicated that generosity can be extended in many ways, such as turning the other cheek, giving away the extra coat, or carrying a soldier's equipment not one mile but two. When we exceed what is anticipated, we can be called generous.

Why should a Christian bear the mark of generosity? By doing so, we demonstrate the lavish nature of God. When we are generous, we acknowledge God's generosity to us. We will seldom do more than is expected if we first are not grateful. Generosity follows gratitude. If we are not truly thankful, we will have difficulty being generous. Generosity received should translate to generosity extended.

_____

_____

_____

_____

October 3
Feed the Fire

Fire has long represented God and the presence of his Holy Spirit. One day, as Moses was tending his father-in-law's sheep, he saw a bush was on fire, yet it was not being consumed. As he approached, he heard, "Moses, Moses." Moses responded, "Here I am." Then, the voice that Moses later discovered was God's said, "Do not come any closer but take off your sandals, for you are standing on holy ground." Out of the burning bush, God called Moses to lead the Israelite people to the promised land.

One of the things I enjoy doing in the winter is building a fire in the fireplace. It is cozy and the perfect place to lose myself in a book. It doesn't take long for me to feel like all my burdens are melting away. However, I am not a very good firebuilder. I have improved over the years, but I still use a lot of newspapers. And talk about blowing. Sometimes, I blow so hard and so long that I think I am about to hyperventilate. But it has been worth the effort when the fire is finally going.

Unlike the average old dog, I occasionally learn new tricks. For example, experience has taught me it is easier to keep a fire going than trying to restart it. So, I will invest time and energy in stoking the fire to keep the flame lit. The same is true of our spiritual fire. We must provide it the things it needs to keep it going and to help it grow. What are the pieces of kindling that stoke the fire of God's presence in your life? In one of his letters to the young preacher named Timothy, Paul encouraged him to "stir up the gift that is within him." Perhaps you sense that your fire is not what it once was or what you would like for it to be. Maybe Paul's advice applies to you. Why not stir up the embers by speaking with God. Poke them a bit by reading your Bible. Or perhaps an invitation to the Holy Spirit is in order— "Come Holy breath of God—and blow! Blow until God's presence is in full flame in me!"

_____
_____
_____
_____

October 4
A Battle-fatigued Life

October 4 is observed as "The Feast of St. Francis" in many churches and communities. It is often commemorated with "A Blessing of the Animals Service." Although Francis is often identified with animals, he is a fantastic example of how God can use anyone to help others grow in faith if they allow themselves to be available.

Pica was alone when it was time to give birth. Her husband, Pietro, a cloth merchant, was on a business trip to France. The lady Pica was left to make decisions, including arrangements for their newborn son's baptism. When the priest asked the child's name, she responded, "Giovanni." If the lad's father had not returned and changed his name, we could be saying St. Giovanni instead of St. Francis of Assisi.

As his father's wealth increased, so did the young Francis' appetite for the so-called pleasures of life. When he left school at fourteen, Francis' reputation as a rebellious teenager who loved to drink and party grew. Although considered arrogant, he could be charming, earning him leadership of the town's young men.

Life in the family textile business was something Francis considered boring. He dreamed of becoming a war hero like the Medieval Knights. When the township of Assisi went to war, he had his opportunity. However, they were heavily outnumbered, and it ended in a massacre. Francis observed mutilated men screaming in agony. As an ill-trained warrior, Francis was quickly captured.

Steven B. Angus

Dressed like an aristocrat and wearing expensive new armor, his life was spared. However, a dank underground cell became his home for almost a year as his captors negotiated a ransom with his father. When the settlement was accepted, Francis returned home seriously ill both in mind and body as a battle-fatigued war casualty.

Disappointment, battle fatigue, and captivity may be fitting words for your feelings. However, Francis's story was just beginning. He was about to discover that God was preparing him for a greater mission. So, it is with us.

_____

_____

_____

_____

October 5
Jesus Calling

Throughout my tenure as a pastor, the first or second Sunday in October has been devoted to pets and their human families. The Church's lawn becomes a safe haven for dogs, cats, goats, and other creatures to receive a blessing. This service often occurs near October 4, the Feast of St. Francis. Someone asked, "Who was St. Francis, and why do we bless the animals?" I love it when people ask questions.

After spending a year as a prisoner of war, Francis returned home, his dream of being a heroic knight shattered. Only 23, he pondered the familiar question, "What will I do with my life?" While he did not know the answer, what he did know was working in the family textile business wasn't for him. Seeking clarity, he took a hike, literally. Wandering the hills surrounding his town, he found a little church that needed repair. He entered the disheveled chapel and saw a painting of the crucifixion. In the center was a large wooden crucifix. Kneeling beneath the scene, he was drawn to the open eyes of Jesus, which seemed to probe his soul. He found the Lord's stare both intimidating and summoning. Even if he wished to look away, it would have been impossible. His doubts, fears, memories of the war, confusion, guilt, and longing for purpose all gushed forth in a petition—"Lord, what do you want me to do? Show me what you want me to do with my life."

Prostrated before the scene, he heard Jesus speak to him by name. "Francis, go rebuild My house; as you see, it is all being destroyed." His heart was changed. He desired to obey Jesus's call as best as he understood it. He began by repairing the run-down chapel and then others nearby. Over time, he realized what Jesus meant wasn't a structure. Francis was to build up the faith of God's people. Francis was to be an example of what following Jesus should look like.

Faith Bytes

Listen. Do you hear your name being called? If there is a yearning within to build up someone's faith, it is Jesus Calling.

_____
_____
_____
_____

October 6
The Sweetness of Jesus

In an ancient text titled "Legend of the Three Companions," three of Francis' disciples speak of the event in their teacher's life that would shape his ministry. They report that as Francis prayed, he felt God saying, "Francis, if you want to know my will, you must hate and despise all your body has loved and desired to possess. Once you begin to do this, what seemed sweet and pleasant will become bitter and unbearable, and the things that made you shudder will bring you sweetness and contentment."

Soon afterward, while traveling, Francis met a leper. Like most people of that era, he had a fear of lepers. When he saw someone with this skin disease, his practice was to look the other way and hold his nose. However, remembering God's words, Francis did not turn away on this day but rode directly toward the man. Dismounting, he walked towards the man, missing parts of his face. Placing a coin in his disfigured hand, Francis paused to kiss it. In return, the leper gave him the kiss of peace. Francis remounted his horse and continued his journey.

Some days later, he took a large sum of money to the leper hospital. Gathering them together, he gave each a coin and kissed each of their hands. When he left them, he realized what had been revolting to him was now something pleasant. In his Diary, Francis wrote, "When I was in sin, the sight of lepers nauseated me beyond measure, but then God himself led me into their company, and I had pity on them." He realized while hugging those who were suffering, he was embracing Jesus.

Today, be attentive to those we often overlook or avoid. In reaching out, like Francis, we may encounter the sweetness of Jesus.

_____
_____
_____
_____

Steven B. Angus

October 7
Away in a manger, No crib for a bed. . .

Did you realize that Christmas is only seventy-nine days away? Some of my favorite memories of Christmas have nothing to do with December. One occurred with a group of Estonian children attending a camp in the Baltic countryside of Northern Europe. For most of these inner-city teens from the capital city of Tallinn, it was the first time they had seen a live cow, fed a horse an apple, or taken a swim in the Baltic Sea. It was also the first occasion some of them heard about Jesus.

The arts are vital to the Estonian people, and the campground had an impressive outdoor amphitheater. With a group of teens eager to present a play, we invited them to create a Christmas drama to share with the other campers and staff. It was amazing to watch their enthusiastic creativity.

Most of us take the annual Nativity pageant for granted. However, did you know the Christian Church existed for 1200 years before someone had the idea to recreate it as drama? It seems a monk returning from a pilgrimage to the humble stable in a Bethlehem cave told a friend, "I want to do something that will recall the memory of that Child who was born in Bethlehem, to see with bodily eyes the inconveniences of his infancy, how he lay in the manger, [as animals] and how the ox and ass stood by."

In 1223, according to an eyewitness named St. Bonaventure, a monk named Francis stood before the manger, "bathed in tears and radiant with joy." The monk told the people about the nativity of the poor King. However, he could not utter His name for the tenderness of His love. Instead, he called Him "the Babe of Bethlehem."

Go ahead. Sing a Christmas Carol. Meditate on the Babe of Bethlehem before commercialism bombards us. Offer a prayer of gratitude for St. Francis.

_____
_____
_____
_____

October 8
Birds Who Share God's Joy in Song

Francis is the Patron Saint of the Environment and Animals in many Church traditions. Although Protestants do not usually elevate individuals to such a status, it does not mean we cannot appreciate their example. Francis of Assisi was an actual person. Based on the various stories and legends, Francis must have been a friend to all God's creatures, humans, animals, and nature.

Faith Bytes

The earliest books about Saint Francis were written by Thomas of Celano, who knew him personally. Thomas reveals Francis' love for animals and his conviction that faith and care for God's creatures go hand-in-hand. The story, which seems to be the source of Francis's love for animals, occurred when he spotted a flock of doves and birds of all varieties. Leaving his traveling companions, Francis ran after the birds. He greeted them, "Beloved birds." Instead of flying away, they remained. Surprised, he asked them to stay and listen to the Word of God. When they lingered, he said, "My brother and sister birds, you should praise your Creator and always love him. He gave you feathers for clothes, wings to fly, and all other things you need." Celano reports that Francis blessed the creatures and sent them forth in all directions to share God's joy in song. When Francis rejoined his companions, he lamented not preaching to the birds before. He said:

"If you have men who will exclude any of God's creatures from the shelter of compassion and pity, you will have men who will deal likewise with their fellow men."

I love my pets and often sit on my porch and invite them to listen to scripture and use their voices to speak to our Creator. I wonder—Does God see me as I see my pets?

_____

_____

_____

_____

October 9
The Peace Prayer

Although Francis lived 800 years ago and was forty-four when he died, he continues to have a profound influence. Today, more than 35,000 Catholic Priests and Nuns are members of the Franciscan order. The Secular Franciscan Order, consisting primarily of the laity, has over 300,000 members worldwide. The sitting Pope chose to be called after St. Francis of Assisi, describing him as "the man of poverty, the man of peace, the man who loves and protects creation." There are numerous Protestant orders of St. Francis as well.

The familiar "Peace Prayer" is attributed to Francis. In 1967, Sebastian Temple wrote a hymn based on this prayer titled "Make Me a Channel of Your Peace." According to Hymnary.org, it has appeared in thirty-seven hymnals. I encourage you to go to YouTube and listen to some of the various presentations of this hymn.

Steven B. Angus

This Prayer of St. Francis was prevalent during World Wars I and II but remains timeless in its message.

> LORD, MAKE ME AN INSTRUMENT OF YOUR PEACE:
> WHERE THERE IS HATRED, LET ME SOW LOVE;
> WHERE THERE IS INJURY, PARDON;
> WHERE THERE IS DOUBT, FAITH;
> WHERE THERE IS DESPAIR, HOPE;
> WHERE THERE IS DARKNESS, LIGHT;
> WHERE THERE IS SADNESS, JOY.
>
> O DIVINE MASTER, GRANT THAT I MAY NOT SO MUCH SEEK
> TO BE CONSOLED AS TO CONSOLE,
> TO BE UNDERSTOOD AS TO UNDERSTAND,
> TO BE LOVED AS TO LOVE.
> FOR IT IS IN GIVING THAT WE RECEIVE,
> IT IS IN PARDONING THAT WE ARE PARDONED,
> AND IT IS IN DYING THAT WE ARE BORN TO ETERNAL LIFE.
> AMEN.

_____
_____
_____
_____

October 10
Comfort Food for Our Souls

When I was a child, when someone was eccentric, we would smile and say, "They are just an odd duck." Some days, this is how I feel about the Apostle Paul. His comments oscillate somewhere between bold and brash. For example, his statement: "We know that all things work together for good for those who love God, who are called according to his purpose." [Romans 8:28] Just where does he come up with this "We know" stuff?

One day, a little boy told his Grandma, who was busy baking a cake, how "everything" was going wrong in his life. His world seemed to be one problem after another. Meanwhile, his Grandmother asked him if he would like a snack, and he nodded yes. She poured cooking oil into a measuring cup and offered it to him. His response was immediate. "Yuck!" "Then how about two raw eggs?" she queried. "Gross Grandma," he said, frowning. "Would you like some flour or maybe baking soda?" she asked casually. "Grandma, those things are nasty," the boy retorted. The Grandma replied, "Yes, all those things seem bad by themselves. But when they are put together correctly, they make a wonderfully delicious cake!"

I have known some Grandmothers like this one. Sometimes, she has been my wife, a friend, a colleague, or someone I talked with while waiting for my car to be

Faith Bytes

serviced. Although worded differently, I needed the message— "God knows how to bake an awesome cake!"

When you sense you are becoming flustered, imagine God folding it into all sorts of life experiences. Each ingredient is required to fulfill God's purpose in our life. Perhaps some "Romans 8:28 cake" will serve as comfort food for our souls.

___

October 11
Gospel in the Batter's Box

When driving, I usually have the radio tuned to a sporting event or a sports talk program. I suppose I could be labeled a sports junkie, and October is the perfect time to feed my addiction. Football is in full swing, hockey season is on the horizon, basketball teams are scrimmaging, and baseball. Let's just say I have penciled in the day the playoffs begin, leading to the World Series [and the Braves winning another championship].

Every baseball season has something to offer, making it a fantastic year for those who love it. The 2022 season was one for the ages when the casual fan checked the box score to track New York Yankee Aaron Judge's pursuit of setting a new American League record that stood for sixty-one years. The week Judge tied Roger Maris's single-season record of sixty-one home runs and then set the new standard by hitting number sixty-two was must-see television. It was thrilling to watch the game and see Judge's mother and Roger Maris, Jr. seated in the stands to witness the historic event. Following the landmark game, the son of the legendary Maris addressed the media and praised Judge's accomplishment. He stated that his father would have been proud that his record was broken by someone who did it the right way without using performance-enhancing drugs.

When I heard his remarks, I was reminded that the goal of every Christian should be to have it said, "He/she did it the right way." Integrity should be the standard every follower of Jesus pursues. Unfortunately, such an endeavor isn't easy. We are surrounded by a seemingly never-ending parade of opportunities that promise to be a shortcut to our goal. However, if we are truly transparent about doing the right thing, borrowing another baseball expression, "we strike out." And let's face it, some of those whiffs are not pretty.

If you watch one of the many baseball games leading up to the crowning of the World Series champions, each time you see a player strike out, pause and offer a prayer of thanksgiving. For what, you ask? How about the fact that with Jesus, the three-strike rule doesn't apply. We may strike out, but we are never off the team. How is that for some baseball Gospel?

Steven B. Angus

October 12
Squirrels, Tarzan, and Trusting One Another

Humans can learn much about ourselves by observing the creatures we share space with. I enjoy where I live because of the wildlife that passes through. Recently, a flock of about ten turkeys has kept our miniature donkey named Jenny company. My wife, Cheri, and I haven't decided if Jenny prefers the comradery of the turkeys, deer, or groundhog best. We do know she isn't interested in the coyotes who sing to her during the night.

Although these are seasonal guests, others appear almost daily. It isn't uncommon to see chipmunks scurrying along the wood line or a clan of rabbits grazing in the backyard, even as they are mindful of the location of our dogs. Then there are the squirrels. I have often referred to them as a "pack" because about six of them interact with each other. I have a squirrel feeder attached to a tree to let them know they are welcome. I also attribute these creatures' trust to the St. Francis statue prominently displayed for them to see.

As a squirrel watcher, I love it when they stand erect and stare back at me or chase each other. Their ability to leap from one limb of a tree to another gives the allusion to miniature acrobats on a flying trapeze. I can only recall one or two times when I saw a squirrel miss the branch it aimed at.

Perhaps what amazes me most about these creatures, particularly the squirrels, is the level of trust they demonstrate. When I was a child, I would watch Tarzan on television and then go outdoors, climb trees, and do the Tarzan jungle yell. Thankfully, it never crossed my mind to jump from limb to limb. However, squirrels never hesitate. They take the leap, trusting a favorable outcome.

Trust. It is the foundation necessary for relationships to thrive. Although possible, restoring a marriage where trust has been violated is tough. Without trust, almost every action is seen with suspicion. The greatest obstacle facing the church is a lack of trust. Society is suspicious of institutional religion. Many congregations, clergy, and parishioners distrust each other and see every action with cynicism and criticism. When we fail to trust one another, we cease to be the church in the world. We allow the world to undermine our greatest strength. If we cannot love (and I would add trust) our sisters and brothers whom we have seen, how can we love (or trust) God, whom we have not seen? Maybe our struggle as people of faith is our resistance to trusting the very things we say we believe.

I marvel at the contentment my squirrel neighbors demonstrate. I wish I could live just one day with the peace they have. Until we can trust God and one another, we will never know "the peace that passes all understanding" that Jesus spoke about. I have no intention of swinging or jumping from one branch to another, but I will try to truly trust God so that I can trust someone besides myself.

_____
_____
_____
_____

Faith Bytes

October 13
Is the Cornerstone Missing?

I keep hoping to find Steve Harvey on my doorstep to inform me that I am a Publisher's Clearinghouse Sweepstakes winner! I doubt that will occur as I have never entered. The astronomical awards advertised make a $500 prize seem relatively insignificant. However, that was the prize back in 1791. Although the value would be $14,000 in today's currency, the contest wasn't about the money. It would be considered a great honor if your suggestion was selected. In fact, one entry included a future president, Thomas Jefferson, who did so under an assumed name. The prize was awarded to James Hoban, an Irish immigrant living in Charleston, South Carolina. His architectural design for a Presidential residence was selected. The home would be named the Executive Mansion. President Theodore Roosevelt officially renamed it the "White House" in 1901.

On this day in 1792, the cornerstone was laid. President Washington had chosen the site but could not attend because he was in the nation's capital, Philadelphia. On November 1, 1801, President John Adams and his wife, Abigail, moved into the new residence. Mrs. Adams's comments should be noted. She said, "I pray heaven to bestow the best of blessings on this house and on all that shall hereafter inhabit it. May none but wise men ever rule under this roof!"

The White House Cornerstone has been the subject of novelists, movies, and historical conspiracy theorists claiming it is missing. It is fun to allow our imagination to wonder. The cornerstone of a building is an integral part of the construction of a building. It determines the position of all the pieces to be laid afterward. The New Testament identifies Jesus as the stone that was rejected by many. However, for those who believe, he has become the cornerstone of our lives. Although Jesus is never missing, we may ask ourselves, "have we misplaced him?"

_____

_____

_____

_____

October 14
An Island Named Quandary

Recently, I have felt as if I am living on an island. Although it isn't deserted, the atmosphere breathes of isolation. The Island has a name; no, it isn't christened after a "little buddy" named Gilligan. Instead, its name is "Quandary." The good news is several ships are ready to sail. However, the various crews refuse to reveal their destination and have published conflicting itineraries. This only adds to the Quandary. And if this weren't as confusing as attempting to work a Rubik's

Steven B. Angus

Cube in a dark closet, each vessel displays on its bow the name "The Right Choice."

Do you feel my Quandary? Do you have such an island for sale? Such occasions occur when something we believe to be accurate, perhaps revered as sacred, is called into question. My most recent Quandary happened when I mentioned Columbus Day and was reminded of allegations of brutality towards indigenous people. Although I was acquainted with this information, I was also familiar with the other Christopher Columbus. The one reported never using profanity and led his shipman in religious rites during voyages. With every turn of the half-hourglass, the crew would pause and pray in unison. When the day concluded, they would join voices and sing vespers. I prefer to remember Columbus as a man of deep religious conviction. However, I understand when he was endorsed for Sainthood by a sitting pope, there were reasons it did not occur. This was a simple quandary to wrestle with on a particular day, reminding me that most of us are human.

As we enter the election season and consider how I will cast my vote, I feel like I am living on an island named Quandary. It isn't deserted, is it? So, as I pray, I am comforted by the words of American Religion Historian Martin Marty, "God affects things in the world in ironic ways."

_____
_____
_____
_____

October 15
The Methodist Preacher from Georgia

I have an old hardback book in my library whose title is mostly faded. Its title page reads "The Sermons of Sam Jones." I do not remember how I acquired it, but I am pleased to have it in my collection. I have kept it because it reminds me of those who came before me in ministry. Although you may not recognize a common name like Sam Jones, it could be a part of your "family tree of faith." He may have been instrumental in leading your great-grandparents to faith or inspiring someone who became your pastor's pastor.

Records indicate Reverend Jones conducted eighteen revivals in Nashville, Tennessee. In 1885, the Nashville ministerial association invited him to erect a tent for 5,000, which was packed three times a day for four weeks. National newspapers reported that the evangelist berated, amused, and compelled his audience to come forward, pledging their lives to Christ. Some claimed that 10,000 responded. He made such an impression he was invited to address the State Legislature.

In those days, Nashville was a riverboat town. These boats transported trade goods but also barrooms, gambling casinos, and dancing girls. Much of this industry belonged to Tom Ryman, who was converted during the Jones meeting. Ryman cleaned up his boats and used his wealth to construct a building where Jones and others could hold revivals. Ryman's Union Gospel Tabernacle eventually became "the Mother Church of country music," the Grand Ole Opry. The year following the Nashville revival, Jones estimated he preached 1,000 sermons to 3 million people around the country.

On this day, in 1906, Sam Jones died. However, the faith of this Methodist preacher from Georgia lives on through us. What will be our spiritual legacy?

_____

_____

_____

October 16
Faith that Perseveres

"(REFRAIN:) IT IS WELL (IT IS WELL),
WITH MY SOUL (WITH MY SOUL),
IT IS WELL; IT IS WELL WITH MY SOUL."

On this date, in 1888, the man who penned these lyrics of the hymn, "It Is Well With My Soul," died of malaria in Jerusalem. The tragedy that led Horatio Spafford to write these words has encouraged many.

Mr. Spafford was a businessman and attorney in Chicago. He had a beautiful home, a lovely wife, and four daughters. Life was good until a devastating fire destroyed most of Chicago. His family stood on a hill and wept as they watched everything they owned perish in the flames. Spafford borrowed money and sent his family to Europe to join their friend, the evangelist Dwight L. Moody. In the middle of the Atlantic, misfortune once again occurred when the ship transporting his family was struck by another vessel. It took less than two hours for the oceanliner and 226 passengers to perish. Among the casualties were his daughters. Fortunately, his wife was rescued and sent a telegram to her husband: "Saved Alone." During Spafford's voyage to join his wife, one night, the captain pointed out the spot where the tragedy had occurred. Retiring to his cabin, he wrote these words.

"WHEN PEACE LIKE A RIVER ATTENDETH MY WAY,
WHEN SORROW LIKE SEA BILLOWS ROLL,
WHATEVER MY LOT, THOU HAST TAUGHT ME TO SAY,
IT IS WELL, IT IS WELL, WITH MY SOUL!"

Steven B. Angus

In his grief, the love of God provided hope and strength for what lay ahead. When we hear stories of faith that persevere, we are reminded that God is near when storms come our way.

October 17
The Bishop and The Sister

On this date, almost 2000 years apart, two vastly different followers of Christ remind us of a Christian quality we typically overlook. Ignatius was an Apostle John student and Bishop of Antioch in Syria for forty years from AD 67-106. During the Roman reign of terror against Christians, Ignatius was arrested and sent to Rome to be executed. During the arduous journey, he was chained between guards who responded to each act of kindness by their prisoner with harsher cruelly. Along the way, leaders from local congregations would meet him to express their love.

Ignatius hastily dictated letters to their communities of faith. Seven of these letters exist today. One was addressed to the Roman Christians, and because the death march moved so slowly, the document arrived before he did. In it, Ignatius pleaded with them not to attempt a rescue, stating, "Nearness to the sword is nearness to God; to be among the wild beasts is to be in the arms of God; only let it be in the name of Jesus Christ. I endure all things that I may suffer together with him since he who became perfect man strengthens me." When the Bishop arrived, his executioners took him directly to the arena and threw him into the lions. Ignatius was willing to make the ultimate sacrifice for his Savior.

Also, on this date in 1979, Mother Theresa was awarded the Nobel Peace Prize for her work among society's forgotten and most vulnerable. Two radically different outcomes remind us that following Jesus is embracing a life of sacrifice.

Faith Bytes

October 18
Teaching Sheep to Feed Themselves

"The Bible is the Church's Book" is a statement often made. Although the church looks to it to organize its life within faith communities, it is also intended for every Christian. Still, even this doesn't tell the entire story. First and foremost, the Bible is God's love letter. It is intended for anyone who opens it or hears it read. The Bible is a gift from God to everyone. The Bible is yours.

The Bible has been a part of my life from birth when my father laid it in my hand with the idea that it would be the first thing I held. A pastor from my childhood delighted in saying he always knew I would be a preacher. According to him, when I was a toddler, he would give me a Bible, and I would stomp my foot and chatter loudly. Some may say I never stopped chattering!

We say the Bible is a precious gift, but why? For one reason. Jesus. The Bible explains why he came, who sent him, and what he did on our behalf. Furthermore, it details what Jesus is doing for us now and in the future.

John Wesley said, "I want to know one thing, the way to heaven…for this end, He came from heaven. He hath written it down in a book. Give me that book! At any price, give me the Book of God!"

One of my bishops said, "As a pastor, you must teach the sheep how to feed themselves. They cannot survive on what you feed them two or three times a month. They will starve to death." I have tried to follow his advice. I hope we can learn to feed ourselves the Word of God in the coming days. In the meantime, take your Bible, thumb through it, and see what it reveals.

_____

_____

_____

_____

October 19
Work the Plan

When Charles Wesley was a student at Oxford University, he realized how easily he was distracted from his studies and faith. Realizing he wasn't the only one with this tendency, he invited a few men to join him in pursuing these things. When his older brother, John, returned to Oxford as a lecturer, he joined them. Their extreme Christian behavior caught the attention of faculty and students and earned them numerous derogatory names. Their systematic code of conduct tagged them, The Holy Club, Methodist, and Bible moths. The Bible was central to their gatherings when the movement only numbered five or six devotees.

Steven B. Angus

John Wesley identified himself as *"homo unius libri,"* which is Latin for "a man of one book." He remarked before it was politically incorrect, "I am a Bible bigot. I follow it in all things, both great and small." In the preface to his 1765 edition of the "Explanatory Notes on the Old Testament," Wesley gave six (or seven) suggestions for personal Bible study. These tips have reached out to us across the centuries.

His first suggestion was to set aside some time in the morning and evening to read God's Word. We must have a plan and then work the plan. Although evident, starting something, even one considered a Holy Habit, is easier said than done. Today, we have so many tools designed to help us accomplish this goal that they have become a distraction. Perhaps the time-honored blueprint of reading a chapter from the Old and New Testament is the best way to begin. Finding a suitable method isn't the issue. It's "the when" that tends to waylay us. Wesley's plan was to read the Bible when your day began and ended. Who can argue with the premise that God should be our first and last thought of the day? Why not plan to read a chapter from the Bible before going to sleep tonight and in the morning when the day is fresh?

_____

_____

_____

_____

October 20
Messy Can Be Fun!

How many photographs do you have of your child's first birthday? Undoubtedly, they are remarkable because the subject is our precious prodigy. However, when it comes to the cake, most of the images are similar. After we sing "Happy Birthday," blow out the single candle, we place a small cake prepared for this occasion before our little blessing. Cautiously, the guest of honor gazes upon the silly adults. Soon, the tiny hand is extended, accompanied by a chorus of "oohs" and "awws." Once the fingers reach their destination, a squishy handful is taken, followed by an entire fist inserted into the mouth so gumming the prize can commence. We refuse to look away as if we were on a whale cruise, not wanting to miss it. And then—Yes! The Birthday girl executes the perfect two-handed shovel technique. Our chest expands as we realize that all those hours of singing "patty cake" have returned dividends as they patty the cake and the morsels fly. Here it comes—Hands to hair. Then, the grand finale, as an index finger laced with chocolate, finds the perfect landing place in an ear or a nasal cavity.

Feeding oneself at age one is an adventure. Just imagine how little Mary will feel when she attempts the same maneuvers at one year and one day. Learning to feed oneself as a Christian can be just as messy. Perhaps we need to be reminded that messy can be fun!

Faith Bytes

In modern English, John Wesley's second Bible guideline is: "If time permits, read a chapter of the Old and New Testament, but it's okay to read less if that works better for you." Remember, a handful is okay. Biting off more than we can chew can result in choking. Before reading the Bible from cover to cover, take a leisurely stroll through one of the Gospels.

_____
_____
_____
_____

October 21
So Many Questions

Why should we read the Bible? This is a fair question. The Bible is an extensive library of Books. Frankly, some of us simply do not enjoy reading about a bunch of dead people. And the names? Gee, whiz! I will confess parts of the Bible are drudgery to read. When my Bible reading plan has as its "chore," I mean text for the day parts of Ezekiel, I inwardly moan. Trying to wade through those prophets is enough to make a preacher want to cuss.

I apologize for my initial question. Asking why we should read the Bible sounds like a chore to be checked off our "Do this to be holy list." The question—no, some of the questions that keep me returning to the Bible are: Do I want to know the God who created me? What is God's will for my life? How can I love Jesus more? Does God have something to say about this problem? How can I be a better husband? How can I finish well with fewer days ahead of me than behind? What is Godly contentment? How can I better listen to God and speak to God?

If I allow the question, "Why should we read the Bible?" to stand, my answer would be I have so many questions, and God may actually answer some of them in scripture. John Wesley's third guideline for reading the Bible was to do so with "a single eye to know God's whole will with a firm resolution to do it."

Why not take a moment and read a section of scripture with three questions in mind. What does this teach about God? What does it say about me? Knowing this, how will I live today?

_____
_____
_____
_____

Steven B. Angus

October 22
Recognizing the Harmony of the Bible

Michael Landon of "Bonanza" and "Little House on the Prairie" fame starred in a movie titled, "I Was a Teenage Werewolf." Well, I was a teenage pastor, serving my first church. I had been invited to Sunday dinner in the home of a widow whose years numbered in the nineties. When the six of us sat down to the meal, it required two tables to hold all the food. The spread included no less than four or five different meats.

I recognized her labor-intensive efforts and said, "Mrs. Kimborough, this is amazing. You shouldn't have gone to so much trouble." She quickly stated that she had been born and raised a Methodist and had no intention of changing. Then she said something that taught me that sometimes grace must trump Biblical exegesis. She said, "I have always had several types of meat at mealtime. The Bible says, 'They did eat their meat with gladness.' The good book tells us to eat meat at mealtime. Isn't that right, preacher?"

My black-and-white upbringing shouted, "Yes, but that isn't what it meant." What came out of my mouth was, "Yes, mam' that's what it says, and we are having a lot of gladness." This dear lady had a relationship with Jesus nine decades in the making. Who was I to arrogantly contradict her?

However, some have been hurt deeply and irreparably because certain verses or phrases have been lifted from Scripture and misapplied. In the Preface to his "Explanatory Notes on the Old Testament," John Wesley instructs us to read the Bible, recognizing its harmony with the grand theological themes. This simply means we should not read a passage isolated from other relevant texts. Scripture interprets Scripture. They can guide us to God's love and care when taken together.

_____
_____
_____
_____

October 23
The Teacher Who Recognizes Our Needs

Who was your favorite teacher? The answer may come quickly or with a disclaimer, "It depended on my need at the time." Miss Woody instilled in me a passion for history, not by emphasizing dates but by emphasizing the narrative. She could paint word pictures and dialogue that would rival John Grisham.

Perhaps the dearest to my heart was Mrs. Moss, my fourth-grade teacher. I assume she taught me all the necessary topics for the grade level; however, I do not remember any particular lesson. At the time, I needed someone to restore my confidence and help me realize I was smart in my own way. It would be several years before I learned she was the wife of a Methodist preacher.

The teacher makes all the difference. John Wesley wrote that serious and earnest prayer should be constantly used when reading the Bible. Scripture can only be understood through the same Spirit whereby it was given. Our reading should likewise be closed with a prayer that what we read may be written on our hearts. Jesus said, "The Holy Spirit, whom the Father will send in my name, will teach you everything and remind you of all that I have said to you." [John 14:26] The Holy Spirit is our tutor who recognizes our needs and uses the Bible to point us to Jesus.

Five hundred years ago, Martin Luther stated that the Bible is like the swaddling clothes wrapped around the baby Jesus and the manger in which he was laid. We do not worship the manger, nor do we worship the Bible. We cherish it because it cradles the Savior. It is Jesus we worship. He is the Savior to whom all Scripture points and to whom the Holy Spirit teaches.

_____
_____
_____
_____

October 24
Sometimes Less Really is Best

How long should a sermon series be? This is a question preachers ponder and parishioners endure. The consensus seems to be four to eight weeks. Rev. Martyn Lloyd-Jones was a medical doctor who became the pastor of Westminster Chapel in London for almost thirty years. He is regarded as one of the finest Expository Preachers to have lived. This is a style of preaching that generally goes verse by verse through a book of the Bible. On Sunday mornings for eight years, Lloyd-Jones preached 232 sermons covering each of the six chapters of The Letter of Ephesians. He delivered 119 sermons from the Book of Acts on Sunday evenings for three years. His most prominent series occurred on Friday nights when he gave 366 messages from the Book of Romans. They were published in a fourteen-volume set. My most extended series consisted of thirty sermons on the life of the Apostle Peter.

Borrowing a phrase from the yellowed-haired theologian Goldie Locks, we are looking for the one that is just right. The truth is when it comes to reading the Bible, we are apt to rush through the experience. Granted, we should aim to read the Bible in its entirety, but sometimes less is best.

Steven B. Angus

John Wesley's guide to reading the Bible stated: "It might also be useful if while we read, we were frequently to pause and examine ourselves by what we read, both with regard to our hearts, and lives." Doing so would provide us with a matter of praise in that God has shown us something for our lives.

As we read scripture, whether it is five verses or five chapters, it is always helpful to ask what this means to my life? What is the one verse or idea that God has for me?

October 25
Oughta....

Recently, I was bemoaning to a friend that my vocabulary is dominated by the phrase "I ought to." Being a product of the South, it generally sounds like, "I oughta." Interestingly, almost every dictionary includes it; if they don't, "they oughta."

Ought expresses the idea of duty. When a Christian uses it, it usually concerns a perceived moral obligation. It is not as forceful as "a must" but more vigorous than "a should." We say we ought to be punctual, or we oughta go to church. When I employ the phrase, it means I have the moral scruples that recognize an action would have been or would be the proper response; however, I neglected to do it, or I am unlikely to do so. It would be interesting to know how often Christians use "I oughta" compared to the general population. Perhaps this is why some avoid church gatherings or even reading the Bible. We do not want to be presented with another "oughta," which we will likely neglect or put off until we forget it.

When reading the Bible, John Wesley recognized this tendency. His closing statement about effectively reading scripture stated: "And whatever light you then receive, should be used to the uttermost, and that immediately. Let there be no delay. Whatever you resolve, begin to execute the first moment you can."

Jesus was never afraid to call people to action. Neither is the Bible. As we read the Bible, we "oughta" ask ourselves, "How does God want me to respond?" And then do it immediately.

Faith Bytes

October 26
Here I Stand

"The Bible is alive; it speaks to me; it has feet; it runs after me; it has hands; it lays hold of me," were the words of a Sixteenth Century German priest named Martin Luther. He is identified as the father of the Protestant Reformation. Churches and some countries commemorate his actions annually on October 31 as Reformation Day.

The movement began as Luther listened to a sermon on indulgences. Indulgences were documents prepared by the church and sold to individuals either for themselves or on behalf of the dead, absolving them of the consequences of sins. Luther was alarmed when the clergyman stated, "Once the coin into the coffer clings, a soul from purgatory heavenward springs!"

The selling of indulgences was just one concern Luther found questionable. He prepared a list of 95 grievances and, on October 31, 1517, nailed them to the Church door in Wittenberg, Germany. He called for reform in what became known as the Five Solas. "Sola" is Latin for slogans: sola Scriptura (Scripture alone), sola fide (faith alone), sola gratia (grace alone), Solus Christus (Christ alone), and Soil Deo Gloria (to the glory of God alone.) Luther sought to return the focus of faith back to its source. . .Jesus.

This action of publicly challenging the Church's authority and statements such as "a simple layman armed with the Scriptures" was superior to both the pope and councils without them paved the way for Luther to be branded a heretic. When given the opportunity to recant, Luther stated, "Unless I can be instructed and convinced with evidence from the Holy Scriptures or with open, clear, and distinct grounds of reasoning ... then I cannot and will not recant, because it is neither safe nor wise to act against conscience." Then he added, "Here I stand. I can do no other. God, help me! Amen."

Perhaps today is a good day to ponder—Where do I stand?

_____
_____
_____

October 27
A One Week Challenge

I hope you are enjoying your adventure with the Bible. Perhaps studying scripture hasn't been something you have tried, and you are ready to give it a test drive. Or maybe you have started only to become discouraged and stopped. If so, John Wesley's tips for personal Bible reading may be helpful. Here is a review.

Steven B. Angus

Suppose you like going to the primary source. In that case, it is located in the preface to Wesley's "Explanatory Notes Upon the Old Testament." You will notice how Wesley, ever the preacher, lists six by number but finds a way to work in a seventh step.

1) Set aside some time in the morning and evening to read.
2) If you have time, read a chapter of the Old and New Testament; however, it is okay to read less if that works better.
3) Read with a single eye of knowing the will of God and doing it.
4) Read in faith to see the connection and harmony of the grand theological themes. In other words, don't proof text.
5) Pray before and after you read the scriptures, asking and allowing the Holy Spirit to be your tutor.
6) Don't rush. Pause and examine yourself while you read. Note your growth in faith and also where you need more grace.
7) Whatever God shows you to do, act on it quickly.

If you are not in the habit of daily Bible reading, try it for one week as you apply these tips. I believe you will see that it makes a difference in your life.

_____
_____
_____
_____

October 28
If You Believe It, Leave It

For his sixth birthday, Joe received a walking, talking robot. Although it was a toy, it quickly became his favorite. Then, the unthinkable occurred. As Joe was about to leave home to go to church, his cat jumped up on the desk in his bedroom, knocking the toy to the floor with a gigantic crash. When Joe picked it up and pressed the power button. Nothing happened. His robot was broken. Then Joe had an idea. He would take it to church, place it on the altar, and ask God to fix it. When he did, God said, "No problem." Joe was thrilled that God would fix it, so he took his toy and went home. The boy woke up excited every morning of that week to see if his toy had been fixed, as God said. However, to his disappointment, the toy was still broken. So the following Sunday, the boy returned his toy to the altar and asked God, "Why didn't you fix my robot this week? You told me you would." God replied, "You didn't leave it at the altar."

I know. Parts of the story are frankly unbelievable. Yet, sadly, this scene occurs weekly. We go to church, lift to God our troubles, and ask God to help us. And then "the Joe" comes out in us. Instead of leaving them with God, we pick them back up to deal with them ourselves. We don't trust God to take it entirely away to fix it.

Faith Bytes

Do you feel like you are carrying thousands of pounds of trouble on your back? Jesus once said to his disciples: "Therefore if the Son makes you free, you shall be free indeed." [John 8:36] Surely, this is what one hymn writer thought when he wrote: "Burdens are lifted at Calvary, Jesus is very near."

_____
_____
_____
_____

October 29
Fragments

Life can be challenging. We hear the alarm clock bidding us to get out of bed. Before putting our feet on the floor, we consider if we have the resolve to face the day. Perhaps the heaviest burden is the notion that we are a failure. We can overcome many trials and tribulations, but the most challenging hurdle to conquer is the belief that we are seen by others as a failure. The American author F. Scott Fitzgerald said, "There are no second acts in American lives." Thankfully, God does not concur. Many, if not most, of the people God chose had personal histories of failure. The list is long: Moses committed murder. David adultery. Jacob deceived his father. Noah was guilty of drunkenness. Peter denied knowing Jesus, not once but three times in one evening. In fact, the Bible is one long story of people who failed, yet God provided a second act.

Perhaps you are attempting to carry the weight of failure. It is never far from the forefront of our minds when it is on our shoulders. We sometimes call them skeletons in our closet. If you are tired of lugging it around, there is good news. God can help us lay the burden down and may even use it for good. We are not the first to have failed or will be the last. The Bible says, "All have sinned and fallen short of the glory of God."

A famous violinist contracted a renowned manufacturer to produce the finest instrument he had ever made. When the violin was delivered, its tone did not please the musician. In anger, he smashed it. The disheartened dealer, carefully gathering the broken pieces, remade the violin and returned it to the violinist. This time, the musician was charmed by the resonance and was surprised to learn that the violin was the one he had broken. The proud manufacturer said, "I have made it out of the fragments."

What do you consider your greatest failure? God can take the fragments of a life shattered by failure, assemble its pieces, and produce in the regenerated soul-sweet melodies.

_____
_____
_____
_____

Steven B. Angus

October 30
Pass the Skittles, Please

If you have a sweet tooth, you're in luck. Each year, during the week preceding Halloween, approximately 600 million pounds of candy are sold in the United States. It is estimated that $10.6 billion will be spent by Americans purchasing Halloween Candy. Looking at 12 years of data, CandyStore.com determined that the most popular candy by state was Skittles, ranking as the number one choice in seven states. A National Confectioners Association poll found that 70 percent of Americans still prefer chocolate candy and will purchase 90 million pounds during Halloween week.

Did you realize the word "Halloween" actually has Christian origins? "Hallows" is just an old word for "saints." So, it is Hallow Evening, the Evening of Saints. Stay with me. In Genesis, the day began at sunset rather than sunrise. So, November 1 was All Hallowed, All Saints Day. Keeping with scripture, the first service occurred the evening before, All Hallows Evening. Some credit the Scots for running the phrase together to sound like Hallowe'en.

But what is a hallow, a saint? We tend to think of dead people. However, the Apostle Paul often wrote such statements as "To all God's beloved..., who are called to be saints." Does this mean we are called to be dead people? The word translated into English as saints meant those set aside for a holy purpose. Saints are individuals made righteous by Jesus and set apart for God's purpose.

When we celebrate All Saints Day, we are reminded that we are connected to every other believer—those who lived long ago, those living today, even those who will come after us. Go ahead and say it. . .Happy Halloween! Happy All Saints.

_____

_____

_____

_____

October 31
"Happy Reformation Day!"

October 31 is often identified with "ghoulish costumes" and children saying, "Trick or treat." However, the date is also referred to as Reformation Day. It is significant to all Christians, particularly those who identify as Protestants. Although Martin Luther isn't considered the Father of all Protestants, his championed principles remain essential doctrines. These include Salvation, not by works, but by faith; the priesthood of all believers; the primacy of Scripture; worship in the people's language; and more.

Faith Bytes

On October 31, 1517, Luther posted his 95 Theses on the door of the Castle Church in Wittenberg, Germany. Although the document addressed many concerns, perhaps the most significant was the belief that salvation is from God and is not based on works or absolution from the church.

Wesley speaks of having his "heart strangely warmed" as he heard the preface to Luther's Commentary on Romans being read as he attended a Bible Study on Aldersgate Street in London. The Songbooks of most denominations include hymns written by Luther, including "A Mighty Fortress Is Our God" and "Out of the Depths I Cry to You."

On my desk, I have a copy of Luther's Sacristy Prayer. I refer to it throughout the day, particularly on Sunday before preaching. It reads:

> **"Lord God,**
>
> **You have appointed me as a pastor in Your Church, but you see how unsuited I am to meet so great and difficult a task. If I had lacked Your help, I would have ruined everything long ago. Therefore, I call upon You: I wish to devote my mouth and my heart to you; I shall teach the people. I myself will learn and ponder diligently upon Your Word. Use me as Your instrument -- but do not forsake me, for if ever I should be on my own, I would easily wreck it all."**

Perhaps you can surprise someone by saying, "Happy Reformation Day!" Yes, you will receive some odd looks, but you may have the opportunity to tell a remarkable story.

_____
_____
_____
_____

NOVEMBER

November 1
For All the Saints

Some hymns are best when accompanied by a pipe organ or an orchestra. Others find their full potential when a congregation blends voices acapella. Rare is the anthem that finds beauty in either. One such anthem is "For All the Saints." Written as a processional hymn for All Saints Sunday, its author, a young Anglican priest, William Walsham How, was known for his kind heart, untiring energy, and genuine interest in the spiritual and physical needs of those in his care. When he became a bishop, he served the slum section of East London. He turned down several appointments to more prestigious bishoprics, choosing to help the people in this ignored area rise above their hopeless and appalling conditions. He stated his only consideration was how much he could make his life count. His mission statement, "Feed with the Word, feed with the Life," was engraved on his pastoral staff. His final sermon was titled "The Ideal Clergyman, The Ideal Layman." The homily began by stating that the first test of a layman, "Is he the sort of [person] I would like to send for to visit me on my deathbed?"

The hymn "For All the Saints" originally had eleven stanzas structured by the Apostles Creed. Whether accompanied by musical instruments or acapella, Bishop How's lyrics stir the heart as we pause to remember those who rest from their labors.

> *For all the saints, who from their labors rest,*
> *who thee by faith before the world confessed,*
> *thy name, O Jesus, be forever blest. Alleluia, Alleluia!*
>
> *O blest communion, fellowship divine!*
> *We feebly struggle, they in glory shine;*
> *yet all are one in thee, for all are thine. Alleluia, Alleluia!*

Faith Bytes

November 2
Vote With as Much Devotion as You Pray

I have never been afraid to discuss politics. In private conversations, I will share my opinions and address why I felt compelled to vote a certain way. I generally vote for the person; when uncertain, I base my decision on the platform.

I agree with Charles Spurgeon, [who, although a Baptist, was considered a political liberal]. He stated, "We are now called upon to exercise one of the privileges and duties which go with liberty, let no [person] be neglectful in it. Every God-fearing [individual] should give [their] vote with as much devotion as he prays."

We all face the great temptation during a hotly contested election to vilify those who disagree with us. John Wesley was concerned about such behavior in the 18th century. In his journal entry dated October 6, 1774, Wesley reported meeting with members of the Methodist Societies who would be voting in an ensuing election. He was never one to avoid addressing a sensitive topic and offered his advice. He encouraged them:

1. To vote, without fee or reward, for the person they judged most worthy:
2. To speak no evil of the person they voted against:
3. And, to take care, their spirits were not sharpened against those that voted on the other side.

This remains good advice for each of us. If you haven't voted, I hope you will do so.

_____

_____

_____

November 3
The President Who Asked For Grace

Those who have served as President have always intrigued me. In particular, I have tried to look behind some of the decisions that defined their presidency and learn how their faith may have guided their choices. Many of these Americans offered prayers that have been entered into the public record. George Washington was such a person. He left a prayer journal containing a treasure trove of inspiration. The following is one such prayer.

> "Almighty God... I yield thee humble and hearty thanks that thou has preserved me from the danger of the night past and brought me to the light of the day, and the comforts thereof, a day which is consecrated to thine own service and for thine own honor. Let my heart, therefore, Gracious God, be so affected with the glory and majesty of it, that I may not do mine own works,

but wait on thee, and discharge those weighty duties thou requirest of me. Give me grace to hear thee calling on me in thy word, that it may be wisdom, righteousness, reconciliation, and peace to the saving of the soul in the day of the Lord Jesus. Grant that I may hear it with reverence, receive it with meekness, mingle it with faith, and that it may accomplish in me, Gracious God, the good work for which thou has sent it. Bless my family, kindred, friends, and country, be our God and guide this day and forever for His sake, who lay down in the Grave and arose again for us, Jesus Christ our Lord. Amen." [Keefauver, Larry. Prayers of the Presidents]

November 4
The Deist Who Asked God's Blessing

The third President of the United States, Thomas Jefferson, was recognized as a deist. A deist believes in a God who does not interact with humans. Jefferson wrote his version of the New Testament, which deleted all references to the miraculous. If this was his belief, the following prayer offered for the nation on March 4, 1805, is miraculous.

"Almighty God, Who has given us this good land for our heritage; We humbly beseech Thee that we may always prove ourselves a people mindful of Thy favor and glad to do Thy will. Bless our land with honorable ministry, sound learning, and pure manners. Save us from violence, discord, and confusion, from pride and arrogance, and from every evil way. Defend our liberties, and fashion into one united people, the multitude brought hither out of many kindreds and tongues. Endow with Thy spirit of wisdom those whom in Thy name we entrust the authority of government, that there may be justice and peace at home, and that through obedience to Thy law, we may show forth Thy praise among the nations of the earth. In time of prosperity fill our hearts with thankfulness, and in the day of trouble, suffer not our trust in Thee to fail; all of which we ask through Jesus Christ, our Lord. Amen."

– *Washington D.C., March 4, 1801* [newoxfordbible.wordpress.com/prayers-of-the-presidents/]

Faith Bytes

November 5
The President Who Led Family Prayer

It has been stated that our nineteenth President, Rutherford B. Hayes, brought dignity and honesty to the presidency. His wife, Lucy, was instrumental in this endeavor. As a young girl, she accompanied her father to Lexington, Kentucky, to free 15-20 slaves he had inherited from his aunt. She was the first first lady with a college degree. She startled a nation by hosting African American musicians in the White House to perform. She was often called "Lemonade Lucy" because she banned liquor and wine from the White House. She also brought morning prayer to the White House staff. She invited cabinet members and congressmen to join her and the President for hymn singing on Sunday evenings. Each morning, President and Mrs. Hayes would gather with their family as the President offered this brief but sincere prayer:

> "O Lord, our Heavenly Father, who has safely brought us to the beginning of this day, defend us in the same with Thy Almighty power. Grant that we may not fall into any danger and keep us from evil. May all our doings be ordered by Thy governance so that all we do may be righteous in Thy sight. Amen."

[Keefauver, Larry. Prayers of the Presidents]

_____
_____
_____
_____

November 6
The President Who Led the Nation in Prayer

Franklin D. Roosevelt was our thirty-second President who led our country through the turbulent years of the Second World War. On June 6, 1944, also known as D-Day, President Roosevelt led the American people in a prayer of almost 550 words through the radio. This is part of that prayer.

> "Almighty God: Our sons, pride of our nation, this day have set upon a mighty endeavor, a struggle to preserve our Republic, our religion and our civilization, and to set free a suffering humanity… Lead them straight and true; give strength to their arms, stoutness to their hearts, steadfastness in their faith. They will need Thy blessings. Their road will be long and hard. For the enemy is strong…."

> "Embrace these, Father, and receive them, Thy heroic servants, into Thy kingdom. And for us at home…help us, Almighty God, to rededicate ourselves in renewed faith in Thee in this hour of great sacrifice…With Thy blessing, we shall prevail over the unholy forces of our enemy. Help us to conquer the

apostles of greed and racial arrogances. Lead us to the saving of our country and with our sister nations into a world unity that will spell a sure peace—a peace invulnerable to the schemings of unworthy men. And a peace that will let all men live in freedom, reaping the just rewards of their honest toil."

November 7
My First Act as President is a Prayer.

During his Inaugural Address on January 20, 1989, the forty-third President of the United States, George W. Bush, stated: "My first act as President is a prayer. I ask you to bow your heads." He then offered this prayer:

"Heavenly Father, we bow our heads and thank You for Your love. Accept our thanks for the peace that yields this day and the shared faith that makes its continuance likely. Make us strong to do Your work, willing to heed and hear Your will, and write on our hearts these words: 'Use power to help people.' For we are given power not to advance our own purposes, nor to make a great show in the world, nor a name. There is but one just use of power, and it is to serve people. Help us to remember it, Lord. The Lord our God be with us, as He was with our fathers; may He not leave us or forsake us; so that He may incline our hearts to Him, to walk in all His ways… that all peoples of the earth may know that the Lord is God; there is no other."

November 8
A Masterpiece!

Joseph F. Girzone wrote an excellent book titled "Joshua." Its popularity led to several other books. The series' central theme is to answer the question, "What would Jesus be like if he lived in our modern world?" Joshua and Jesus come from the same Hebrew word, so Joshua is Jesus in this story.

In one episode in the original book, a wealthy man watches Joshua. He is amazed at his simple lifestyle and lack of concern about money and possessions. Finally, the rich man named Aaron asks Joshua how he became

Faith Bytes

the way he was and believes the way he did. Thoughtfully and with genuine kindness, Joshua explained it to Aaron. He said: "Each person looks at life through a different vision. Three men can look at a tree. One man will see so many board feet of valuable lumber worth so much money. The second man will see it as so much firewood to be burned to keep his family warm in the winter. The third man will see it as a masterpiece of God's creative art, given to man as an expression of God's love and enduring strength, with a value far beyond its worth in money or firewood. What we live for determines what we see in life and gives a clear focus to our inner vision."

What is the vision you have of yourself? How about your neighbor? Do we measure value based on bank accounts or what someone brings to society? We tend to measure a life's worth (our own or another) based on such things. When we do so, we miss the masterpieces God has created in us and around us. A Masterpiece! This is how God sees you and, lest we forget, how God sees those we tend to deem less than lovable. No one is beyond the love of God.

Throughout the day, consider this question, "Is there anything you or someone else has ever done that will prevent Jesus from entering the home of our hearts if we invite him?"

_____

_____

_____

_____

November 9
Worship: Overtures of Love

Several years ago, I attended a worship service at the St. James Armenian Church in Jerusalem. It was constructed in the 12th Century. When I entered the ornate sanctuary, I was taken by all the incense burners, candles, and beautiful chants sung by the choir of priests. Having been exposed to 800 years of rising smoke, the murals on the walls and ceiling were covered in layers of black soot. What I remember about the worship, besides the fact it lasted three hours, was how the priests did everything that happened. This included the reading of scripture, the prayers, hymns, lighting candles—everything. A rope was around the chancel area separating the priests from those who attended. Congregants would enter a pewless corridor, gaze upon the scene briefly as if it were a driveby nativity scene, drop a few coins into an offering box, perhaps cross themselves, and leave. Although it was likely unintentional, what was being conveyed was worship is a spectator event and not intended for participation.

What is worship? I have yet to find a better explanation than Richard Foster's in his book "Celebration of Discipline." He described worship as "our responding to the overtures of love from the heart of the Father." Isn't that a beautiful image? Don't you find it—I can't think of a better way to express it—rather, romantic?

Steven B. Angus

Contemplate the fact that God is making overtures of love to us. Do you remember what it feels like to have someone declare their love for you? There is nothing like it! In those moments, we may smile or even laugh. We may have the urge to sing or dance. Sometimes, all we can do is to sit quietly and soak it in.

Worship isn't the overtures of love. Worship is our response to this love. Worship is realizing that God loves us so much that we have no alternative but to answer. God's overture is like the courting calls of a love bird that waits for its' mate to respond to its advances. Returning the call is our worship. We are compelled to answer. Does this understanding of worship cause you to appreciate these words from the Psalms?

> *"As the deer longs for streams of water, so I long for you, O God. I thirst for God, the living God."* [Psalm 42:1-2a, NLT]

November 10
Dr. Livingstone, I Presume?

David Livingstone has been described as Mother Teresa, Neil Armstrong, and Abraham Lincoln rolled into one. However, he may have spent his life working fourteen hours a day in a cotton mill had he not heard an appeal for medical missionaries to China. Soon after committing to China, the door suddenly closed because of the Opium War. Then he heard about the unexplored continent of Africa and felt the call to open "God's Highway" to these unreached peoples.

Eventually, Livingstone wanted to demonstrate the connection of Africa to the Bible and began searching for the source of the Nile River. Five years passed with scarcely a word, followed by two without any. This would have been the end of the story had it not been for a young American journalist whose pen name was Henry Morton Stanley. Stanley embarked on a seven-month, seven-hundred-mile journey to find the man or his remains. Enduring smallpox, savage lions, the spears of natives, and hungry cannibals. Then, on November 10, 1871, Stanley extended his hand to a sickly physician and asked the legendary question, "Dr. Livingstone, I presume?" The two remained together for five months. Livingstone refused to return home with Stanley and continued his work. Within a year and a half, he died in a mud hut, kneeling beside his cot in prayer.

When Livingston's remains arrived in England, they were greeted by a hero's 21-gun salute. His Westminster Abbey tombstone reads: "For 30 years, his life was spent in an unwearied effort to evangelize the native races, to explore the undiscovered secrets, and to abolish the slave trade."

Faith Bytes

Livingston described his life this way: "[I am] serving Christ when shooting a buffalo for my men or taking an observation, [even if some] will consider it not sufficiently or even at all missionary."

_____
_____
_____

November 11
Psalm 91

It has become an American custom that the observance of a holiday occurs on a Monday to ensure we can enjoy a three-day weekend. Veterans Day is not one of those occasions. Veterans Day, formerly known as Armistice Day, was set to honor the end of World War I [WWI], which officially occurred on the eleventh hour of the eleventh day of the eleventh month, in other words, November 11, 1918.

In 1938, it became a legal holiday honoring World War I veterans. In 1954, the term Armistice was replaced with Veterans to honor primarily living American veterans who have served honorably in times of war and peace. The distinction between Memorial and Veterans Day is that the latter honors those deceased veterans, and today, it expresses gratitude primarily for the living.

Sometime today, pause and read Psalm 91. It is often referred to as the Soldiers Psalm. It is said that soldiers in WWI recited this psalm daily. The classic story reports that the general of the 91st Brigade gave his troops a small card with Psalm 91 printed on it. He asked, and they agreed to recite it daily. The story goes that after they began praying this prayer, they were involved in three of the bloodiest battles in WWI without any casualties. In contrast, other brigades suffered losses of as much as ninety percent.

True or not, the story demonstrates the mystique of Psalm 91. It has been printed on the bandanas of those undergoing surgery and engraved onto military dog tags. As was the case of our son, who served in Iraq, sewn into flak jackets. The psalm is identified as a prayer of protection offered by those who place their trust in God. In a sense, we are all Veterans encountering personal battles. Before we enter the trenches, let us call upon the one who is our refuge and strength.

_____
_____
_____

Steven B. Angus

November 12
Time Spent For Some Good Purpose

The renowned preacher Charles Spurgeon had a personal library of 12,000 volumes. Although my library pales by comparison, it contains books I cherish. Tucked away in my forest of bookshelves is a six-volume set of commentaries that I open maybe once every four or five years. However, it isn't for research purposes but to read the inscription. It states, "Presented to Steven Angus by the Lydia Sunday School Class, 1973." I value them because of the precious ones who thought enough of me to give me my first set of commentaries, "The Matthew Henry Bible Commentary." This was my only set of commentaries for many years, seen by the tattered binding.

On this day in 1704, the forty-two-year-old Henry recorded his intention to prepare a commentary on the entire Scripture in his journal. A couple days later, he adds, "I set about it, that I may endeavor something and spend my time to some good purpose and let the Lord make what use he pleaseth of me." He had completed most of the project when he died ten years later at forty-two. It would be the standard for over 300 years.

John Wesley quoted Henry in his "Notes on the Bible." Charles Wesley had the set in his personal library and consulted it as he wrote his hymns. The lyrics of "A Charge to Keep Have I" are taken verbatim from Henry's commentary. When George Whitefield was short of time for sermon preparation, he would kneel on the floor with Henry's commentary and outline his sermon.

I wonder, what is God prompting you to begin? It is only too late to start, well, when it is too late.

_____

_____

_____

_____

November 13
I Commend to You, Our Sister

An NPR article stated that when Vice President Kamala Harris delivered her victory speech to the nation, she spoke directly to a specific slice of the population when she said, "Every little girl watching tonight sees that this is a country of possibilities."

It was a momentous occasion for our nation as it acknowledged that gender should never disqualify someone from pursuing their goals nor our acceptance of them. We would be wise to recognize this does not instantly make things as they should be. Just as electing an African-American president did not suddenly end racial bias, selecting a woman as Vice President will not automatically eliminate sexism. However, it is a start. As Christians, we can reclaim leadership in promoting society's need for the talents of women.

The Letter to the Romans may be the most essential book in the New Testament. John Wesley, Karl Barth, and Martin Luther are a few whose lives were transformed by reading Romans. In his commentary, Martin Luther identified it as "the purest gospel."

Realizing the significance of his message, Paul would not have placed it in the hands of just anyone. In concluding his letter, Paul ended with a personal note and mentioned twenty-nine people by name. He sent greetings to twenty-eight of them while commending one. To commend someone is to vouch for their character and ability. Paul throws the weight of his personal endorsement to this individual, stating, "I commend to you our sister Phoebe, a deacon in the church." He placed this labor of love into the hands of the person he felt most qualified to deliver it safely to the church.

I hope those who are girls and boys today will reflect and say, "My church taught me values that transcend gender or race."

_____

_____

_____

November 14
The Fighting. . . ?

In the South, the second Saturday in November [not to mention every Saturday in the fall] can mean only one thing: It's football time. Allow me to tell you about eleven young men who decided to field a football team for their small college. Coincidentally, it was also the second Saturday in November. However, the year was 1888. The mascot chosen to identify these gallant collegiates was "the Methodist." If fans were feeling feisty, they were "the fighting Methodist." The name must have been inspired by the school's first president, the eldest of twelve children, six of whom became Methodist ministers. The team may never have run onto the field had it not been for the leadership of quarterback Arthur Carroll, who enticed his teammates by volunteering to make the pants for each player. Carroll later became a tailor. The team won 16-0 and ended the season with a perfect record of 2 and 0. From 1888 until 1910, the Methodists amassed sixty wins, twenty-six losses, and eleven ties. That is not bad for a team primarily led by player-coaches.

1911 brought change for the school as a new Athletic director replaced football with Rugby and suggested a new mascot to reflect the school's new direction. And, after all, being called "Methodist" didn't intimidate an opponent. By 1914, football returned with a fresh identity. They were now the University of Southern California Trojans.

Steven B. Angus

As I reflect on these gridiron Methodists, I find similarities with today's church, such as our reliance on player-coaches who share their unique talents and being told we do not intimidate, which is code for irrelevant. Despite or because of these qualities, we courageously enter the field and offer our best to Jesus. Give me an M! Give me an E! Give me a T! Give me an…..

_____

_____

_____

_____

November 15
Pandemic

I have a library with resources on just about any topic you could imagine. I have listened to innumerable hours of lectures. Before 2020, I am confident the word pandemic did not appear in a book title, nor was it listed in a seminary course syllabus. Whatever our profession, nothing prepared us for what we experienced during the COVID years. I vividly recall kicking back in my recliner for a nap, hoping I would awaken as a modern Rip Van Winkle to a pandemic-free world. As much as we longed for the epidemic to pass, life would never return to how it had been.

I may have unfairly characterized my previous education as inadequate for what we endured. If I have, that was not my intent. My training, all that I have experienced, the good and the unpleasant, enables me to state firmly—that Jesus is still Lord. Life has taught me that the Bible is the word of God because it continues to speak God's truth into our circumstances, whatever they may be. Shortly after our country received the "all clear" announcement, something occurred that made the pandemic appear like a blip on the radar for me. My wife at the time died. Again, I longed to be Rip Van Winkle and would awake from my nightmare. Following her death, some days, I felt as if I would live out my life trapped in Egypt or destined to an endless loop of wilderness wandering. In time, God helped me to see what could be. God demonstrated his care by bringing to me the precise people I needed. The chief among these is Cheri, the woman who is now my wife. As widowed people, we have joined hands and trust God to lead us into a new land.

As I have tried to listen for God's guidance, I have continually returned to the story of the wandering, recently liberated Israelites of Exodus. For 430 years, they were accustomed to living a certain way. Once on the Red Sea's opposite shore, they were enamored with looking back and could not move forward.

During the following days, I want us to join Moses and the Israelites in the Wilderness and identify some lessons they discovered that can encourage us. But for today, ponder this question—Am I looking back to the determent of seeing God's future?

_____

Faith Bytes

November 16
Back to School

Late on a Friday afternoon, a young man applied for a job at a logging company. The foreman asked him if he could bring down a tree with an axe. The fellow walked over to a tree without saying a word and began chopping like an old pro. Soon, he yelled, "Timber." The foreman told him to be back on Monday morning.

On his first day on the job, the young man outdid everyone else on the crew. But, as the week progressed, he got slower and slower until Friday, he struggled to bring down just one tree. He went through all the motions, swinging his ax, hitting the tree, and repeating it, but it didn't work well. Exhausted, he laid down his axe and sat on a log, shaking his head in confusion. The foreman came over and began to talk to the novice lumberjack. He said, "I believe I know what the problem is." The young man's demeanor became hopeful as the experienced foreman said, "You have been so busy all week doing the things that a logger does that you forgot one of the basics of the trade. You failed to sharpen your axe, which has become dull and worthless because it has not been kept in good condition."

Sometimes, we are so busy as individuals and possibly as a church that we have forgotten to take care of the basics and struggle in our walk with Jesus. Like the young man and his axe, we do not need new equipment or even to necessarily work harder. What many of us need is a refresher course on how to keep our axe sharp. Moses spent forty years in the wilderness before he returned to Egypt to confront Pharoah. He needed this time in God's classroom to prepare him for the journey to the Promised Land. What lesson is God teaching you for your faith to be sharp?

_____

_____

_____

_____

November 17
When God says, Woe

The photographer says, "Don't move. Be perfectly still." Instantly, we develop an itch in our ear that needs to be scratched. "Hold it. Smile and look natural." Thankfully, the photo opp lasts only a few minutes unless we have a toddler with no concept of smiling or being still on-demand. Is our aversion to stillness an American thing? We tend to equate movement with progress and progress with value. Therefore, if we aren't moving, our personal worth is diminished.

For 430 years, the only motion the Israelites experienced was the bidding of their Egyptian masters. Now, they can move away from their former life for the first time. The march out of slavery must have seemed easy until they ran smack into the Red Sea. Like the trail boss leading the old western wagon train, the call "Woe" echoes down the procession, and forward progress grinds to a halt. Soon,

Steven B. Angus

they realize that the cloud of dust to the rear isn't of their own making. It is the entire Egyptian army. It would be futile for the Hebrews to circle the wagons.

Have you considered how "pandemonium" sounds like "pandemic?" Moses assumes command, instructing them to do three things humans struggle to accomplish. He said, "Don't be afraid. Just stand still and watch the Lord rescue you today."

This is the reoccurring lesson God would strive to teach his wilderness wandering, woe is me, whining children—which brings us to today. God wants us to see what God is doing. He will halt our movement one way or another, so we have no choice but to observe it. Instead of resisting the stillness, we should take the opportunity to see what God is doing. What do you detect God doing around you?

_____

_____

_____

_____

November 18
When Words Fail

Some days, when I am alone with Jesus, finding words can be difficult. I am uncertain what to say or feel, so I am sharing thoughts I spoke previously. On those occasions, I try to be still and listen—listen to the ideas that pass my mind, the sounds surrounding me, the birds, my dogs playing, the silence. Words seem to be a distraction that gets in the way.

Moses must have felt this way. I doubt any human, even someone like Moses, could continuously experience the adrenaline rush, which is sometimes God's presence. In Exodus 15, Moses and the liberated Jewish slaves are safely on the Red Sea's opposite shore. God had parted the waters, allowing them to cross on dry land. When they looked back upon their pursuers, they witnessed God's fantastic and frightening power as their former captors were destroyed in one swipe of the Almighty's hand. Now, safely on the quiet side of God's redeeming action, what could a mortal say? Yesterday had passed, and tomorrow? Tomorrow was the inauguration of the wilderness.

Maya Angelou titled her autobiography "I Know Why the Caged Bird Sings." Facing the daunting wilderness, all Moses and the Israelites could do was sing. The opening lyrics of their song declared, "I will sing to the Lord, for he has triumphed gloriously." [Exodus 15:1] The newly formed Gospel group, "Moses and the Harmonizing Hebrews," sang to God about his glory. The lyrics were,

> "The Lord is my strength and song, And He has become my salvation; He is my God, and I will praise Him; My father's God, and I will exalt Him." [Exodus 15:2]

Faith Bytes

When I need to speak to God and struggle to formulate my thoughts, all I know to do is sing. Here is a lesson for wilderness living: when words fail, Sing. Sing to Jesus.

___

November 19
Streams of Bitterness

"Lions, and tigers, and bears, o my!" This familiar cadence reminds us of Dorothy and her entourage traveling through a wilderness filled with an assortment of visible perils. They, however, are about to discover that the most dangerous foes are the invisible ones within.

God heard the plea of the Israelite slaves for deliverance. God led them out of Egypt and through the Red Sea. Moses led them in a hymn featuring original works by the former Prince of Egypt and his sister Miriam. Then, it was time to enter the wilderness. After traveling for three days, they camped by a water spring. Someone sampled it, and word spread that the water was bitter and unfit to drink. They express their frustration to Moses about their dissatisfaction with God. God instructed Moses to toss a piece of wood into the spring, transforming the bitterness into sweetness.

At this point, God says what we expect God to say, such as "Remember I delivered you" and "Keep my commandments." However, in the end, God includes a statement that seems odd for the present circumstances. He says, "For I am the Lord who heals you." [Exodus 15:26] Healing? The issue is water, isn't it?

Just as the travelers to Oz were confronted with personal unseen demons while in the wilderness, so it was with the Israelites. So, it is with us. How long does it take to overcome 430 years of painful bondage? God saw a need for healing, which the Israelites did not know they had.

When spending time in the wilderness, we discover places within ourselves we did not know existed. We may encounter streams of bitterness in the form of sin, self-centeredness, and injury. The good news is Jesus speaks sweetness into this bitterness, saying, "I am the Lord who heals you."

November 20
Who Has the Remote Control?

How many *"teleautomatons"* do you have? This was the name Nikola Tesla gave the invention he used to maneuver a miniature boat in 1898 at Madison Square Garden. Financially, Tesla's remote-controlled boat was a flop. However, his creation is considered one of the ten most significant inventions ever.

The remote control. Have you considered how many uses we have for it? We use them to control everything from garage doors to automobiles. We use our smartphones to operate our HVAC system's thermostat and adjust the house lights while on vacation. As I stare at the CTRL key on my laptop, I realize the remote has become our version of Peanut's character, Linus's comfy blanket. Control, conveniently nestled in the palm of our hand.

Leaders, even the best ones like Moses, have trouble relinquishing it. During a visit, Moses' father-in-law observed him attempting to do everything to the point of exhaustion and the determent of the people. As fathers-in-law are prone to do, he offered his unsolicited advice. He suggested Moses teach the people God's instructions and train leaders. Jethro summarized: "If you follow this advice, and if God commands you to do so, then you will be able to endure the pressures, and all these people will go home in peace." [Exodus 18:23, NLT]

Did you zoom in on the last part of Jethro's statement, "Do this, and you will endure the pressures, and the people will know peace?" Which meant peace for Moses as well. Great advice! However, the first one-third of his statement is the most crucial part. "If God commands you to do so." Until we release control to God first, the other is unlikely. The wilderness demands us to ask: Who has the remote control of my life?

_____

_____

_____

_____

November 21
Finding the Sweet Spot

If you played baseball or softball, you likely understand the meaning of the phrase "the sweet spot." Once experienced, it becomes the ballplayer's quest to achieve it again. The sweet spot is the precise moment when the ball, bat, and swing align perfectly. Nothing is so pleasant as when a five-ounce sphere becomes a submissive projectile.

The sweet spot is what we hope for in our homes, at work, the church, and even our politics. Most of all, we want to be in that place with God. However, we soon realize it's not always easy, which explains why we hope for it. We forget there can be a fine line between casual familiarity and respect. Recently, I read two

Faith Bytes

articles. One stated too much familiarity can lead to a breakdown in a relationship. The second said the opposite: familiarity builds trust. The sweet spot with God combines familiarity and respect, giving birth to intimacy.

As the Israelites wandered in the wilderness, they arrived at Mt. Sinai. Following a visit with God, Moses informed the people they would have a meeting with God in three days. They needed this time to become familiar with God. However, the people were expected to get ready. Moses consecrated them, and then they washed all their clothes. Meeting God wasn't to be taken casually. When the day arrived, thunder and lightning rattled the mountain, followed by a trumpet blast so loud the people trembled. Then Moses led the people to the foot of Sinai to meet God.

Wilderness living seeks the sweet spot, where God is the Father in whose arms we find rest, yet is so awesome we approach him respectfully.

_____
_____
_____
_____

November 22
A Wooden Peg

I have the browser on my computer opened to worldometer.info. It contains information about what is occurring on planet Earth in real-time. Included is a counter recording the growth of the world's population. The numbers are ticking so frenzied that I cannot mentally count. When I click on a hyperlink, I am taken to a page of miniature humans, as others are added to represent births. This occurs at such a rate I might assume someone is holding down a character on the keyboard. During two minutes, the world's population grew by 314 people, 2.5 individuals per second. Watching, I became mentally overwhelmed and understood the Psalmist's query, "What are human beings that you think about them?" [Psalm 8:4 CEB]

The question isn't farfetched when we are in the wilderness. We can understand the Israelites thought process: "God may have seen our misery in Egypt, but he has certainly lost sight of us in this wilderness." Responding, God instructed Moses to build a portable house of worship called the Tabernacle. God was specific about the details. Listen for the significance intended for every weary wilderness wander. "There will be two bases under the first board for its two pegs, two bases under the next board for its two pegs, and so on." [Exodus 26:18-19 CEB]

Did you hear it? God is mindful of the most minuscule detail of His work, even a wooden peg. When we feel like a wooden peg, we can rest assured that God is mindful of us. Remember, without the peg, the building would collapse.

_____
_____

Steven B. Angus

November 23
Relationships Are Like Socks

If you want to know what a relationship with God can be, read Exodus 33:12-23. Relationships like socks come in a variety of assortments. We have a relationship with our elected officials, although we have never visited their homes. We have a relationship with the CFO who signs our check, but her children's names are a mystery. However, we are prepared to hear embarrassing reports when asking after a parent. For most of us, our relationship with Jesus tends to fall between the extremes. And if we are brutally honest, we may be content with this arrangement as long as the checks keep coming.

Although we must be careful not to treat God as if he is one of our golfing buddies, God created us for intimacy with him. God knew all there was to know about Moses and said to him, "I will personally go with you, Moses. I will give you rest." [33:14, NLT]

Granted, Moses was at a disadvantage and recognized his limitations. He said to God: "You have told me, 'I know you by name, and I look favorably on you.' If it is true that you look favorably on me, let me know your ways, so I may understand you more fully and continue to enjoy your favor." [33:12b-13a, NLT]

Moses' phrase, "So I may understand you more fully," speaks volumes. The takeaway for Moses was—there is always more to know. He did not bother asking to know God absolutely. This would have been ridiculous. However, Moses understood he could learn more because of his time with God. Because of his wise use of time in the wilderness, he recognized God's eagerness to teach him. How much do you wish to know about God? Ask.

_____

_____

_____

_____

November 24
Let Go of My Cookie!

An essential part of being thankful is remembrance. In Deuteronomy 8:11, Moses told the Israelites, "Take care that you do not forget the Lord your God." [NRSVUA] He then lists things God had done for them [8:12-16]. And concludes: "Do not say to yourself, 'My power and the might of my own hand have gotten me this wealth.' But remember the Lord your God." [8:17-18]

After a tiring morning of shopping at the local mall, a woman felt she needed a break. She bought a bag of cookies and put them in her shopping bag. She then purchased a cup of coffee and found a place to sit at one of the crowded tables. Taking the lid off her coffee, she took out a magazine and began to sip her beverage and read. Across the table was a man reading a newspaper. After a few minutes, she reached out and took a cookie. As she did, the man also

Faith Bytes

reached out and took one. This put her off, but she did not say anything. A few moments later, she took another cookie. Once again, the man did also. Now, she was dismayed, but she still did not say anything. After a couple of sips of coffee, she again took another cookie. So did the man. This upset her, especially since now only one cookie was left. Apparently, the man also recognized the dilemma. Before she could say anything, he took it, broke it in half, offered half to her, and proceeded to eat the other half himself. Then he smiled at her and, putting the paper under his arm, rose and walked off. She was steamed as her coffee break had been ruined. She was already thinking about how she would tell this offense to her family. She folded her magazine, opened her shopping bag, and discovered her own unopened bag of cookies.

When it comes to our blessings, do we treat God this way? Moses said, "Remember the Lord your God." He is the source of all good gifts.

_____

_____

_____

_____

November 25
A Tenderized Heart

Most likely, you have begun making plans for your Thanksgiving feast. The clock is ticking regardless of the number of place settings at the table. The gobbler must be thawed and cooked according to weight. However, everyone knows the secret to a moist, savory bird is proper attention to the rubbing and tenderizing process.

When I was young, I was often told I was too tenderhearted. I soon believed this was a character flaw, and because of it, I was soft. So, I set about proving that I was tough and could dish out hurt with the best of the bad boys. Thankfully, I abandoned this roughhousing and chose something unhealthy and more dangerous. I learned to hide my feelings to the detriment of being able to share them. At least I wasn't being called tenderhearted. This became my wilderness.

I have learned that God appreciates a tender heart towards him and others. God's great tenderizer is the Holy Spirit, who targets the throne room of the human spirit—the heart. Notice the common thread in these phrases from Exodus 35 and 36:

> 21 Everyone whose heart was stirred, and everyone whose spirit was willing...brought the Lord's offering
> 22 all who were of a willing heart brought. . . an offering of gold to the Lord.
> 26 all the women whose hearts [were] moved. . . used their skill [and] spun the goats' hair.
> 29 [Those] whose hearts made them willing to bring anything for the work that the Lord had commanded [did so]
> 36:2 Moses then called....every skillful one to whom the Lord had given skill, everyone whose heart was stirred to come to do the work.

Steven B. Angus

As you smell the savory aroma of the turkey cooking, invite the Holy Spirit to tenderize your heart to God.

_____
_____
_____
_____

November 26
The Lord Has. . .

Moses had his hands full. Those grumbling Israelites never seemed to appreciate what God had done for them. As Moses tried to guide them safely through the wilderness, he used every opportunity to help them stop complaining and to "Praise God from whom all blessings flow." In Exodus 35-36, Moses presented to the people Bezalel and Oholiab as project managers for designing and constructing the interior of the Tabernacle. Listen to how Moses introduced them and how he repeated one phrase five times.

Moses said:

> "The Lord has specifically chosen." [35:30]
> "The Lord has filled them with the Spirit of God" [35:31]
> "The Lord has given both... the ability to teach their skill to others." [35:34]
> "The Lord has given them special skills as engravers." [35:35]
> "The Lord has gifted them with wisdom and ability." [36:1] [NLT]

In each incident, Moses said: "The Lord has." It was a lesson the wilderness wanders needed.

As we sit down to our Thanksgiving meal, it is a time to reflect upon the countless ways God has blessed us. Some will pause and allow a moment to name specific blessings for which they are thankful. Perhaps Moses can assist us as we invite each to complete this sentence: "The Lord has. . ."

_____
_____
_____
_____

Faith Bytes

November 27
Stoke the Fire

Have you noticed how the wilderness can be chilly? This is true of houses as well. I recall living in a charming home with a lot of character. Of course, we know "charming" and "character" are code words for "it had issues." Not only was it drafty, but its only heat source was a wood stove. But the real kicker was it was a frigid winter. I quickly learned the necessity of getting up two or three times during the night to keep the fire going if I hoped to avoid frostbite when my toes touched the floor at daybreak. Needless to say, my stay in this dwelling was brief.

As Moses led the people through the wilderness, fire was crucial. It represented God's presence among the people. There had been the fire in the bush that was not consumed from which God spoke to Moses. God also provided a pillar of fire that guided the Israelites at night. When it came time for Moses to teach the people how God expected to be worshipped, it included fire. A fire was to be maintained on an altar at all times. When Moses shared this with the people in Leviticus 6, he implored the people three times, "The fire on the altar shall be kept burning." This wasn't an easy task. The embers would need stirring, wood added, and the ashes that represented past sins had to be removed. Each was necessary to keep the fire of God's presence burning.

As we journey through our wilderness, we must not forget that God has an altar today. No, not in the church building. It is our heart. Although God's grace never burns out, our inattention can allow the embers to lose their glow. When this occurs, life can become deathly cold. What must you do to stoke the fire of God in you?

_____
_____
_____
_____

November 28
Happy New Year!

Happy New Year? Perhaps I should explain. I grew up in a church tradition that did not include words such as Advent or Lent. It was assumed since these words were not in the Bible, they had no significance for us. Although Christmas was acknowledged, it was clearly stated, "We don't know when Jesus was born." And it is true we don't know; nevertheless, many church traditions have recognized the richness these seasonal tools can offer our faith. On the other hand, those of us who grew up with this vocabulary may not be clear about their meaning. Think of this information as a tool, such as a Sunday School quarterly, provided by the church to help us experience God's love.

We order our lives by a secular calendar, but did you realize the church has its own? The secular calendar identifies January 1st as New Year's Day. For centuries, the Christian New Year occurred on the first Sunday in the Season of

Steven B. Angus

Advent. This day isn't a set date but is always the Sunday between November 27th and December 3rd. It is easier to consider it the fourth Sunday before Christmas Eve. This means the Christian New Year is upon us! If you want to confuse your non-liturgical friends, greet them with a "Happy New Year!"

Advent comes from a Latin phrase that means arrival, coming, or comings. It is a time of preparation that looks forward to Christmas but also, and this is important, the Second Coming of Christ. When Advent was first observed, the emphasis wasn't on Christmas but on the Second Coming of Jesus. In many churches, the first two Sundays in Advent tend to focus on Jesus' second coming. The last two Sundays emphasize how the Jewish people looked for the arrival of a Messiah and how Jesus is that Messiah. The goal is to remember to be on the lookout for all the ways Jesus comes to us. The question that always accompanies Advent is, Are you looking for Jesus?

_____

_____

_____

_____

November 29
Ready or Not

I can still hear my cousin Terry as he counted, "97, 98, 99, 100." Then he called out in a loud voice, "Ready or not, here I come!" All the cousins had scurried off in various directions, trying to find the ideal hiding spot to keep Terry from finding us. We each realized that if we were located, it would be our turn to close our eyes and count as all the others sought a place to hide. The game was called "Hide and seek." On this occasion, I ran into my grandparents' barn. I quickly rearranged several hay bales so I had my own little fort to hide in. Special care was taken, so I had just enough gap between the bails to peek out and watch for my cousin. After a while, I heard him. I held my breath, listening, looking, and wondering, "Would he find me?" I waited. I was ready, and on this particular occasion, I avoided being found.

Advent is about being ready. It is about looking for the ways God comes to us. We remember with joy how God came to us in Jesus at Christmas. We recall that Jesus promised that he would come again one day to receive his people to himself. But Advent is not just about remembering how God came to us in the past or how God will come to us in the future. It is about being ready for the ways God comes to us now. Advent is God's way of saying and, simultaneously, asking, "I am coming! Are you ready? Are you looking for me?" So Jesus reminds us in Matthew 24:44: "Therefore you also be ready, for the Son of Man is coming at an hour you do not expect."

God often comes to us in surprising ways; therefore, we must look for him in unexpected places.

Faith Bytes

November 30
The Right Tools

My youngest daughter and I assembled a piece of furniture she began at college. She brought it home, hoping we could figure it out together. As I removed an assortment of hardware from the grocery bag, in addition to the screws, I discovered several butter knives and a hand-operated can opener. I immediately recognized these as the tools of last resort. Although I was slightly baffled by the can opener when she explained, it made perfect sense.

As I was embracing our bonding moment, she asked if I enjoyed this sort of thing. I said, "I do, provided I have the right tools. If not, it could be frustrating." She then inquired how much my electric drill cost. Seeing how my investment in her higher education wasn't for naught was nice.

The correct tools make a task more manageable and can transform the dreaded into something anticipated. As Christians, we have a toolbox two thousand years in the making. The Christian calendar is a remarkable gift with various seasons, such as Advent. In the coming days, I hope we can learn some of Advent's tools and how they can help us anticipate a meaningful Christmas.

If we were to identify one passage of scripture that expresses the importance of Advent and the purpose of such tools as the Advent wreath and the Chrismon Tree, it would be these words:

"The people who walked in darkness have seen a great light; those who lived in a land of deep darkness—on them light has shined." [Isaiah 9:2, NRSV]

The significance of Christ's coming is captured in two words: "darkness" and "light." As you begin the Season of Advent, what do "a land of deep darkness" and "a great light has shined" mean to you?

Steven B. Angus

DECEMBER

December 1
The Light Shines in the Darkness

Poor Shepherds, gift-bearing kings, a dreaming groom, a singing expectant mother, a birth in a barn, and a father awakened from sleep to hastily escape with his family to Egypt each has something in common. Darkness. When life seemed darkest, God pierced the murkiness with light.

The Gospel of John introduces Jesus, saying: "The light shines in the darkness, and the darkness can never extinguish it...The one who is the true light, who gives light to everyone, was coming into the world." [John 1:5, 9, NLT]

What better way to symbolize the life of Jesus than a candle? A lit candle has been a staple in Christian worship for millennia. Today, an Advent wreath is familiar in most churches and many homes. It is a recent practice when we consider the church has been around for two thousand years.

The inventor of the modern Advent wreath was a German protestant pastor, Johann Hinrich Wichern (1808–1881). During Advent of 1839, excited children at his church's mission school would ask daily if Christmas had arrived. He built a large wooden ring with twenty small red and four large white candles in response. A small candle was lit each day, and on Sundays, a large white candle was lit.

The practice gained popularity in Protestant homes but with only four or five candles. Families would light a candle for each past Sunday in Advent at their evening meal or prayer time. It did not matter the color or how the candles were arranged. What mattered was the visual marking of time and the increase of light as Christmas approached. Your mission—should you accept it, is to secure five candles, and during your quiet time or with your family, read John 1:5 and 9 above and light one candle.

Faith Bytes

December 2
The Gospel In a Candle!

Preachers, teachers, politicians, and most public speakers continually try to balance sharing information while influencing change. One of my preaching professors said the thirty-minute sitcom and the sixty-second commercial had altered the sermon forever by reducing the listener's attention span. Today, we live by the Tweet and the Soundbite.

Often, life-altering events like a diamond engagement ring come in small packages. Who would have thought a handful of candles in a circular ring could cast so much light on a loving God? What began as a tool to help underprivileged German children understand Christmas became an instrument that brought families together for prayer.

By the late 19TH century, churches in Europe and America had adapted the Advent wreath for congregational worship. Larger spaces required larger candles, and soon, purple candles became the norm. Purple often represents repentance and fasting. It is also the appropriate color for a king. A white central candle was added to be lit on Christmas day, representing the birth of Jesus. Protestants have traditionally used four purple candles. Catholics replaced a purple candle with a rose-colored one to express joy.

As the wreath became a regular part of congregational Advent worship, the candles not only represented the four Sundays before Christmas but were assigned a theme for each week. In progression, they are hope, peace, joy, and love. Of these themes, it has been said that Advent Hope moves us, Advent Love leads us, Advent Joy stirs us, and Advent Peace stills us so that we can affirm Jesus as our King. In Jesus Christ, our hope is fulfilled, love consummated, joy completed, and peace sealed. [Derek Weber, umcdiscipleship.org]

Wow! The Gospel in a simple candle! Don't forget to light your Candle of Hope.

_____
_____
_____
_____

December 3
Hope Has a Twin Sister

The nice thing about the Advent Wreath is it is never too late to begin lighting candles. On the first Sunday in Advent, worshipers in countless churches will gaze expectantly at the circle of candles strategically placed in the sanctuary. The scene will be similar regardless of location. As the flame approaches the candle we call Hope, we will witness the first miracle of Christmas when it is not extinguished by the collective body simultaneously inhaling a breath and holding

Steven B. Angus

it. As the candle flickers to life, worshipers will feel a charge of expectancy. The first Sunday will mark the beginning of Advent and a week of trying to understand Christmas and Christian hope. Sometimes, the first candle is called the "Prophet's Candle," as we allow the Old Testament's prophets, especially Isaiah, to encourage us to wait in hope for the Messiah's arrival.

Hope is a word frequently used in our conversations. However, it often comes across as wishful thinking about things beyond our control. We say, "I hope it snows tonight" or "I hope my rich uncle gets out of the poor house and gives me a million dollars." The Hope represented by the flicker that finds life on the wick of the Christmas Advent Candle is different. Christian Hope is expectant. Christmas Hope is confident. Why is it so? Because God kept his promises to the Prophets.

G.K. Chesterton said, "Hope means hoping when things are hopeless, or it is no virtue at all... As long as matters are really hopeful, hope is mere flattery or platitude; it is only when everything is hopeless that hope begins to be a strength." Even when circumstances suggested otherwise, Mary, Joseph, the shepherds, and the Wise Men responded with hopeful confidence that God could be trusted.

I believe Hope has a twin sister, and her name is Faith. As you reflect on the confident characters of the Nativity, what are some of God's promises that kindle the flame of Advent Hope in you?

_____

_____

_____

_____

December 4
Hope Waits

A woman and her friend stopped at a convenience store to purchase milk. When the friend completed her transaction, she handed the cashier $2 and asked for a lottery ticket. Knowing her friend's modest circumstance, she chastised her for wasting her money. In her defense, the friend responded, "Two dollars isn't much to pay for 24 hours of hope." How much are we willing to fork over for a pinch of hope this Christmas?

Hope. When I consulted the dictionary, I was surprised to find it described as a "feeling." The prevalent definition typically states that Hope is the feeling that what is wanted can be had or that events will turn out for the best. Not bad. Am I the only baby boomer suddenly hearing Doris Day singing in the background? Do you recall the lyrics?

> "When I was just a little girl,
> I asked my mother, 'What will I be?
> Will I be pretty?

Faith Bytes

Will I be rich?'
Here's what she said to me:

"(Kay) Que sera, sera,
Whatever will be, will be;
The future's not ours to see.
Que sera, sera,
What will be, will be."

Is there a distinction between "Advent hope" and the passive, "What will be, will be?" As you read these lyrics from Psalm 33, can you hear the songwriter's understanding of hope?

"Truly the eye of the Lord is on those who fear him,
  on those who hope in his steadfast love.
   Our soul waits for the Lord….
  because we trust in his holy name." [33:18, 21, NRSVUE]

Christmas hope has no illusion that every question will be answered. But neither is it a game of chance. Although uncertain about the future, the Psalmist, Mary, Joseph, and Elizabeth demonstrated hope, anchored in the declaration: "Our soul waits for the Lord."

_____
_____
_____
_____

December 5
Hope Expects

Authentic hope isn't a wish we make upon a star or what we do as we blow out the candles on a birthday cake. Hope is more substantial. It is built upon the firm foundation that God's love is unshakable. The Psalmist sang:

"Our heart is glad in him,
because we trust in his holy name.
Let your steadfast love, O Lord, be upon us,
even as we hope in you" [Psalm 33:21-22 ESV]

Beneath the dictionary's definition of hope is a suggested synonym, "expectancy." Isn't it exciting to hear a couple share the news that they are going

Steven B. Angus

to have a baby? They joyfully utter, "We are expecting!" The best analogy of Advent hope in the Christmas story is so apparent we almost miss it. But it is there. We only need to listen to the prayers and songs of Elizabeth, Zechariah, Mary, and Joseph. Although the couples are uniquely different, each expectantly awaits the fulfillment of God's promise.

When a family expects a child, the entire experience is adorned with hope in a paradoxical way. Although it is a season of waiting, it is also a time of knowing a baby will be arriving. This knowledge propels us to plan, but we soon realize there is more we don't know than we do. We feel sure, but then we find ourselves unsure. We are expecting the arrival, but when? We pencil the delivery date on the calendar. Still, as with my oldest child, he woke us early Sunday instead of Monday, saying, "Nope—it's today, guys!"

Advent hope is what exists amid the questions—How? Why? Advent hope seems to thrive on uncertainty. What do you mean there is no room in the inn? Hope is the feeling of great anticipation, but ultimately, we cannot force it. We must allow it to occur.

It is no wonder the first candle of Advent is hope. Each that follows takes its cue from it.

_____
_____
_____
_____

December 6
The Elusive Peace of Advent

The first of its 2,000 performances occurred in 1905, and British audiences loved it. Its popularity prompted the playwriter Baroness Orczy to write a series of historical fiction novels about the protagonist, "The Scarlet Pimpernel."

The setting was the French Revolution, and the hero was a chivalrous Englishman who rescued aristocrats before they met their end at the guillotine. Sir Percy Blakeney leads a double life: apparently, nothing more than a wealthy fop but is actually an eighteenth-century Bruce Wayne. Only those in his inner circle know his true identity. He is known only by the simple flower he leaves behind, a scarlet pimpernel.

I love actor Anthony Andrew's portrayal of Sir Percy. He taunts his foes at social gatherings with the poem:

> *"They seek him here,*
> *they seek him there,*

Faith Bytes

those Frenchies seek him everywhere,
Is he in heaven? Is he in hell?
that damned [cough] elusive Pimpernel."

With the lighting of the second candle on the Advent wreath, we mark our entry into the second week of preparing for the coming of Christ. This candle may represent the most elusive of the traits associated with his coming—that of peace.

Some congregations observe a moment during worship when they greet one another with the words, "The peace of Christ be with you." We often conclude worship with the same statement. We receive the blessing as if it were some sort of wish we all make just before extinguishing the altar candles as if they were sitting atop a birthday cake. Jesus must have known we would struggle with the concept of peace. He said, "Peace I leave with you, My peace I give to you; not as the world gives do I give to you." [John 14:27] Now that we are one week closer to Christmas, what do you believe Jesus meant when he said, "My peace?" When have you experienced it?

_____
_____
_____
_____

December 7
Peace—Mercy to Forgive

Light a candle in an otherwise dark, empty room, and its space is transformed. What was hollow and cold became warm and tranquil. What seemed frightening is swept away as light brushes it aside to lay claim as the occupant. This is why we light an Advent Candle and call it peace.

Mary stopped by my office to share some exciting news. I recently gave a sermon on Jesus' teaching, "Blessed are the merciful, for they will receive mercy." I had stated that forgiving someone often extends mercy to someone who may not warrant it. She noted that the comment caused her to do some soul-searching. She felt burdened and at a loss about what to do. She said, "One morning, while home alone, I laid down on the floor and begged God for his mercy--mercy to forgive, as well as the mercy of his forgiveness." When she finished this prayer, she said, "Afterwards, I felt a peace I had not known in a long time."

Peace seems elusive because we limit it to the absence of war, conflict, and discomfort. Of course, these should be the goal of all sane citizens. However, we have known when the state of affairs around us has been described as "peaceful," yet we did not feel peace. We have known war, natural disasters, and a pandemic. Each, by the world's standards, should stomp out peace. Yet we

Steven B. Angus

light the candle in the darkened room and name it peace in honor of the one who restores our relationship with our merciful God—Jesus, the Prince of Peace. As a follower of Jesus, shine today as a candle of peace in your part of this tumultuous world.

_____
_____
_____
_____

December 8
The Baby Jesus Lullaby

Although President Franklin Roosevelt led the United States through the Second World War, he did not wish this to be his legacy. He wanted to be remembered as the architect of lasting peace among the nations. The night before his death, the President was planning to attend the organization of the United Nations and was writing his speech. Although never given, they were the last words he wrote, including the following.

> "We seek peace--enduring peace...We must cultivate--the ability of all peoples, of all kinds, to live together and work together, in the same world, at peace."

The effectiveness of the United Nations has been debated. However, Roosevelt hoped this League of Nations would become the great peacemaker of society. International conflicts have been resolved, but not all of them.

In his book, "The Christian Salt & Light Company," the late Haddon Robinson wrote:

> *"No peace will exist between nations until peace reigns in each country. And no country will have peace until peace dwells with the people. And no people will have peace until they surrender to the prince of peace."*

We forget that Jesus entered the world as a choir of angels sang him a lullaby. The lyrics reverberate across the ages in a peace-starved world. "Glory to God in the highest and on earth peace [good will toward men]."

We watch nations quarrel, listen to neighbors speak hate to one another, and wonder if God seriously thought we could attain peace. Perhaps God was being sarcastic. However, when we consider that five times in the New Testament, God the Father is identified as the "God of peace." [Hebrews 13:20] God the Son is the "Prince of Peace"[Isaiah 9:6], and the Holy Spirit is called the "Spirit...of peace." [Ephesians 4:3] We realize God's character is about peace. Do you recall how Jesus referred to the children of God in the Beatitudes? As peacemakers. [Matthew 5:9]

Take a moment and pray that you and I can be instruments of peace in our circle of influence.

_____

_____

_____

_____

December 9
The Shepherd's Presence

Although Philip Keller is the author of over thirty-five books, he will be remembered for one in particular: "A Shepherd Looks at the 23rd Psalm." Drawing on his experience as a sheep rancher, he leads his readers through this cherished song. In one section, he explains a pecking order among these wooly creatures. If the Shepherd fails to recognize this inclination, it can create conflict within the flock. He chronicles it this way.

> "Hundreds of times, I have watched an old, austere ewe walk up to a younger one which might have been feeding contentedly or resting quietly in some sheltered spot. She would arch her neck, tilt her head, dilate her eyes, and approach the other with a stiff-legged gait. All of this was saying in unmistakable terms, 'Move over! Out of my way! Give ground or else!' And if the other ewe did not immediately leap to her feet in self-defense, she would be butted unmercifully. Or, if she did rise to accept the challenge, one or two strong bumps would soon send her scurrying for safety. But one point that always interested me very much was that whenever I came into view, and my presence attracted their attention, the sheep quickly forgot their foolish rivalries and stopped their fighting. The Shepherd's presence made all the difference in their behavior."

Over the years, I have collected numerous creches. In my eyes, I consider each unique and beautiful. However, despite an artisan's exquisite talent, the scene leaves me feeling cheated as I gaze upon an empty manger, which is a characteristic of a pre-Christmas display. The picture painted is anything but serene. Then Christmas arrives. The baby is born and placed in the manger. The Shepherd King is in his temple. The other figurines take their cue and come to life as if sprinkled with pixie dust. And there is peace.

_____

_____

_____

_____

Steven B. Angus

December 10
Brokenness Leads to Peace

Peace and Bethlehem go together like ham and eggs or peanut butter and jelly. In fact, the second candle of Advent, the Peace candle, is often called the Bethlehem Candle. With its gentle lyrics, the greatly loved carol "Silent Night" is seen as a lullaby about Bethlehem. Although the familiar lyrics do not mention the village's name, there is no doubt about where the babe was sleeping in "heavenly peace."

Although we do not usually associate this gentle carol with brokenness, its origin is firmly rooted in it. Its first performance occurred on Christmas Eve in a small village located in the Austrian Alps in 1818. When the church's organ was damaged by flooding, its young priest, Father Joseph Mohr, had to consider other options. He presented the lyrics to the schoolmaster and organist in a nearby village. He asked him to compose an arrangement Father Mohr could play on his guitar to be sung during the Christmas Eve mass.

Later, an organ builder servicing the church's instrument heard the tune and was enamored with it. He took it home with him and shared it. The first American performance occurred in New York City in 1839. It was published in its current English form during the Civil War and became a favorite of both Armies. Over time, the original manuscript was lost, and Mohr's name was forgotten. It wasn't until 1995 that a document in Mohr's handwriting was discovered that authenticated he wrote it. Imagine composing something that inspired countless multitudes with the peace of Christ, and no one knew it.

When life is tumultuous, remember how God used a broken organ, a novice priest with a guitar, and a music teacher who lived most of his life in an apartment over his schoolroom so that our spirit could be lifted as we sing—

"Silent Night, holy night,
All is calm, all is bright…
Sleep in heavenly peace."

December 11
The Missing Jesus

When I was a much younger preacher, a friend and I traveled to a large city to make a hospital visit. It was the season of Advent, just a few days before Christmas. As we made our way down the corridor, we could not help but notice

Faith Bytes

a stunning Nativity scene. The figurines were about two feet tall, inside a stable of split wood. In silence, we paused to absorb the scene. We noticed it simultaneously. As if reading from a script, we spoke frantically, in unison, "Jesus is missing!" Everything one would expect to see, including a manger. What wasn't there was the main character, the infant Jesus. To say I was mortified would be a gross understatement. I simply couldn't believe it. Jesus was missing. I felt a hollow spot in my stomach. I said, "Surely no one would steal Jesus, especially in this place!"

We continued our stroll down the hallway. As I passed the receptionist at the information desk, I blurted out, "Did you know that Jesus was missing?" She recognized the concern in my voice. Calmly, she said, "It's not Christmas. He has not been born yet." Continuing, she added what I suppose was her attempt to ease my embarrassment, "I bet I have ten people a day report Jesus is missing."

However, I still felt silly for not remembering this was the reason Jesus was missing. I turned to my friend and said, "Hmmm, if Jesus hasn't been born yet, I suppose the shepherds and magi are standing around to be Mary's Lamaze coaches."

Things are just not the same without Jesus. Whether we are talking about a crèche, a church, or our life, nothing is the same without him. I still remember the empty spot when I witnessed the Jesus-less nativity scene. But I will be honest. This wasn't the first or last occasion I felt that hollowness. Whenever I have forgotten that my life is built on Jesus, I have experienced that void anew. When Jesus is missing, worship will be a performance, ministry a duty, and the Church, another civic organization.

Is Jesus missing? It's all about Jesus!

_____
_____
_____
_____

December 12
When You Care Enough to Send the Very Best

"We received our first Christmas card!" Hopefully, you or someone in your home has made the announcement. It was in 1843 that Henry Cole of London had the idea of sending a Christmas greeting card to his friends and, in doing so, created the first Christmas card. It was a three-panel card. The center one pictured a family enjoying a Christmas party. The side panels depicted the acts of feeding and clothing the needy. The inaugural caption has never been surpassed: "A Merry Christmas and a Happy New Year."

The idea caught on, and by 1860, several greeting card firms had sprung up throughout England. Then, in the middle 1870s, Louis Prang of Boston entered the field with religious Christmas cards. Finally, in 1944, the Hallmark Card company solidified its position in American history with nine simple words written on a three-by-five-inch notecard by Ed Goodman, a sales and marketing executive. Who hasn't heard the slogan— "When You Care Enough to Send the Very Best?"

It is remarkable how something that had humble beginnings became an instrument that touches the lives of so many. And yet, that is what Christmas is about. It is about humble beginnings. The story of Jesus' birth surrounded by shepherds, cattle, and straw is modest. Yet, it continues to bless the lives of countless individuals day in and day out, all because God cared enough to send his very best.

As you mail your Christmas cards, perhaps you can take a moment and pray for those who will receive your gesture of thoughtfulness. Indeed, we can take the additional step of offering a prayer of gratitude and blessing for those who took the time to send us Season Greetings.

_____

_____

_____

_____

December 13
From Mean to Clean

In August 1868, in a Western short story titled "The Luck of Roaring Camp," Bret Harte introduced a baby who changed the hearts of a community. Roaring Camp was the meanest, toughest Mining Town in all the West, recognized as having more murders and thefts than any other place. The camp was inhabited entirely by men except for one woman who made her living the only way she knew how. Her name was Cherokee Sal. Eventually, she became pregnant but died in childbirth. No one knew who the father might be, so they put the baby boy in a box with some old rags. Somehow, this didn't seem right, so one of the men rode 80 miles to buy a Rosewood Cradle. When they put the rags in the beautiful new cradle with the baby, it didn't look right. So, another man rode to Sacramento and purchased a new blanket to put around the little baby. But then someone noticed that the floor under the cradle looked dirty. Soon, those tough men got down on their hands and knees, scrubbing the floor, bringing attention to the awful state of the walls, ceiling, and windows. Before long, things were looking better.

But they soon realized they had to give up their carousing and fighting. After all, the baby needs a lot of sleep and can't do so during a brawl. Besides, the baby didn't like angry voices or frowning faces. So the men started smiling and talking in pleasant, cheerful tones. Since babies shouldn't be left alone, they set the cradle by the entrance of the Mine so one of the men could watch him. Then somebody noticed what a dirty place that was, so they planted flowers and made a lovely garden there. Before long, they realized that when they put their hands down next to his, their hands looked so dirty. Very quickly, the general store was sold out of soap, shaving gear, cologne, etc.

Little did they realize it, but the baby changed how they lived and gave them a purpose and joy to accompany it. When we make Christmas about Jesus, we will see a change in ourselves and experience joy.

___

December 14
Scene Stealing Shepherds

When the third candle is glowing on our Advent wreath, it signals the beginning of something akin to Homecoming week. Although lacking a parade with floats, it does represent the exciting days leading to the big game—in our case, Christmas. It is the candle of Joy, often called the Shepherds Candle.

Shepherds. Seldom has a Nativity Pageant Mary not been overshadowed by a wayward lamb making faces at the audience. If not a sheep, it was probably a bored shepherd who notices the chain supporting an ancient low-hanging light and suddenly tosses his head covering into the air to—? Well, who knows the intention of a four-year-old shepherd, only one year removed from "sheep-dom?" Frankly, shepherds and sheep can be scene-stealers, and that's okay. This role is the closest we came to Broadway for most of us.

Why do we associate shepherds with the candle of Joy? We have Luke's Gospel to thank for introducing us to a band of sheepherders doing what they had been doing for generations—tending sheep. This night began like thousands of others before it. However, the appearance of an angel has a way of changing the script, even one who assures you that you have no cause to be frightened.

What occurred was like our watching an episode of Law and Order for the sixty-third time. Just when we are about to figure out who did it, a voice breaks in, saying, "We interrupt your life to bring you news of great joy!" And we, like the shepherds, try to understand how the birth of a baby, not even related to us, warrants an interruption, much less joy. There again, maybe, just maybe, that is God's lesson. Joy is what occurs when we allow God to interrupt.

Steven B. Angus

December 15
The Christmas Docu-drama

The message to the shepherds is as familiar as the recent Christmas pageant. Nestled in the center of the Nativity narrative is the message delivered by an angel that brings clarity to all that came before it and afterward. "Behold, I bring you good news of great joy." We read the words tucked inside the recently received Christmas card, wishing for once the message was intended for us. Although hopeful, the words seem more like an inner office memo designed for shepherds, holy folks, and kind people. We cannot help but feel we have been caught reading a note left on the copy machine addressed to everyone but us. It seems Christmas is for children, merchants, and the Hallmark Channel movie producers. Each gobble up their little piece of "tidings of great joy" as we are left in our small three-by-five cubicle to suffer and rot.

An event or story can be reported in many ways. If the intent is to be impartial and only provide information, we would expect only a newspaper reporter's who, what, when, and where posture. Although Luke's Gospel addresses these four W's, his narrative isn't petry dish reporting. He wants to draw us into a docu-drama, where we are a part of the story. He includes a fifth W—Why? Why is this Savior born? This explains his use of such words as "you" and "for all the people." The news is good because it embraces us.

We are not to be intimidated by the shepherds. The story encourages us to identify with and applaud them. You see, the average "Josephs," not the big shots back in Jerusalem, got it. We overlook that the angel did not tell the shepherds to go and see the Savior born to all the people, only where he could be found. After the angel departed, the sheepherders discussed it and decided to go to Bethlehem. Read the story in Luke 2:8-20. Notice it was after they met the Savior that joy settled upon them.

_____

_____

_____

_____

December 16
Joy Depends On It!

Terrified shepherds. I suppose an angel has that effect. Gabriel sought to ease their anxiety. Like the wingless Clarence in "It's a Wonderful Life," he reported he was on a mission from God. If we hope to embrace the glow of the Advent Candle of Joy, we would be wise to consider this messenger's exact words. He prefaced "joy" with "I bring you good news that will bring great joy."

Joy would be the response to the news. This may cause the rub for many of us. Information is only good news if we believe it matters to us. If we see a report about someone five hundred miles from home receiving a transplant, our

Faith Bytes

response is negligible. However, our heart is grateful if a church friend on our prayer list is the recipient. Suppose the beneficiary of such a precious gift is our child, spouse, or even ourselves. In that case, our internal Good News monitor will blast into orbit! And the accompanying joy? Let's just say the gauge explodes! The closer the news applies to us, the greater the joy we experience.

As Jesus visited the home of a religious teacher, a woman came and anointed his feet with perfume. When the leader questioned this, Jesus said, "I tell you, her sins—and they are many—have been forgiven, so she has shown me much love. But a person who is forgiven little shows only little love." [Luke 7:47, NLT]

We are in the home stretch towards Christmas. If we are struggling with a lack of joy, is it possible we haven't made the connection with our need for a savior? News is only good, bad, or neutral as we associate it with ourselves. Which is it? Your joy may depend on it!

_____

_____

_____

December 17
Reasons to be Joyful

Each lead actor in the Nativity narrative has this in common: Life was hard, but they found reasons to be joyful.

Life seemed to deliver one bad break after another for this young man. At the time of his birth, his father was in prison. He never forgot his mother's stories of nursing her children on the jail steps. He demonstrated genius early as he learned Latin by age four, Greek at nine, French at eleven, and Hebrew at thirteen. He declined scholarships to Oxford and Cambridge because he would not agree to enter the Anglican ministry.

As a youth, he complained that church music was dull. His father grew tired of his criticism and challenged him to write something better. The following Sunday, he presented his first hymn to glowing reviews and launched a church music career.

Later, he became pastor of one of London's most influential independent churches. Due to various physical and psychiatric illnesses so severe, he eventually could not preach. Although his body was frail, his spirit seemed to soar as he wrote encouraging letters to his parishioners. He was not considered an attractive man, described as skinny and pale, with a disproportionately oversized head atop a five-foot frame. One biographer noting a rejected marriage proposal wrote, "Though she loved the jewel, she could not admire the casket [case] which contained it."

He wrote more than six hundred hymns. Yet one stands out above the others and has graced many Christmas Eve Candlelight services. The opening measure bursts forth. "Joy to the World; the Lord is come. Let earth receive her king."

Steven B. Angus

It has often been discussed whether Isaac Watts could have written so powerfully if his life journey had been easy. Of course, no one knows, but it does seem joy resides with those who look for reasons to rejoice. What reasons can you identify that stirs joy within you?

_____

_____

_____

_____

December 18
Bubble Gum Joy

Joy has such a pleasant ring to it. It sounds nicer and seems weightier than its counterpart happiness. For some, they are the same. However, when I hear happiness, it sounds conditional. In other words, it is usually dependent on external factors to signal an emotional response. Joy seems to be generated inwardly and becomes hotwired into our emotions, impacting our reactions. Is this scientific? I am not sure, but it does reflect my observations.

The angel told the shepherds, "I bring you good news of great joy." The Greek word for great is "megas". We recognize its English usage. We have mega-markets, mega-bites, mega-bucks, and our favorite, we order our french fries, mega-sized.

The angel's message would produce enormous joy that could only be described as "mega joy!" Perhaps you are thinking, give me a mega dose of joy in this instance. A teaspoonful is more than I have presently.

I remember such an Advent when I ran into Brittany. She was always doing stuff in a big way, and at that moment, her big thing was a massive wad of bubble gum. She paused her chewing momentarily and blew a bubble about the size of a softball that burst on her face. Laughing, she removed it and returned it to her mouth. Knowing how busy things are around the church at Christmas, she asked if she could do anything to help out. I jokingly said, "You can write me a sermon, preferably on Christmas Joy." This young woman, barely twenty, said, "Why don't you get some bubble gum and start blowing bubbles. It will put you in a more joyful mood." Such wisdom!

I thought of Jesus' teaching about being like a child. It's not childishness but more like the innocence accompanying those who do not take themselves so seriously. A child finds joy in the moment. Perhaps we should seek out the nearest gumball machine and invest in joy.

_____

_____

_____

_____

Faith Bytes

December 19
I Triple Dog Dare You

Although the hymn was not written with Christmas in mind, we should not shy away from singing it, particularly on the Third Sunday of Advent, characterized by Joy. On second thought, I am glad it isn't deemed a Carol, as it is too splendid to limit our singing of it to one Sunday a year. The lyrics and Beethoven's arrangement, "Ode to Joy," usher my soul into the manger. I could be a barefooted shepherd, a dust-weary Wiseman, or the guy who rakes out the cattle stalls; it would not matter as long as I could kneel before my savior and sing:

"Joyful, joyful, we adore Thee
God of glory, Lord of love
Hearts unfold like flow'rs before Thee
Op'ning to the Sun above

Melt the clouds of sin and sadness
drive the dark of doubt away
Giver of immortal gladness
fill us with the light of day

All Thy works with joy surround Thee,
Earth and heaven reflect Thy rays,
Stars and angels sing around Thee,
Center of unbroken praise.

Field and forest, vale and mountain,
Flowery meadow, flashing sea,
Chanting bird and flowing fountain,
Call us to rejoice in Thee.

Wow! In fact, "I triple dog dare you!" No, this has nothing to do with Ralphie or frozen flag poles. Go ahead and sing or hum a few bars of this hymn and allow yourself to experience some Advent Joy!

Steven B. Angus

December 20
Christmas Demands Change

I knew the day would eventually come. A part of me looked forward to it. Another dreaded it. I suppose I had tried not to think about it because I realized my life and household would never be the same once it occurred.

My eldest son bounced into my bedroom, plopped across from me, extended his arm in an arm wrestling position, and said, "Okay, Dad. Let's go!" I had been challenged. It had barely been six weeks since I received a similar challenge and rose to the occasion. This time, something seemed different. Was it the toned muscles that had appeared since Matt had started lifting weights? Or maybe (I prefer to believe this) I simply realized how tired I was from being up since 5 a.m.

We began with the left arm, my weakest, of course. Two bulls worthy of the name Angus could not have strained harder. After a few moments, down the arm went. It was a first. It was mine. Matt had leaped the first hurdle. Now for the real test—the right arm. More groaning as testosterone levels reached epic proportions. I thought my wrist would break. And just like that, the eldest Angus had been unseated as the arm wrestling champ.

This ego-deflating moment gave me insight into myself and my expectations about Advent. I know Christmas is coming, just as I knew the day mentioned above would eventually occur. I want to rejoice in Christmas because it reminds me that God expressed his love for me by sending his son into the world. Yet, I also know my life can never be the same if I take Christmas seriously. I must be willing to approach God differently; truthfully, some days, I don't want things to be different. Part of me would have been content for Matt to remain my "little boy" because I knew what would be expected of me. I would happily approach this Christmas as I have all the others. However, I know I can not. Things have changed. The world has changed. My life has changed. Knowing that Christmas is coming, how will it change your life?

_____

_____

_____

_____

December 21
To Love and To Be Loved

The Danish theologian Soren Kierkegaard compiled a story that has been told in various forms but generally goes something like this.

One day, while running an errand for his father, a prince passed through a poor section of a village. As he looked out of the carriage window, he saw a peasant girl so beautiful he looked for excuses to pass that way daily, hoping to catch a glimpse of her. Eventually, he realized he had fallen in love with her and longed to meet her. However, he wondered how he could gain her hand in marriage and simultaneously know she had agreed not because he was heir to the throne but for love.

Obviously, he could order her to marry him. But he didn't want a bride through coercion. He could put on his royal robe and crown and drive up to her front door in his carriage, drawn by six white horses, escorted by foot soldiers. This would undoubtedly capture her attention. However, the issue remained: Did she love him, or was she overwhelmed by the splendor? He wanted to love and be loved. He hoped she could forget that he was a king and she a humble maiden and allow a shared love to forge their marriage.

After careful reflection, the prince devised a plan with all the charm and romance of a Hallmark Christmas movie. He would exchange his royal garment for the garb of a peasant, leave his castle, and live in the village. As he lived with his people, he learned their ways and language. In time, the maiden grew to love him as he had first loved her.

The Fourth Candle of the Advent Wreath is Love. This simple, fairytale-like story captures Christmas's message and demonstrates God's heart that longs to love but also to be loved.

_____
_____
_____
_____

December 22
Forgive Us Our Christmas

Christmas Eve is almost here. Does the thought invigorate you or leave you feeling exhausted? If you are perplexed, perhaps you can relate to Christina, who, although only four years old, was caught in the pre-Christmas swirl of activity. It all seemed to be coming to a head on Christmas Eve. Her dad was overburdened with worries of his own. Her mother was overwhelmed trying to get everything ready for the season. The pressure she felt gave way to episodes of weeping throughout the day.

The little girl tried to help but often felt in the way. Sometimes, the usual kindness of her parents wore thin. Finally, near tears, she was hustled off to bed. Before crawling under the covers, she knelt beside her bed, intending to pray the Lord's Prayer. As she spoke the words to God, her tongue betrayed her. When she came to the section about forgiveness, she said, "Forgive us our Christmas as we forgive those who Christmas against us."

Does the child's prayer ring true for you? As Christmas draws near, it seems life becomes hectic, and we struggle to remember the season's significance. With all the rushing around, trying to get all the gifts purchased, as we elbow our way through the long lines, perhaps we need to pray and ask God to forgive us for what we have turned Christmas into. Indeed, it seems that Christmas has

Steven B. Angus

become something we do to others or what they do to us instead of remembering the precious gift God has given to us. Christmas is about Jesus! Christmas is the autobiography of a loving God! Let's enjoy hearing the nativity story once again.

December 23
Christmas Mice and Some Sage Advice

I recall the delight I felt as a child whenever I heard the poem attributed to Clement Clarke Moore, "Twas the Night Before Christmas." Interestingly, it was about one hundred years ago today that the poem was first published on December 23, 1823, in the Troy Sentinel newspaper in upstate New York. Yet, as I prepare these words, it is quiet and restful throughout our home, and the line, "not a creature was stirring, not even a mouse," seems appropriate.

I remember something my preaching professor, the late Reverend David Buttrick, said in his introductory course on homiletics. He said, "If someone falls asleep during worship or your sermon, do not chastise them. They have extended to you and your congregation the highest compliment. People will only sleep where they feel safe." He may have been full of himself, which he was known to do. However, some four decades later, I still remember his advice. I feel the weightiness of his statement so earnestly this Christmas. The church must intentionally provide a safe environment for neighbors and families. For some, this could be the need to be safe from physical harm, but I believe most of us need a place that allows us to feel the freedom to rest. We need a harbor that will enable our soul and body to recuperate from the trials, the busyness, the meanness, and the hardness of day-to-day living. Have you ever taken a nap in a church sanctuary? Perhaps you should try it sometime. There is nothing quite like it. A safe place becomes a familiar place, and vice versa.

The lyrics of a seldom-sung Christmas Carol offer sage advice and an invitation.

> *"God rest ye merry gentlemen*
> *Let nothing you dismay*
> *Remember Christ our savior*
> *Was born on Christmas day."*
> *O tidings of comfort and joy, comfort and joy;*
> *O tidings of comfort and joy."*

Find a place of worship for Christmas Eve and Christmas Day services. Perhaps by embracing the familiar sights and smells of the stable of Bethlehem, you can find some much-needed rest.

Faith Bytes

December 24
Where Love is Extravagant

We watch poor shepherds leave their sheep to glimpse a promised child. We see kings following a star great distances to kneel before a peasant girl and offer their gifts. We have a good man risking his reputation and marrying a pregnant girl with someone else's child. Each of these did what they did at a cost. They risked their lives in the pursuit of love.

The Scottish theologian William Barclay wrote, "Love is not love if it calculates the cost. It gives all, and its only regret is that it has not still more to give."

The Christmas story, from beginning to end, is a display of extravagant love. We see it as a young woman freely presents herself to become the handmaid of God, offering her body and soul to give birth to the child of God. Mary was so uninhibited about her love for God that she didn't care what others thought or what it would do to her reputation. But this is our first lesson about extravagant love. It is not afraid to express itself regardless of what others think.

Do you remember your first love? If so, you probably recall their name and the intense feelings associated with it. You did not mind holding hands in public or giving the appearance of two people driving a car. She would wear his class ring, and he would plaster his notebook with her name. Our love was extravagant.

There may have been a time when we felt the same about Jesus. Sure, we love him but prefer to express it in a little less embarrassing way. No more Amens, emotion, or anything extreme. Mary's and each of these persons' love was extravagant in that they were willing to show their love for God no matter what it cost or what anyone thought. Jesus wants us to have this kind of love for him now. How far are you willing to go to love Jesus extravagantly?

_____
_____
_____
_____

December 25
An Invitation to Respond

The women and men who witnessed the Christmas story of the Bible found it incredible. In fact, it was so profound it elicited a response from them. The angels could not resist singing. The Magi were compelled to follow the star. The shepherds yearned to go and see what a great thing God was doing. Mary pondered all that occurred and sang a solo, the Magnificent, to an audience of ONE. Even the yet-to-be-born John could not refrain from leaping within his mother's womb when in the presence of the expectant Mary. This was precisely what God hoped would occur then and what God desires from us when we discover that God has come to us. Great things demand a significant response.

Steven B. Angus

What does the Christmas story call forth in you? I can identify with the shepherds when they hear the news. Initially, they found it difficult to believe that God knew them. Then, overcome with joy, they had to see what God had done for them. When they saw what God was doing, they had to be still and worship. Recognizing that God is still active in our world calls forth the same response: we must worship.

The Christmas story invites a response from each of us. As you celebrate the birth of Jesus, be sure to see what God has done for you. Come to him and worship.

_____

_____

_____

_____

December 26
A Hallmark Christmas

I have had the opportunity to visit Bethlehem on two occasions. The first can only be described as a Hallmark Christmas card moment. It was January. Earlier in the day, as we made our ascent to Jerusalem, the temperature dropped, and soon, large snowflakes were floating down and blanketed the city. Although it was a beautiful scene, it required a change in our itinerary. So, it was decided this was an ideal time to go to Bethlehem.

As we approached our destination, we came to a check station armed by Israeli troops. We were told the city had been closed because of rioting earlier. Our Jewish tour guide knew some of the soldiers and persuaded them to allow us to enter the city. Because of the curfew, the city seemed like a ghost town. However, we were not going to let this deter our excitement. We began singing Christmas carols and could not believe we were approaching the city of the nativity during a snowstorm! Several inches of snow were on the parking lot when we arrived at the Church of the Nativity. However, because the village was closed, we did not have to wait in line to enter the Church. We had the 1800-year-old cathedral to ourselves.

Once inside the Church, we entered the cave that had served as a stable. Usually, due to large crowds, pilgrims would quickly file by the cave. We had the place to ourselves and had a worship service with carols and a reading of the Nativity from Luke 2. Then, one by one, we knelt and looked under an altar and placed a hand on a mosaic star that marked the spot reported to be the place where Jesus was born. It was one of my life's most meaningful and reverent moments, and I will never forget it.

Now that Christmas day has passed and the crowd has thinned, perhaps you will revisit it without rushing and take in its meaning for you.

_____

_____

Faith Bytes

December 27
Shepherds' Hill

My second visit to Bethlehem was entirely different from the previous one. The streets were congested, filled with vehicles and pedestrians. Before going to the Church of the Nativity, our Palestinian Christian guide took us to the traditional Shepherds' Hill. This is where the Angels were said to have announced the birth of Jesus.

Whereas the ancient Church of the Nativity reflected Greek Orthodox, Armenian, and Roman Catholic worship, Shepherds' Hill had no icons or incense burners. Just a bunch of sheep on a rustic hillside. The ground was mushy from use and because of the winter rains. We had to walk carefully to maintain our balance and avoid stepping in something whose odor would have remained with us the remainder of the day.

As I looked down to ensure I did not step where a sheep had preceded me, I saw a ram's horn. It had not been surgically removed but knocked off by some scuffle with other sheep. It was scarred, battered, and still very fresh. I pulled a plastic bag from my waist pouch, picked it up, securely wrapped it, and placed it in my pouch. Whenever I look at the horn, I am fascinated by its raw roughness and jagged edges.

Our snow-globed nativities, candle-lighting services, and pageants can enhance our anticipation of Christmas. As essential as it is for us to sing carols gathered around our crèches' if we are to experience the authentic Christmas message, we must visit Shepherd's Hill. We need to smell the stench of the sheep with their broken horns and the dirty wool. We must never forget when Jesus was born, innocent children lost their lives, leaving behind weeping parents. Its harsh earthiness helps us to see how Jesus's coming intersects with the rawness of our own lives. Remembering Shepherds' Hill makes the purpose for Jesus' coming authentic and relevant today.

Can you identify the Shepherds' Hills in our world? In your life? Calling them by name is a vivid reminder of our need for God.

_____
_____
_____
_____

December 28
Deployed to Deliver

The History Channel broadcasted a docu-drama about a decisive battle on Nazi lines near the end of World War 2. An American unit of rough and tough New Yorkers charged up a hill, moving much farther than their flanking units, and were surrounded by the enemy. Unaware of what had happened, a substantial number of casualties occurred among the unit when the Allied forces began pounding the enemy position with artillery. The stranded troops attempted to send messengers but were unable to get through. Finally, desperate to report their plight, they deployed a courier pigeon. As the bird took flight, it appeared wounded in the firefight. All hope seemed lost.

Sometime later, a grazed, slightly wounded pigeon landed at Headquarters. Word was immediately sent down the line to cease fire. If the message had not been delivered, more lives would have been lost!

Thankfully, the message the deployed Angel was to deliver reached those who needed to hear it. It wasn't for the shepherds only but for the entire world. However, what they declared was never intended to be a one-time soundbite. It was to be a message sent up and down the line repeated by those who genuinely believe it. As the Angel prefaced, "Behold, I bring you good news of great joy." What he was about to impart would always be good news and the source of great joy. Lives depend on our faithfulness in delivering the message: "For unto us has been born a Savior, which is the Messiah, Jesus Christ our Lord."

_____
_____
_____
_____

December 29
Our Point of Reference

In the retail world, Christmas is over on December 25. According to the traditional Church calendar, December 25 signals its beginning. The celebration continues until January 6, the Twelfth Day of Christmas. The Twelfth Day is called the Epiphany. You may know the phrase "Experienced an Epiphany" to describe an "Aha" moment. Old comic strips often demonstrated those incidents with a light bulb over a character's head. The Church associates Epiphany with the Wise Men, who followed a star to where the infant Jesus was. This was their Aha moment. The Star of Bethlehem has a significant role in the Christmas Story. However, this isn't the only occasion a star is associated with Jesus.

In Revelation 22:16, Jesus says, "I, Jesus, have sent My angel to testify to you these things in the churches. I am the Root and the Offspring of David, the Bright and Morning Star." Jesus identified himself as the "Bright and Morning star." This fulfilled a prophecy by a reluctant prophet named Balaam, best remembered for conversing with his donkey. One of his final prophecies found in Numbers 24:17 Balaam said, "I see him, but not now; I behold him, but not near; A star will come out of Jacob; a scepter will rise out of Israel."

Notice that Jesus did not refer to himself as merely a star but as a particular star: the "Bright and Morning Star." Is there significance for us as we celebrate Christmas while looking to a new year?

Faith Bytes

In ancient astronomy, the Morning Star was the name given to the brightest star in the sky just before daylight. For thousands of years before the Magi, mariners, and travelers used the stars as a reference point. Perhaps this is intended to be the first implication for us. Jesus wants us to remember that he is our point of reference. When we need help knowing what we should do or what direction to take, we should always look to him. Just as the wise men followed a star, just as that Bright Morning Star pointed travelers the way west, Jesus is not a point but the point of reference. In John 14:6, Jesus said, "I am the way, the truth, and the life. No one comes to the Father except through Me."

If our point of reference is faulty, our arrival at the intended destination is in jeopardy. How are you looking to Jesus as your point of reference?

_____
_____
_____
_____

December 30
Morning has broken!

It turns out that the star ancient mariners referred to as The Bright Morning Star isn't a star after all. It is the planet Venus in the western sky, reflecting the sun's light just before dawn. Many folks still refer to it as "the morning star."

According to Astronomers, Venus is distinctive among the planets of our solar system. Although it is not the closest planet to our sun, it still has the hottest surface temperature, about 900 degrees Fahrenheit. Venus has no moons and no rings. However, there is more. If we could somehow look down on all of the planets in our solar system from above, they would all be turning counterclockwise. That is all except Venus, which turns in a clockwise position.

Just as Venus is unique among the planets of our Solar System, so it is with Jesus. He cannot be compared to anyone, for he alone is the only begotten Son of God. Things change as Venus, the Morning Star, becomes visible around 4:00 a.m. in the western sky. The birds awaken and begin to sing their welcome to the sun as it appears in the eastern sky. Morning has broken! The bright morning star represents the promise of a new day. The darkness is overcome by the light. Hope emerges.

We seem to be being swallowed up in darkness when we suddenly glimpse the Bright Morning Star on the horizon. Jesus has come to us. Something better is possible because Jesus is indeed with us. Jesus is the Bright Morning Star because, in him, there is newness. Every day has the potential to be uniquely new. In him, we can always start fresh!

_____
_____

ABOUT THE AUTHOR

Steven B. Angus preached his first sermon when he was thirteen years old. He has continued doing so for over fifty years. Although retired, he serves as the pastor of Kingston Springs United Methodist Church in Kingston Springs, Tennessee. He is married to Cheri Clyde Angus. They live on their farm outside of Nashville, Tennessee, and enjoy spending time with their four dogs, two cats, miniature donkey, eleven grandchildren, eight children, and six daughters and sons-in-law. Steven and Cheri are newlyweds meeting after both became widowed.

Dr. Angus is a graduate of Martin Methodist College [now known as the University of Tennessee, Southern], Middle Tennessee State University, and Vanderbilt Divinity School. He also has attained the Doctor of Ministry degree from The School of Theology, University of the South, Sewanee, Tennessee. This is the author of two previous books, *No Greater Inheritance: The Last Will and Testament of Jesus Christ* and *Guess Who is In God's Family Tree*. Steven can be contacted at stevenbangus@gmail.com.

Faith Bytes

BOOKS BY THIS AUTHOR

No Greater Inheritance: The Last Will and Testament of Jesus Christ

Perhaps the title intrigues you. The notion that someone like Jesus would have a Will and Testament seems out of character. In fact, those who recorded his story in the New Testament make it clear that Jesus was not a man of means. Today, we would consider Jesus as homeless. To suggest that a poor person actually had something of value to include in a will seems ludicrous. Although Jesus never used the precise words, Will and Testament, he did believe that he had some priceless treasures worthy of bequeathing to those he loved. The portion of scripture recorded in The Gospel of John, chapters thirteen through seventeen, has been referred to by various titles. I suggest another: The Last Will and Testament of Jesus Christ.

The treasures he offers to us are not only to be acknowledged on the occasion of death or even at a funeral service. The inheritance is intended for us today. What is contained in these chapters reaches beyond the hope of a future eternity. We shall discover that Jesus, by his death and resurrection, has bequeathed to us many other gifts intended for our enjoyment now. Our goal is to discover, perhaps for the very first time, what our inheritance encompasses. As we learn to love him, we soon discover that there is so much more that comes with that relationship. The message of the Last Will and Testament of Jesus Christ is very clear: Whoever receives the Son receives it all. And there is NO GREATER INHERITANCE!

Surprise! Guess Who is in God's Family Tree

One might presume that the women in Jesus the Messiah's genealogy would include only the finest Jewish women, but they weren't. Instead, the five women were primarily poor, mostly misfits, widows, and unimportant, unknown, sinful women by society's standards. Most weren't even Jewish at all. Except for Ruth and Mary, they had tarnished sexual histories, although to some, even their background would have been called into question. They were everyday women living ordinary lives tainted by sin—just like us! But to God, they were beautiful because God created them. They were precious to God, and because of their inclusion in God's Family Tree, God extends us hope. Jesus came from a long line of broken people who foreshadow the kind of people he came to save.